Child Potential

Child Potential

Fulfilling Your Child's
Intellectual, Emotional, and Creative Promise

Theodore Isaac Rubin, M.D.

CONTINUUM · NEW YORK

1990

The Continuum Publishing Company
370 Lexington Avenue
New York, NY 10017

Copyright © 1990 by El-Ted Rubin

Printed in the United States of America

Library of Congress Cataloging-in-Publication Data

Rubin, Theodore Isaac.
    Child potential : fulfilling your child's intellectual, emotional,
and creative promise / Theodore Isaac Rubin.
        p.   cm.
    Includes index.
    ISBN 0-8264-0489-8
    1. Child development. 2. Child rearing. 3. Self-realization.
I. Title.
HQ767.9.R83   1990   E
649'.1—dc20   90-38666
                                                       CIP

To Ellie, my wife,
the best enabler I know

The Child is father of the Man.
William Wordsworth

Contents

Part IV: The Enablers

Preface

In *Compassion and Self-Hate* I wrote about how we relate to ourselves and about development of the compassionate way of life.

In *Reconciliations* I wrote about the impact of culture and society and how we may struggle fruitfully to retain our humanity as members of a less than compassionate world.

In *One to One* I described relating processes between ourselves and other people and how our relationships can become more compassionately productive and are to some extent predictable.

In *Real Love* I described love and its great value when used constructively.

In *Child Potential* I am concerned with a specific area of early development. The area I speak of is that of *intellectual*, *emotional*, and *creative* potential and its becoming activated and fulfilled. I treat these as one area because as I shall describe a little later on, their impact on each other really makes them inseparable.

My concern in this book is helping the parent to help the child to realize a high percentage of his or her potential. This not only makes for personal satisfaction or self-realization in adult life. It also contributes enormously to mental health and to a compassionate life-style replete with loyalty to self and caring about others. There is little as corrosive to self and to confreres as unrealized potential or unused innate inner resources.

13

The age group I am interested in here ranges from infancy through young adulthood. I do not divide this book into segments by age. It will be readily apparent which material is applicable to particular ages. Most of the subject matter is applicable to children of all ages and much of it to adults, too.

Hopefully, children, the adults they become, and the children they have, will benefit as well as relationships between parents and children.

Quiogue, NY October 1990

I
Basic Considerations

In this section I want to describe what I mean by intellectual, emotional, and creative fulfillment as well as self-esteem. Their description and elucidation will help to clarify what it is we are striving for in our children. I feel that it is not enough simply to refer to intellectual, emotional, creative fruition, and self-esteem. We must have sufficient understanding of them so as to be able to see how both destructive and constructive forces work. Additionally, I feel that this understanding serves as a powerful motivating force in helping children toward self-realization.

I include in this section a first chapter about the origins of this book because I feel that it will help to understand the formulations of my point of view relative to the issues we discuss.

How This Book Came into Being

More than thirty years ago when I was a resident psychiatrist in a New York State hospital, I was responsible for a young patient who claimed that he was maltreated as a child.

I investigated as thoroughly as I could, questioning him, his parents, his siblings, and other relatives, too, for many hours, but came up with no hard evidence of abuse or deprivation of any kind.

I thought perhaps there were subtleties that escaped me due to lack of experience and skill.

My patient was very sick, too disturbed to function outside the hospital. But he was clear about his complaint of childhood abuse and deprivation, though he could not substantiate his claims.

Years later, in private practice, I saw many patients not nearly so sick as my young hospitalized patient. But they, too, had in no way lived up to their potential and had not used their innate assets fruitfully. In time, it became evident that they were in fact emotionally and intellectually stunted. Though they did not know it initially, this stunting and its consequent chronic frustration was intimately linked to the anxiety and depression that brought them to me for help. These people functioned but they were not happy about what they were doing and about how they were doing it. They related to other people in a much healthier way than my hospitalized patient, but solid satisfactions in their relationships were largely lacking. I believe these people are not at all unusual. They surely represent a

17

very large population of the "silently frustrated" who unfortunately may not develop symptoms that signal the need for help.

Some of my patients also claimed childhood deprivation. Some did not. All of them were aware of a deep, unsatisfied, emotional hunger for "something." I became aware of a huge gap between innate potential and self-realization. Here, too, there was usually lack of overt childhood deprivation or obvious abuse.

These kinds of "underachieving patients" became my major interest in psychoanalytic practice rather than people suffering from overt clinical symptoms. But eventually I learned that lack of self-realization, underachievement, and symptoms such as depression and more than usual anxiety were intimately related and often presented themselves simultaneously.

I also learned that I was right thirty years ago in believing that subtleties escaped me at that time. I found out that devastating assaults and deprivations in childhood that block the possibility of full development and use of assets and inner resources are often subtle indeed. Of course, overt abuse, total lack of love, calloused exploitation, lack of parental sensitivity, and sexual assaults are catastrophic but fortunately less common.

I also learned that so-called subtle deprivations are particularly harmful to potential in children who are especially sensitive. In fact, I believe that the stunting and crippling effect of deprivation is directly proportional to the innate capabilities and potential of the person in question. While every child is vulnerable and will profit by constructive input, this is particularly true of children with more than usual potential. They stand to lose more and to profit more, relative to the treatment they receive.

Interestingly, I also found out that these children are often damaged more by what they do not receive than by the assaults they do receive. They are like plant seeds that, lacking water, never blossom into the beautiful plants that could have been. Additionally, I came to realize that the greater the unused potential, the greater would be the self-hate and self-corrosion and devastation to all areas of living and to the possibility of happiness.

I worked with these patients as adults. Three have become

lawyers. One has become a social worker psychoanalyst. One has become a psychologist psychoanalyst. Fifteen have become physicians and several of them are now psychiatrists or are in training in psychiatry and other specialties. Several became expert professionals in the business world. Their socioeconomic status improved radically in all cases as did work interest and satisfaction. This would not have been possible without considerable emotional and intellectual growth and development. In turn, their new work has contributed to more satisfying emotional, intellectual, and creative living.

Yes, there had been many subtle assaults and deprivations in their early lives and many of them not so subtle, but all of them were devastating in their effect on healthy growth. But adults, too, can be motivated to change and grow. However, people do need vehicles to get through life's heavy traffic. For many of my patients, their vehicles turned out to be the professions they never dreamed they could have.

In working with these people I learned a great deal about childhood and adolescence. Much was consistent with what I learned about myself from my own psychoanalysis many years earlier.

What if what I learned was applied to children before they got into grievous trouble like the young man I treated in the state hospital?

What if parents were tuned in so that "replacement therapy" did not have to be given, as in the case of my patients, by a psychiatrist when they became adults?

It was these ideas that motivated me.

I want to share these ideas with you, the subtleties and the not so subtle, the don'ts and the dos, so as to motivate and to enable healthy children to fulfill their potential without professional help.

Intellectual Fulfillment

Intellectual fulfillment, or arriving at the fruition point of one's intellectual development, includes for me a considerable number of abilities. Even the most fortunate of us does not develop any ability, let alone all abilities, 100 percent. In a way this is good because it means that healthy growth and development can continue all of our lives. Of course, each of us has different and highly individual inherent possibilities. But remember, we are interested in fulfilling whatever our potential is in a given area as fully as reasonably possible. Let me list several important ones for our purpose here:

• The ability to perceive fully and accurately that with which we come into contact through our various senses. A live curiosity is a prime motivating force here and if it is deadened or destroyed in childhood the child will have limited motivation to observe and will have fewer and damaged perceptive abilities, making him or her appear to be inherently dull. I shall discuss curiosity fully in section 4.

• The ability to conceptualize. This means the ability to understand the central focus of an idea or concept. I include in this ability the capability of integration—to be able to put together several concepts and to see what they have in common, how they contrast, and how they may apply to various issues. I also include abstraction ability and the use of symbols beyond their concrete value. This is essential for mathematical and

20

successful scientific work. Without it, even the interpretation of the simplest proverb may not be possible.

• Memory plays a significant role here. It is particularly valuable when we not only remember what we have observed or experienced but also understand whatever it is we remember. Memory and conceptualization feed each other endlessly because the better and more we understand, the easier and better we remember. The more we can call up material from memory, the better we can apply knowledge to concepts we desire to understand. Memory is intimately connected to perceptive ability. Aside from fantasy memories, we simply do not remember what we do not experience. Remembering perceptions that are clear, precise, and real is very valuable, but this in large part depends on perceptive ability.

• The ability to use logic so as to be able to arrive at valid conclusions is extremely valuable. As with so much else that defines intellectual ability, the use of logical thinking comes from both inherent roots and early exposure. Training and habitual usage or multiple opportunities and experiences in applying logic to various situations play a large role.

• Judgment is largely constituted of the abilities that have preceded, and lack of development of any of the above abilities is reflected in poor judgment.

Good judgment may not seem directly connected to memory, logic, conceptualization, etc., because we are often not consciously aware of using them in arriving at a conclusion. But we do use them always, albeit on an unconscious level and often with greater rapidity than can be easily observed. Judgment, for me, here also includes the ability to discern reality as differentiated from fantasy and plays a great role in all aspects of adult life.

• The ability to think clearly (which is part of conceptualization) and then to be able to express these thoughts and to verbalize ideas, beliefs, and feelings through the use of expressed language is invaluable. Teaching ability is usually an extension of clear thinking and being articulate, and largely consists of being able to help other people to learn and conceptualize.

• Learning and the ability to apply what is learned for pleasure, profit, and life enrichment is absolutely crucial in any serious discussion of intellectual potential and its fruition. This ability guarantees continuing intellectual change and growth, and usually contributes to and extends intellectual curiosity. This often accompanies love of *learning and knowing,* which further guarantees a continuation of intellectual development. I also include here the ability to profit from what is learned and experienced in any way whatsoever—and even to profit from the wisdom and experiences of other people.

• I do not list or describe special gifts that people have in lesser or greater supply—such as total recall memory, foreign language ability, mathematical genius, etc. In large part they would also come under the umbrella of creative endowment and fulfillment. In any case, these special abilities are especially sensitive to upbringing and suffer or profit as a consequence of either neglect and damage or awareness and appropriate respect and nourishment.

We can readily see that all aspects of intellectual ability overlap and feed each other. Perception supplies memory, and being able to tap a good memory is vital to the application of knowledge for the purpose of understanding or conceptualization.

I see the mind as being developed and shaped by the information it contains. A full mind is one that is most useful in intellectual pursuit and activity. This reminds me of a bird whose gullet is useless unless filled with the gravel or small stones it uses as grit to digest its food. The mind uses its information to process still more information effectively. In so doing it continues to become increasingly developed as it fulfills its potential capacity. Filling the mind takes place through exercise of all of one's intellectual abilities or multiple processes as applied to life's encounters and experiences.

It is very important to differentiate here between lack of intellectual endowment and ignorance. One is a genetic condition. The other is the result of ignoring knowledge. As exposure to knowledge is increased and richness of experience takes place, intellectual ability increases regardless of genetic endowment or early damage.

It will soon become apparent that intellectual, emotional, and creative fulfillment not only overlap and supplement each other but are also interdependent. Indeed, any kind of modification in one area invariably alters development and function in the others. This is why complete batteries of psychological tests are crucial in determining intellectual endowment. IQ tests without examination to evaluate the possibility of emotional blocking are useless and even destructive. This bonding between intellect, emotionale, and creativity makes me believe that they are in fact one process taking place in one person.

We break the process into separate entities in order to clarify and to understand human behavior. But we must not lose sight of the more than intimate ties between these somewhat different aspects or uses of the same mind.

Emotional Fulfillment

In keeping with the closing statements of the last chapter let me say that the connection between one's emotional condition and development and intellectual development and function is always apparent to clinicians who work with people in psychotherapy. This applies to acute reactions, chronic conditions, and changes in emotional development and fulfillment.

In short-term acute emotional depressions, intellectual impairment and function is quickly in evidence. Memory suffers, attention span is poor, perception is dulled, thought associations are often slowed and in some *phases* they are sometimes so rapid as to render them useless.

In chronic conditions concentration of self and emotional investment in self may be so preoccupying as to obliterate the ability to function intellectually on any constructive level. Every practitioner sooner or later experiences the ravages to intellectual function present in severe hypochondriases, manic reactions, schizophrenic reactions, chronic hysteria, etc. Many workers believe that where emotional stunting has taken place due to severe deprivation of love in infancy there is a loss of abstraction ability so that even the simplest proverb cannot be interpreted. This was discovered in otherwise normally intellectually endowed and functioning adults who spent their infancies and early childhoods in large, mechanical kinds of institutions. Interestingly, this inability to abstract is often found in certain schizophrenic conditions (e.g., often the patient cannot interpret the simplest proverb). Every therapist also experiences the satisfaction in seeing vast improvement in intellectual function as emotional disturbances are remedied.

Therapists are especially gratified to witness the acceleration of intellectual development and consequent function as the individual improves emotional development. People who become increasingly in touch with how they feel seem to come to life intellectually, too. This is especially true of people who have been unconsciously deadening their feelings and alienating themselves from feelings for years. As they "feel more," they seem to "think better." Their motivation to learn increases, their curiosity enlarges, as does the depth, breadth, and acuity of their perceptions and insights.

The improvement of intellectual development and function has an ameliorative effect on people emotionally. They feel better about themselves, know and feel more about themselves, others, the world, as their insights take root and amplify on a feeling as well as on an intellectual basis.

I remember patients who with the improvement of emotionale began to notice, look for, understand, and appreciate on all levels (intellectual and feelingwise) the colors of rainbows, leaves, flowers, buildings, etc., as well as people's facial expressions, music, odors, etc. They were coming to life in all aspects of themselves as they became increasingly interested in the world around them, evidenced by the growth of intellectual and emotional involvement with that world and existence in all its manifestations and ramifications. This increased intellectual curiosity and further seeking of experiences that enhanced both emotional and intellectual growth.

As healthy growth takes place in people, there is increased emotional and intellectual integration. When sickness, stagnation, and regression occur, disparity between intellect and emotional development may be present. The individual here may show appropriate intellectual function, albeit limited and inappropriate emotional output, including flattened emotional response.

From my point of view the fulfillment or actualization of emotional development or what we may call relative full development centers about two areas. These two areas are: (1) The range and depth of feelings and degree of aliveness as well as the being in touch with feelings or being consciously aware of them and (2) the ability to invest feelings in other people or to get appropriately involved with people emotionally. This includes the ability to sustain and to commit to adult relationships without undue anxiety and with at least some emotional satisfaction and enrichment. In short, this includes the ability to love as well as the ability to receive love with a constructive outcome. Of course, much here will depend on the first aspect of emotionale, the intensity and in-touchness with one's own feelings. The ability to empathize, sympathize, and identify with is crucial. They make bonding and exchange of feelings possible as well as the availability and use of other people's experiences. Having an appropriate conscience and knowing right from wrong in any cultural framework is vital to getting along with people at any level.

Where proper development and fulfillment of emotional development takes place, the individual feels more strongly and represses less feelings than in stunted development. Let me say at once that this does not mean that feelings are out of control and run rampant. Quite the contrary! When we are in touch with how we feel, our feelings come under our central conscious control and we decide and have the ability to choose how we act. When feelings are repressed, they escape our central conscious control and often unexpectedly explode to the surface. When this happens, feelings dictate behavior without benefit of choice based on logical considerations and experience. This in large part explains why people sometimes seem to do things, especially highly destructive actings out, without logic and seemingly out of character. The fact is that the angry man who knows and fully feels his anger expresses it in a nondangerous way. Repressed rage often leads to unpredictable violence.

Feeling strongly about things, issues, ideas, and people means being fully alive. It also provides the possibility of real individuality, real priorities, real choices and decisions, real self-assertion and creativity. These are enormous contributors to joy and help to sustain a strong sense of identity (who we are and what we stand for) and self-esteem.

When stunting and aberration have taken place, we suffer in all the above areas and tend to become repressed, conforming automatons. How can it be otherwise if we deaden our responses and feel minimally? How can it be otherwise if we repress feelings we do have so that we are out of touch with them? This, of course, must happen in early childhood when children are for any reason taught to be afraid to feel, let alone to express what they feel. If we do not feel fully and consciously, we become exceedingly vulnerable to peer pressure, to the inordinate need to be liked at any cost, and to conform to any influence, however destructive.

The death of feelings means the death of real values and surrender to outside forces, including counterproductive, malevolent ones. This signals serious aberration of the ability to identify with, to empathize with, to sympathize. In essence and in pure form (which fortunately seldom takes place) this largely accounts for aberrations ranging from drug addiction, gangsterism, utter ruthlessness to self and others, and even to Nazism. The individual relatively devoid of feelings, in a desperate attempt to feel, often resorts to drug stimulation, near suicide attempts (speedy boats, cars, etc.), and dangerous liaisons of all kinds. They are also particularly given to sadomasochistic relating in which pain is used in an attempt to feel something—anything at all—in order to fill the sense of emptiness. As successful treatment takes place, the reduction of dangerous activity is marked. The same is true of diminishment of the compulsion to form cruel, self-destructive relationships.

Obviously, the dearth of feelings and lack of emotional development are particularly destructive to the ability to relate successfully.

We are relating creatures! When we are forced in isolation experiments to be absolutely alone, without any stimulation from other people—sight, sound, or smell—most of us hallucinate or dream up fantasy people. It is as if we simply cannot get along alone. This is equally true of children. Lonely children very often dream up imaginary playmates with whom to relate. Playing is a form of relating and begins very early when parents start cuddling, tickling, and playing with their infants.

Very sick people, especially highly narcissistic people (people who are inordinately self-preoccupied), have great difficulty in relating, and this difficulty further complicates their emotional illness, producing a continuum of vicious cycles. In a way, the inability to relate produces at least some of the results of isolation because emotional isolation invariably has profound deleterious effects on all areas of being. Psychoanalysts are well aware of the truth of the statement that "Relating brings out the best and the worst in us." This is especially true in close and sustained relationships in which levels of maturity and the ability to exchange feelings, to communicate, and to give and take services, attention, support, and all the stuff of life will be surely tested.

In people of healthy emotional development—where potential in this area has been relatively fulfilled—love is possible. This provides the possibility of partaking in and enjoying the satisfactions and rewards of human encounter for which there is *no* parallel in the human condition.

The love and exchange I speak of here is much more than the excitement of infatuation and sexual encounter, though these, too, are not without considerable benefit. May I caution at once, I do not believe that love solves all ills but it certainly helps enormously.

The love I speak of here is only possible when potential has been realized to at least some healthy extent. This love consists of cooperative and creative relating. I described this process in considerable detail in *One to One—Understanding Personal Relationships*—but let me say just a few appropriate words in this regard here. Cooperative relating is characterized by mutual acceptance. It is replete with kindness, trust, openness, intimacy, tenderness, and everything we call real caring. Creative relating means a growing ability to communicate feelings and ideas to each other with increasing accuracy and ease. Creative relating also consists of high motivation, input, and satisfaction in helping each other to attain self-realization—the acceptance and healthy development of self, especially in any creative enterprise. All of these ingredients of love are interdependent and augment each other.

Let me close this chapter by saying that satisfaction in all areas of life—educational, social, sexual, economic, intellectual, aesthetic, and creative—in very large part is directly proportional to emotional development in its two aspects: amplitude of feelings and relating ability.

Creative Fulfillment

There have been many works written about creativity and especially about its relationship to unconscious process. A recapitulation here would be impossible and inappropriate. But it is important that we go over some aspects in this area so that we are on common ground when we talk about creative fulfillment.

Karen Horney believed that unfulfilled creative assets do not simply sit there without effect. She believed they eventually cause self-corrosion and are invariably damaging. I agree. I believe that creative potential, unfulfilled, creates enormous self-hate and contributes to a chronic sense of emptiness and shaky self-identification.

I do not believe that creative ability will manifest itself regardless of how poor influences on a child may be or that "talent will out no matter what." Proper nurturing in this regard has effects unparalleled in any other area of life. I think this will become apparent in later sections of the book. Suffice it here to say that I believe all of us are born with different kinds and degrees of creative potential but that none of us are born devoid entirely of possibility. *But* there is no area in childhood more vulnerable to neglect and damage and more needy of recognition and nourishment if it is to flourish. It is no accident that so many "creative geniuses" in all areas—art, music, economics, etc.—have had their patrons, mentors, and muses.

In this context I like to think of creativity in the broadest terms and include development of our own selves or persona as we grow through various ages and stages of life—business creativity; artistic creativity; any and all kinds of inventiveness; designs for living; political invention and development; philosophies; and so on.

In order for an act or a product or theory or idea to be creative, originality is less important than conceptualization, integration, and synthesis, and these are directly proportional and intimately connected to richness of association ability. Before I explain, may I say that this bit of technical discussion is to show further how inextricably connected are intellectual, emotional, and creative functions. Without the first two, the last—creativity—would be impossible. In fact, there is the rare "autistic savant" with severe intellectual and emotional damage who nevertheless demonstrates exceptional skill in one or another areas—music, painting, sculpting, mathematics. But I believe here, too, the product is more the result of rare skill sometimes born of genetic genius than one of creativity characterized by the criteria I have listed. In any case, the creativity involved, further proves the point that even the severely maimed can be creative and were they not maimed, perhaps their production would be still richer.

Also, I am not of the belief that creative process is the result of neurosis and is hurt by removal of neurosis through treatment. My own experience evidences the contrary. Neurosis impedes creativity. Health increases creativity. Creativity is therapeutic and aids change, growth, and the development of self. My own experience indicates that creativity springs from the healthiest aspects of ourselves, and in some very sick people, their creativity may be evidence that at least some health and real self exist and need further development.

By association ability I mean the simple process of being able to generate thoughts and ideas freely. Psychoanalysts make great use of free associations because they know that all associations are eventually linked. Therefore, one association leads to others, which lead to still others, eventually producing all kinds of insights of personal value. This is an excellent way to break through the repressive mechanism and to put one's self in touch with old memories as well as with feelings that may otherwise not be readily available. For example, a patient of mine, lying on the couch, said he just had the thought of his brother being hit by a car. This led to the thought of his mother favoring his brother in "every fight we ever had." This patient was fifty-five years old and had not fought with his brother in forty years. Through free association old memories were revealed, repressed anger surfaced, insight about still trying to gain parental favor was established. The unconscious was stirred up and what was repressed became unrepressed or freely experienced. This means that the energy used to repress could be used more constructively. The process also contributes to the individual's becoming more in touch with himself and his feelings. It must be understood that repressed feelings do not go away. They develop autonomies of their own, fragment us, and create anxiety. When we become conscious of them we become free to handle them as integrated adults and free ourselves of hidden impulses derived from them. I shall discuss free association further in the section titled "The Enablers."

When the creative process is less burdened by repression, associations become richer and freer. They are assigned less judgment value and in the presence of sufficient self-esteem they are taken seriously even as questions of their being good or bad are discarded. Thus, ideas, thoughts, dreams, sounds, concepts, and fantasies that come up from the unconscious are looked upon as having potential value even though they may not immediately fit into the context of immediate practical living. This is the way, I am convinced, that great works of art, scientific theories, and economic theories are born.

But an idea left as such will go nowhere. The idea must be viewed as serious and this will only happen if the individual takes him/herself seriously enough to have relatively high self-esteem. As we will discuss later, this will depend largely on the experiences of the person as a child.

If the idea, image, series of sounds, etc., is taken seriously and adequate motivation exists (again intimately related to self-esteem), conceptualization, synthesis, and integration will be applied.

The idea will bring on a series of other ideas, information gleaned from experience, and memory and extension of the idea will take place as a concept develops and becomes clearer.

Eventually the concept will, through the application of logic, become developed and synthesized or honed down into a theory or song or painting as its parts are integrated or put together into a recognizable form.

Of course, the use of memory and clear vision in understanding old ideas is invaluable here as is the use of all other aspects of intellect and feeling. Healthy emotionale is vital in having a free flow of associations. Healthy intellectual function provides the fabric for logical, useful, and comprehensible organization. Healthy self-esteem insures taking the entire process seriously and guaranteeing the maintenance of the flow of association and continuation of the whole process. Joy in the process and in the product produced also provides continuing motivation that contributes to further fruition.

The actual process of going from free association to full development may in large part take place on a less than fully conscious level. But eventually an integration takes place between material that was held unconsciously and material of which we are conscious. There is also an integration of unconscious and conscious synthesizing and logical activity.

The value of creative activity cannot be overestimated. Creative process exercises the intellect and emotionale as it uses and integrates all aspects of ourselves in the most unique and productive ways. Indeed, we may look at creative process as the rewarding product of integrated intellectual and emotional activity as well as a great contributor to that activity.

Creative process, in its tapping of ourselves on our deepest levels and in our totalities, has the therapeutic effect of attacking and diluting alienation from our feelings. As we create, we get to know what we feel and thus who we are to a greater and greater extent. Combining increased *in-touch-with* feelings with intellect makes us whole persons and has a profound therapeutic effect.

The fruition of creative effort, while it is obviously not the only one or even the most important reward (the process is more important than the product), nevertheless gives great satisfaction and can aid self-acceptance and self-esteem. Those of us who experience joy through creative effort and fruition are blessed indeed.

I do not believe that the well dries up. Indeed, I believe that each effort primes the pump for still more production and joy. If *drying up* takes place, this is the result of a pathological process—emotional depression, hopelessness, neurotic resignation, alienation, undue perfectionism, etc.

I believe that creative effort is the epitome of self-assertion and communication. When we create (regardless of medium or form), we are tapping and putting forth the essence of ourselves and in so doing we assert who we are. In putting forth a painting, book, ceramic, song, etc., we are through the artwork communicating on the deepest and most holistic level with people who involve themselves with that work. In a paper I wrote for the *American Journal of Psychoanalysis* some years ago, I said art is a relating process between artists. Yes, the viewer becomes an artist, too, and must exercise his/her own creative machinery in order to understand, communicate, and relate to the producing artist through the artwork.

Again and again I've heard people say that particularly creative people are sick and narcissistic. I believe uniqueness is often mistaken for sickness. Where sickness does exist, we often find creative affectation present in which manner is more important than substance. There is much that passes for art that is actually fraudulent pretense. When the artist, the real artist, is sick, I believe his work neutralizes his illness and is an effort to get well. The artistic work is always an attempt to communicate. However reclusive the artist may be, his work is an antinarcissistic effort.

Creative process breaks through repression as it makes for ideas and observations that are new to us regardless of originality. As this happens, we become more vital and alive and even passionate. We become more interested in ourselves and others. We become more interesting to others and have much more to offer others as we use this most effective antialienating, antiboredom, anti-self-rejection, uniquely human device.

Self-Esteem

Self-esteem, self-worth, or the evaluation of ourselves by ourselves or the conglomerate attitudes we have toward ourselves, or in short, how we feel about ourselves, is absolutely crucial.

High self-esteem is a virtual guarantee of trusting one's feelings sufficiently so as to be able to apply them (how we feel) to judgment ("I do not like thee, Dr. Fell, / The reason why I cannot tell, / But this I know and know full well, I do not like thee, Dr. Fell") and to creative work. Our feelings often give us faster and more accurate and more meaningful messages than our logic. But we ignore our feelings if our self-esteem is poor and may also abandon our logic as well.

Self-esteem refers to how we *really* feel about ourselves and is not the stuff of any kind of cover-up of self-inflation, affected behavior, self-glorification, arrogance, or outward appearance. Indeed, the higher the self-esteem the less arrogance and affectation will be present. I may point out in this connection that in arrogance we arrogate or ascribe to ourselves qualities that do not exist and make claim to special treatment on the basis of those qualities. (I will speak more about arrogance in the next section under "Liabilities.")

Self-esteem is the genuine article and is invariably based on genuine feelings that are connected to real inner resources and assets. Self-esteem is intimately connected to feelings of identity and security. Poor self-esteem makes for insecurity, a poor sense of who we are, and is often associated with alienation from

34

our own feelings as well as poor anxiety and frustration tolerance.

More often than not, we are not directly in touch with self-esteem on a fully conscious level. This means that we know little about how we really feel about ourselves even though the results of how we feel are all about us. This means that even though how we feel about ourselves is unconscious, almost everything we do—consciously—is in large part predicated on self-esteem. This is obvious when we realize that self-acceptance and self-confidence are directly proportional to self-esteem. Without self-acceptance, in a state of self-rejection and self-hate, it is impossible to make good use of ourselves in coping with the world we live in on any level. With self-acceptance we are comfortable with ourselves and our integrated energy and assets can be applied to all of life's business.

Of course, self-confidence largely determines the activities we involve ourselves with (social, economic, etc.) and the outcome of that involvement. Secure, self-accepting, self-confident people are in an excellent position to fulfill themselves in all areas of life. Indeed, their expectations of themselves will almost invariably be appropriate. They are neither exorbitantly grandiose nor inappropriately low due to a poor self-regard. While people with poor self-esteem sometimes do well economically and may form constructive relationships, the odds are against them and the burden they bear robs them of the derivative joy. In fact, poor self-esteem often results in inappropriate relationships and also highly destructive ones. It must be remembered that hollow bravado and affected posturing have nothing at all to do with real security and high self-esteem or self-worth. They exist in direct proportion to esteem that is poor and to real underlying feelings of inadequacy.

I like to see self-esteem as existing on two levels or in two ways or parts.

(1) One is the self-esteem that produces the lifelong image we have of ourselves. This image consists of all kinds of feelings, ideas, and thoughts. Some of them are realistic, others are not, regardless of their aberration from reality in either a nega-

tive or positive way. *But,* regardless of reality, the overriding feelings we have about ourselves, the persistent conglomerate feel of ourselves, and the image produced are real. Self-esteem—high or low—is real. Of course, to the extent that evaluation is based on any kind of a real value scale, our view of ourselves in this world will be realistic. But this is not the issue here. Real or otherwise—regardless of anyone else's objective evaluation of us and regardless of criteria used—we have a subjective conglomerate esteem of ourselves and an image of ourselves based on that esteem—high or low. Real high self-esteem is always based on a sense of ownership of real inner assets. Having inner assets is not enough if we do not feel we own them. Feeling temporarily that we own what we don't have may produce exhilaration but not real and long-standing self-esteem.

This part of self-esteem and the image produced, however realistic or unrealistic, is powerfully persistent and strongly resistant to change. In fact, if self-esteem is low, accomplishments in adult life may make for temporary changes that are characteristic of the second kind of self-esteem, which we will soon get to, but will not alter the overall feeling about self. When self-esteem is high, accomplishments are enjoyed and tend to sustain ownership of assets and may make some contribution to continuing self-esteem. To alter that feeling after childhood invariably involves an examination, reevaluation, and struggle with childhood-based experiences. This is usually the work of psychoanalytic psychotherapy.

(2) The second kind or part of self-esteem, not to be confused with self-puffery, is of a more immediate and temporary nature. It is based on fluctuations in ownership of assets and temporary changes in viewpoint as regards one's self-worth. This is often connected to "defeats" and "victories," the so-called ups and downs in life. These changes are not permanent and do not affect the overall image of self but only modify it temporarily. The overall self-esteem and image, having roots in early childhood, can be modified in adolescence, but changes in status quo in adulthood do not change it. This is true even when feelings about one's self change on a conscious level for a considerable period of time. Interestingly, assets, which I shall

describe in the next chapter, are owned in high self-esteem even as ownership contributes to raising self-esteem. In low self-esteem, they are not owned. Pointing them out usually has little effect. The individual simply does not feel connected to them.

Self-esteem of both kinds in large part determines mood and attitudes generally. How we feel about ourselves has to affect how we see others and the world. It impacts powerfully on our expectations of ourselves both in terms of their appropriateness and fulfillment. Obviously, in high self-esteem a plentitude of hopefulness, optimism, and motivation will exist. Curiosity, stick-to-itiveness (so dependent on hopefulness about outcome) and responsibility will flourish. In high self-esteem, we tend to be more responsible because we feel that our input counts and our optimism prevents fear of outcome, which makes for shirking responsibility. Choice and decisions are easier and judgment is good because vision and perception are clear. Relationships are clearer and tend to be more fruitful.

In poor self-esteem, self-delusion, roller-coaster moods, pessimism, affectations, and pretense to counter feelings of fragility, and fear of outcome of one's participation flourish. This results in poor perception, difficulty in making choices and decisions, inhibition in taking action—sometimes to the point of paralysis and lack of satisfaction in both the various processes involved in attainments and even in goals and accomplishments that come to fruition. Relationships are complex and stormy as projections of one's own supposed shortcomings and fears are projected to others and as claims are made on others to take over dropped responsibilities and to compensate for feelings of inadequacy. People of low self-esteem tend to be more dependent, angry about their dependency, and are sometimes arrogant to cover up feelings of fragility and fear. Obviously, this complicates and often destroys the ability to relate fruitfully.

In high self-esteem there is satisfaction of *doing* and *getting*—process and product—and this adds to contentment. In low self-esteem process and accomplishment never seem to be enough, seem to be better with other people, do not accrue to the feeling of betterment, and leave the person feeling "outside of things" and "still having missed the boat" as satisfaction, let alone pleasure, is stunted and short-lived. People of low self-esteem chronically feel that anything *they* do is diminished in value in all areas because *they* do it. This validly follows the Groucho Marx story of "I wouldn't want to join any country club that accepts me."

Recent work, especially in Great Britain, demonstrates that children are aware, receptive, and responsive to their environments from the moment they are born. Experiments indicate that infants only several weeks old can tell the difference between their mothers and fathers as well as strangers. Long before their central nervous systems (brain and spinal cord) are completely developed, in the first weeks following birth they respond appropriately to good and bad treatment—indeed, their gurgling and grimacing and flaying about constitute their language long before they can verbalize "words" used by adults. Not only that—parents who are "tuned in" unconsciously respond to that language and in this way provide the child with what he requires long before he or she can *talk* with words. It is obvious that a great deal of communicating and relating goes on in normal intercourse between parent and child from the very beginning of a human being's existence.

The simple fact is that people are born with an exquisite capacity to respond to feelings of the individuals to whom they relate. This is never as true as with infants and is especially true of the child's response to those people on whom his very life depends. Indeed, most of us feel that in the first weeks of life the child cannot fully differentiate his nurturing parent from himself and feels his environment as part of himself. If that part of himself (mother) feels good about him, he feels whole, comfortable with himself, and this is the beginning of good self-esteem. If part of himself (mother) is chronically out of touch with his signals and needs, is irritated, etc., then he feels at odds with himself, anxious, and this may well be the earliest origin of poor self-esteem.

The parental influence in determining self-esteem cannot be overestimated. Remember, the child responds more to what the parent feels than to what the parent says. The child can seldom be fooled. How the parents feel about themselves, how they feel about each other, how they feel about the baby is absolutely crucial. Even though she may never consciously verbalize it to herself, the child feels herself as the creative offspring of her parents' union. If that union is "good," she is "good." If it is "bad," she can still feel she is good if her parents feel she is good and if that feeling knowledge is conveyed to her.

Parental influence does not stop in early childhood. It continues for many years—indeed this is one of the great values of family therapy. The intensity of parental influence is particularly strong and long in children whose dependency is inappropriately prolonged. We shall discuss this kind of damage in a later section. The child learns from the parents continuously. More is sometimes learned from example, what the parent does, and often more from what the parents say to each other than what the parent says to the child. But, of course, verbal communication is also vital, especially active conversation in which parent and child are both complete participants. The child also learns from benevolent verbal instruction. Of course, parental influence is augmented by other environmental factors—educational experiences, peer influences, extended family influences, and, in fact, all aspects of the times and places we live in and people we live with. But parental influence is paramount.

To conclude, self-esteem—how we feel about ourselves—affects us in all areas of life. It is a reflection of all of our early experiences, especially how our parents feel about us and how they convey that feeling.

Good self-esteem is the enzyme in whose presence emotional, intellectual, and creative enterprise flourishes. Self-esteem determines degree of sense of ownership of ourselves—the continued feeling that we really do own our own inner assets. This provides for appropriate independence and serves us well in all areas of life.

II
Assets and Liabilities

In this section I will discuss human assets and liabilities. Their importance relative to a basic understanding of our goals will be apparent.

Assets, Constructive Forces, Inner Resources

Assets, constructive forces, and inner resources are in some cases one and the same thing. Sometimes one gives birth to another. Sometimes they overlap and extend each other. An asset may be innate—for example, the ability to see forms and color very acutely. This asset may develop into a constructive force—artistic ability—and may thus become an inner resource. Which is which, how they interact, what we call them has little importance. Of great importance is their capacity to germinate and in large part provide the basic ingredients for intellectual, emotional, and creative development and fruition.

Early ownership (feeling that they are indeed our very own) and development of assets will convert them to inner constructive forces applicable to all areas of life. These inner resources are particularly powerful in the development and nourishing of real self-esteem. Some inner constructive forces are innate. Some are acquired. Self-esteem is an asset and one that is crucial to development and ownership of others, which I believe is acquired. Having innate qualities (good looks, outstanding memory, quick reflexes) in a culture that values those qualities or assets may make self-esteem easier to acquire. But it is acquired. It is not innate. And, however blessed with innate qualities, self-esteem can be destroyed along with innate assets and the possibility of using them from the very beginning of one's life. Some are never heard from or used and are lost forever. There is a host of assets that relate to our earliest history and will be present or missing relative to what happened early in our lives. Some of this history cannot be changed once childhood is over. For example, the death of a parent early on, healthy parents with good longevity, parents who divorced early, etc. In some cases compensatory steps can be taken at various stages of development. For example, parents knowing that geographical stability is an asset as well as a family kept intact will not move a child out of a school and neighborhood if divorce must take place. They have preserved and sustained at least one asset.

I have described many of these assets in other places. There is no area of human behavior in which their role isn't important. But their importance in this frame of reference cannot be overestimated. The child does, after all, give birth to the adult and the adult cannot be understood fully or deeply unless we see him/her as a continuum from birth. These assets and their atrophy or development into available inner constructive forces do in large part explain the outcome of his/her life. Therefore, it is relevant that we describe some important ones here in this particular context. We must not overlook them in children or for that matter in anyone who interests us—including ourselves. Recognizing these assets as assets and cherishing them is crucial to not taking them for granted, to fully owning them and ourselves, to developing and using them, to augment self-esteem, to actualize potential, and to the whole process of *humanization*—getting to know what people and ourselves are really all about.

Let me point out at once—nobody has all of them. To the extent that our parents provided them genetically and environmentally we are fortunate. Chance plays a role, too. Not all of us are born in the United States or in good health. But we all have some of them. Few of us recognize assets for what they are. Many are taken for granted. Many are unused, misused, neglected, and damaged before they can combine into self-strengthening inner resources. In describing one's assets and liabilities or destructive forces, we are really describing a significant part of an individual's early history. This kind of history accounts in large part for the outcome of one's adult emotional, intellectual, and creative life, even though change and growth are always possible. Therefore, understanding what they are in large part tells us what some of the building blocks are that we wish to use in helping our children to realize their potential.

The assets that follow are not arranged in order of importance. All items here are important. All of them interconnect, overlap, and feed each other. Where one has been damaged, this affects others adversely. All of them affect our lives regardless of the degree of our conscious awareness of their existence. But being fully conscious of them is itself a valuable asset.

• *Normal birth and having a history of having been a normal baby physically and psychologically.* This asset is probably taken for granted more than any other. Of course, there are any number of people who transcend physical and even early emotional difficulty. Those whose energies do not have to be used in compensatory ways have a splendid opportunity to develop and make use of the enormous possibilities inherent in having normal physiologies.

The healthy baby's potential for constructive growth throughout its entire life is unparalleled by any other entity on earth. But appropriate nurturing along the way will aid and largely determine the outcome.

• *Physical care.* Under this asset I include parents who provide the basic necessities of life. This includes proper food, shelter, medical care, and protection. This is an entity that may or may not be accompanied by emotional nourishment. These basic necessities cannot be taken for granted in a culture where there is great use of drugs and a proliferation of teenage pregnancy. Teenagers on drugs cannot provide adequate parental care. Lack of proper physical care (let alone abuse of any kind) leads to lifelong emotional scarring, recovery from which requires enormous struggle.

• *Life affirmation and value.* Having been taught early on that the preservation of life is absolutely vital is an enormous asset. Life affirmation as a top priority protects the child and adult from disastrous enterprises involving self and others.

• *Vitality* is an inner resource whose parents are normal

human physiology combined with appropriate physical and emotional nurturing. This constructive force cannot be overestimated in its value in all areas of life. There are a great many people who despite normal physical health seem to lack vitality as well as a zest for living. This is usually the result of hopelessness, depression, cynicism, resignation, and forms of neurosis that can be traced to early life.

• *Curiosity* I believe is a natural characteristic of healthy infants and young children and combines with vitality into one of the most important constructive forces. Curiosity provides motivation to explore, to learn, to observe, and makes us vital and alive even as it feeds vitality.*

  • *Sensitivity and responsibility.* There are some children who are particularly sensitive and responsive to any stimulation they receive. This complements curiosity and can provide considerable impetus to the learning process. *But* these children are also more vulnerable to environmental disorder and trauma of any kind.

  • *Parents who love themselves, each other, and their children* are providing an inner constructive fore that will be unparalleled by any other gift they can give their children. People who lack the experience of being loved in early life find it extremely difficult to feel love in later life either as recipients or givers.

These parents are providing the example of relating on the most constructive level. Even as they relate to themselves with love, their love of each other precludes any contribution to destructive narcissism. In loving themselves and each other they are providing enormous contributions to security, self-esteem, and education in cooperative relating. The messages they convey are that (1) our home is a stable one in which all of us, children included, are cherished and taken care of without possibility of sudden dissolution and destruction; (2) since we think very highly of and feel good about ourselves, each other, and you, it is entirely appropriate that you feel the same about your antecedents and yourself. This is a hallmark of self-esteem.

---

*I shall have much more to say about curiosity as an enabler in section 4.

May I point out in this connection that children of divorced parents will gain immeasurably in self-esteem if their parents do not hate each other. They may not be compatible. Their values and priorities may dictate incompatible desires for different life-styles. They may no longer be infatuated with each other. But hatred for each other and vindictiveness are highly destructive to children who feel themselves as being the product of these divisive forces. Unfortunately, where hatred exists, children inappropriately feel responsible for the divorce and this generates guilt as it contributes to poor self-esteem. "They don't love each other but do they have to hate each other?" is a pertinent question here. Where friendship between parents is sustained regardless of marriage or divorce, self-esteem— the great enzyme in emotional development—will be enhanced in their offspring.

Additionally, the communication and relating characteristic of cooperative relating is exemplified. This includes nonjudgmental, nonmanipulative, mutual acceptance, and respect, regardless of individual differences. It includes learning the lessons of openness, tenderness, intimacy, kindness, and trust, and their consequent rewards and joys. It provides a groundwork for satisfaction derived from each other and other people's attainments in self-realizing creative enterprise. It is a bulwark against many of the destructive forces I shall describe in the next chapter.

• *Parents who recognize children as whole people.* By this I mean having had parents who see their children as being separate from themselves rather than as extensions of themselves.

• *Early history of familial respect for individual differences.* This one speaks for itself. In this one there is little or no pressure for familial conformity. *Differences* are not viewed with alarm or as being abnormal, eccentric, or perverse. Pressure to change can be grievous here. I believe that left-handed children who are pressured into being right-handed are often pressured into other more important personality changes. This kind of thing can result in shaky identities over a lifetime.

• *Consistency and stability.* Early consistency in terms of geography, social contacts, and familial relationships contributes to feelings of inner security so helpful in sustaining interest in one's own involvements and productions.

I went to eight elementary schools. I view this as a liability. I had to make new friends and adjust to new curriculums chronically. This did not make for ease with new adaptations. On the contrary, change of place and position has always regenerated the insecurity I felt then. In fact, I remember feeling quite resigned. "What's the use of making new friends when I would have to leave them soon anyway?"

But the consistency that particularly makes for stability and feelings of security and strong self-identification has little to do with geography. I speak here of a consistent set of values. This means what is and isn't important to a family and the location different issues occupy on a scale of priorities. These include family, friends, fun, intellectual activity, social responsibility, integrity, sex, money, power, prestige, and all other entities we consider important or unimportant as the case may be. Our feelings about these items may exist largely on an unconscious basis but they exert powerful influence on our daily lives.

Consistency in this regard means a relative absence of duplicity, hypocrisy, and favoritism. Values are not juggled around for convenience. They do not change from child to child. They are not subject to manipulation. Values can change. Flexibility is desirable. But there is a vast difference between a prejudicial, hypocritical change and a change due to a genuine struggle with self. Of course, different children are treated differently relative to their ages. *But* treatment is essentially consistent as applied to siblings at the same age level. Where there are differences, they exist relative to need rather than as the result of prejudice or preference.

• *Healthy parents whose own parents were healthy and long-lived* and who treated *their children appropriately*. Genetic longevity and physical health obviously provide time and energy to relate and to create. Long-living parents also provide the possibility of appropriate care for children as long as they need it. Of all the creatures on earth our realistic dependency lasts the longest.

Parents who died early do not always indicate genetic-related poor longevity. There are generations of people who have had short lives because of poor health habits (high fat diets) that have been passed on from generation to generation. Medical science continues to give increasing possibility of transcending poor familial historical backgrounds.

Parents who have a history of relatively good emotional health are invariably a boon to their children. Parental emotional good health is a virtual guarantee of considerable contribution of the same to offspring. This is so because good emotional health includes the ability, desire, and high motivation to care for and to relate to children healthily. These parents often have had the example of constructive parent-child relating in their own lives. These kinds of parents, often traceable through generations in particular families, take their children's assets and their development most seriously and respect their children as separate people, each of whom has individual and unique qualities. In any case, this kind of parental application of their own constructive forces is largely what this book is all about.

• *Having had life-loving, joyful, fun experiences.* Those of us who have early on come from life-affirming households are fortunate indeed. The experience of joy, especially as felt through familial communal living, gives an enormous impetus for optimism, hope, constructive involvements, and continued capacity for joy throughout one's life. The self-esteem that flourishes as a result of this kind of early experience further feeds joy in constructive relating and creative enterprise of all kinds.

• *Early familial history of a combined peaceful atmosphere and emotional freedom.* I have written about this asset in books and magazine columns. I have lectured about it in public lectures and I've stressed it in teaching psychoanalytic students.

A peaceful home atmosphere is helpful indeed to the establishment of inner serenity and feelings of security. This is an atmosphere always derivative of a cooperative group. It is not to be confused with the terrified, frozen silence of a dictatorship. It is further usually characterized by contribution of the various family members of their particular skills and abilities. Unlike sick households, where leadership is often maintained by the sickest and loudest members, here the healthiest people determine policy relative to their experience and ability.

This is the antithesis of the peace at any price philosophy that contributes to lack of expression of feelings and an emotional vacuum.

This is a household in which feelings are appropriately expressed and exchanged without fear of reprisals of any kind. These feelings include love as well as warm anger. Human emotions here are accepted, understood, and the environment is secure and optimistic. This means that everyone feels secure enough about mutual love so that fear of retaliation does not exist. It also means that optimism exists as to the outcome of self-expression. The individual knows that the expression of any kind of feelings will increase good feelings about each other and better communicating and an increased sense of well-being for all concerned. This experiential background is of enormous importance in contributing to adult acceptance of one's own feelings, others' feelings, and their fruitful exchange.

• *The early experience of having had privacy.* This includes having had one's own room, bed, clothes, toys, etc. This contributes to a sense of self-identity, individuality, independence, and self-reliance. This aids the ability to be alone with one's self and not to be overwhelmingly lonely. "When I am with myself I am not alone. I am with a person, *me.*" This is an asset to people who need to be alone to do particular work—writing, painting, rehearsing, etc. Adolescents often exhibit their need for privacy and for their own possessions and friends. This is an appropriate transitional step to the adult world where security of being a separate, whole self is necessary for success in any area. Later on in life it is appropriate to want one's own spouse, children, and place in the world. I will discuss this at greater length as an enabler later on.

• *Gender identification.* Having a well-defined sense of being a boy or a girl from an early age is a great contribution to a general strong sense of self. It also aids considerably in acquiring experience in constructive relating with both sexes.

• *Sexual feelings.* This is evidence of a well-functioning physiology and emotionale on a very important level. Sexual feelings and desires are experienced at different ages in preadolescence in different people. Having a history of these feelings early is an asset. Coupled with the ability to speak openly about them and parental acceptance and appropriate education makes them an even greater asset. This asset contributes to the important linkage of sex and emotional investment—sex and love later on in life.

• *Pleasant appearance, charisma, unusual good looks, and sex appeal.* These are all valuable assets to any child but can be made destructive if preoccupation on this level makes for neglect of other areas. This can contribute to shallow and superficial living as well as considerable narcissism. Some people get to hate their looks as an early source of prejudice against their intellectual ability—"so beautiful she must be dumb."

• *A history of healthy function.* This in kindergarten, grade school, small jobs, anything, contributes to esteem and is particularly valuable in early life. I know one man who still remembers the good feeling engendered by himself in building a simple model boat when he was eight years old.

• *Early sustained friendships* are a source of excellent experience for later life and provide memories of pleasure in exercising the give and take with peers as a child. This is especially valuable in relationships with children of the opposite sex. This makes for ease of relating later on and militates against the feeling that the other gender is alien. It also has the effect of diluting the process of idealization of the opposite sex, exorbitant expectations, and disappointment. These add to self-esteem, so necessary to emotional development and encounters throughout life.

There are some fortunate people whose early friendships continue during their entire lives. These can function as an extended family and may be highly supportive to efforts of any kind.

• *A sense of humor.* This one starts very early and is a remarkable asset indeed, especially if given free reign and supported to full development. I have seen remarkable evidence of this asset in children only two years of age. Their perception, their sensitivity to incongruities and ironies, and their capacity for responsive fun and humorous invention, too, was already in much evidence. A sense of humor as with other assets requires development. These beginnings in childhood grow to fuller and deeper fruition as life experiences increase.

A sense of humor requires high development and use of intellect, emotionale, and creativity in order to grow and to be sustained. But I speak here of the real adult thing in which humor is much more than mechanically repeated lines but is rather the product of spontaneous invention.

A highly developed sense of humor does not disappear even in severe depression. I have seen evidence of it in many people who were for the moment very sick. As a clinician I view this asset as one of the most hopeful prognostic signs. It always indicates a quick and inventive mind and a high ability to make abstractions. It is nearly always evidence of at least some insight about people and an indication of at least some experience of real relating with people. It is often the first aspect of the patient I can use in reaching him or her quickly so as to neutralize a crisis situation. Properly used by therapist and patient, this asset can be lifesaving.

A sense of humor is invariably enormously useful in relating to ourselves, others, and the world generally. It serves as an important form of communication. It makes the most difficult experiences bearable. It increases humility, helping us to take ourselves seriously without pretentious solemnity.

Children in whom this valuable asset was not snuffed out are fortunate indeed. Those in whom it has been fostered and for whom it has flourished are blessed with an extremely vital human inner resource that will serve them well all of their lives. It helps compassion with ourselves and others. Even as we take ourselves and the world seriously, humor helps to reduce solemnity, pretense, affectation, and the pain of realistic difficulties.

• *Intellectual endowment.* Normal intelligence or the inborn ability to learn and develop is, of course, part of being born a healthy baby.

As already indicated, most of us are born with a healthy capacity for intellectual development. The potential is there. Its activation is determined by what happens from the time of birth. We've already discussed this area earlier as well as emotional endowment. But I only want to note here that clinics for pregnant mothers and fathers-to-be that provide therapy—usually group encounters—during pregnancy can serve an enormously constructive purpose. Orientation and information regarding early emotional needs and possibilities for the newborn infant can be very valuable. It can also reduce anxiety in parents that is otherwise transmitted to the newborn, thus making life easier and more fruitful for all concerned.

I have not seen sufficient evidence to indicate that infant intellectual development can be enhanced in the womb by out-loud reading and other activities of the parent-to-be. But I do believe that it is entirely possible that the emotional and physio-logical (actually there is no separation) well-being of the mother during pregnancy will aid the developing fetus. I do not believe that genetic endowment of the developing fetus can be changed. But "just normal" potential is enormous and, again, behavior of parents after birth will largely determine the outcome.

• *Abstraction ability.* I've already talked about this aspect of intellectual ability. This one aids enormously in being able to get to the heart of issues. The ability starts early and seems to be highly related to adequate emotional nourishment. Ab-straction ability is particularly useful in being able to use symbols to aid conceptualization, especially in mathematics, physics, any of the exact sciences, music, and I believe in art, too. So much of art and music is highly symbolic and abstract, and abstraction ability—to be able to connect symbol with feelings—benefits artist and viewer as well as composer, musician, and listener.

• *Memory.* We've discussed this asset earlier. Let me say that this one, too, is highly affected by one's emotional develop-ment and condition. In blocking out much that is painful to us we also cut off much that could be useful to us but can't remember. As emotional blocking is removed, this inner re-source is often resuscitated and made available once again.

• *Orientation.* Some people from a very early age have partic-ular ability to know who, where, and when they are. There are organic conditions where this asset is missing. But one's emotional state of health plays a considerable role here. I have always envied people with a good sense of direction and suspect that too many changes of address as a child destroyed mine. I think that unconsciously I stopped paying attention to where I was since I wouldn't be there very long. In this way I did not exercise this ability and it atrophied.

• *Insight*. I speak here of an ability to understand people
or what I have called in the past "a feeling for psychological
phenomena." There are people who early on have an ability
to understand cause and effect in people. They understand more
about fear, anxiety, defensive arrogance, etc., than other people
do. This ability is often related to the abilities to empathize
and to identify with that I spoke of earlier. This ability, if allowed
and encouraged to develop (unblocked by cynicism, bitterness,
chronic hostility), is extremely useful in personal growth and
all areas of relating. This ability occurs in particularly sensitive,
perceptive, and sometimes introspective children, who often
also have a natural ability to be alone.

• *Imagination*. This asset is helpful in feeling out situations
in ways that give more information than logic. In fantasizing
a situation we can "see" how it would feel. (Of course, this
asset also helps enormously in creative enterprise of any kind.)

• *Early history of appreciation for and interest in beauty,
nature, and mechanical intricacies*. These serve obvious uses
and also increase interest in life on all levels.

• *The ability to articulate thoughts and feelings*. I spoke of
this asset earlier. Some people have an inborn ability here and
some don't. Emotional blocking will destroy it. Training will
aid even those of us who were not born to be particularly
articulate. Verbal expression is seldom regarded as a form of
self-expression and assertion, but it is probably the most important form of all. However much we are emotionally equipped
to assert ourselves, in a complex society the message is poorly
delivered if the expression is poor. Articulation plays an increasing role in accomplishment involving intercourse with other
people.

• *The ability to know right from wrong*. This means having
developed a healthy conscience so as to be able to get along
in society with a good degree of social conscience and appropriate ethical and moral judgment. This includes awareness and
sensitivity to other people's rights as well as a healthy desire
to share "skills," information, energy, and time. This corollary
of empathy makes the relating part of emotional development
a possibility. An impoverished conscience as well as a castigating one makes for highly destructive relating. Rebelliousness

and puritanical conformity can be crippling to self-realization on every level.

• *Integrity.* This is a wonderful asset in two ways. First and most important, this asset, which is born of a solid sense of self, guarantees a continuing strong sense of self. This contributes to taking one's values, thoughts, feelings, and creative ideas seriously. Secondly, integrity makes for healthier and more fruitful relationships and an emotionale unburdened by manipulative rationale of all kinds. Of course, carried to the extreme this asset coupled with a puritanical conscience may lead to the extreme in which perfectionistic demands on self and others kill the possibility of constructive compromise when needed.

• *Stick-to-itiveness and goal direction.* These are assets that some of us learn from our first year on. Some of us never learn how to do it, flit all over the place, and are totally unaware of the value of struggle or patience.

• *An early history and development of associating struggle and goal achievement.* This one speaks for itself. The earlier this begins, often the more fully developed is the asset.

• *The ability to wait.* This inner resource is I believe largely acquired despite the fact that we are born with different temperaments and somewhat different levels of urgency as regards physiological needs.

• *Patience.* The real and deep understanding that evolution of a theory, development of a skill, and that change and growth take time is an enormous gift. Being able to wait feeds the ability to postpone gratification. The postponement of gratification is an absolute necessity for training, fruition of skills, or high achievement of any kind. I will discuss the postponement of gratification at greater length in section 4.

• *Frustration tolerance.* This asset is an extension of the last three and also makes the last three possible. I believe this one, too, is largely acquired and is enormously influenced by early family relationships and experiences. Intellectual fulfillment, emotional fulfillment, and especially creative fruition are invariably accompanied by at least a moderate degree of frustration. The degree of tolerance to frustration will largely determine the ability to see processes through to goal fulfillment. This is true also of all communicating and relating processes between people. Instant understanding is simply not characteristic of the human condition.

• *Anxiety tolerance.* This asset is also largely acquired though some of us are innately more physiologically prone to develop anxiety and less able to tolerate it. Since just about all enterprise involves the generation of at least some anxiety, tolerance level in large part determines degree of stress. When tolerance is good, "chances" can be taken. Where it is poor, relationships, intellectual challenges, and creative activity are often avoided or easily abandoned.

• *Early educational satisfaction.* This experience early on is invaluable in the encouragement it provides for more complex and challenging experiences in later life.

• *The early experience of tranquillity.* This asset is inborn and if developed it is useful all one's life but is often lost as growing up takes place. Tranquillity and inner peace enormously aid the learning process and the necessary ability to concentrate.

• *The capacity for joy.* As indicated earlier, this is one of life's most important inner resources. We have all seen it in action in even the youngest babies. We have also known adults who demonstrate near total loss in this area.

• *A capacity for enthusiasm and excitement.* This resource is part of joy and an extension of it. This one helps sustain interest and involvement in involved, long-term projects as well as aiding the experience of one's own aliveness.

• *Hope and optimism.* These are invaluable inner resources and natural human characteristics. I believe people are naturally hopeful and optimistic. Those who are not have been damaged along the way. Optimism is helpful in any struggle for intellectual and creative achievement.

• *Attention span.* Long attention spans make for ease of concentration and the ability to sustain continuity necessary for completion of complex tasks. Children demonstrate different spans at various ages. But parents can help, hinder, or ignore this important asset. I suspect this one also helps in getting to know someone long and well enough to want to sustain a relationship. This inner resource is a blood brother of the ability to wait, stick-to-itiveness, and frustration tolerance and struggle ability. I shall discuss extension of attention span later on in section 4.

• *Self-assertion and expression.* We are all born with this most obvious asset. Every baby is born expressing himself with his very first scream. In large measure it is an umbrella for all other assets since it represents self, our experiencing of self, and our contribution to other people's experience of our selves. This asset is crippled or enhanced along the way and in large part is the substance of this book.

• *History of variety of interests.* The healthy infant is interested in everything. Interests, nurtured, can produce a multifaceted adult who is never bored or boring. Of course, not all interests can be sustained or developed. To a large degree this is an age of specialization and concentration on particular areas is necessary for fruition to take place. Scattering and lack of focus can lead to superficiality and lack of development of a skill necessary for good economic survival. But lack of nourishment can make for constriction and can lead to dull narrowing and killing of spirit, aliveness, development, fun, and joy.

• *Spontaneity.* This asset is an extension of aliveness and vitality. It exists where we are in touch with our feelings and springs from emotional health. It is the antithesis of impulsivity, which does not come from real feelings. Spontaneity is linked to independence and aids enormously in creative enterprise. We are all born with a capacity to develop the ability to tap our assets and to confront issues with originality and appropriateness as needed. But damage of this valuable resource is quite prevalent and often replaced by compulsive conformity. Impulsive behavior is often an attempt to break through the rigid constraints of conformity.

• *Independence.* We start out dependent but in a healthy atmosphere become appropriately independent as our development proceeds. Disturbances of the process of growing up (emotionally and intellectually) make for more than normal dependency. This *morbid dependency* (normal exchange of services is not morbid) is highly destructive to spontaneity and use of self.

• *Healthy independence.* This simply means the ability to take care of one's self appropriate to age and condition. One of its surest signs is the ability to relate and cooperate with others and to retain one's own values. Independent children can play alone but are not unduly withdrawn or reclusive.

• *Flexibility and accommodation.* These assets are invaluable in activity involving every area of living. These are the antithesis of rigidity and constriction. They make new solutions, points of view, and adaptations possible. Children start out with high potential in this area. No other organism on earth has the adaptational range of people. *But* these inner resources that are part and parcel of the ability to change and grow are in large measure evidence of all-around good health and development. Change and growth are possible whatever our age but are more difficult where excessive damage has stunted our flexibility in childhood.

• *Humility.* This asset is the antithesis of feelings of humiliation, depreciation, and grandiosity, which are feeders of illusions and unreality. Humility is the enzyme that is fed by reality even as it helps us to discern reality. Reality in this context includes our own assets, limitations, and liabilities as well as those of other people and the world and its contents.

This asset is highly vulnerable to the onslaught of some of the most prevalent liabilities in our culture, which I will describe in the next chapter. They include hierarchical striving, glory seeking, sick pride fulfillment, and compulsive competition.

• *Reality as concerns human condition.* This asset is invaluable. It is acquired. The level of its development affects every area of life, especially our mental health. It largely determines the validity of our expectations. Many people I see in treatment as adults require years of education as to what being a person is about. They do not know that all people are good, bad, altruistic, generous, stingy, clear-minded, confused, conflicted, indecisive, decisive, etc.

Exorbitant expectations lead to grievous disappointments, self-hate, and depression. Self-acceptance—including acceptance of all that we are—leads to compassion, awareness, healthy change and growth, and constructive relationships. The combination of self-esteem and understanding what being a real person is really all about provides *self-acceptance,* a mental health asset par excellence and a feeder of intellectual, emotional, and creative development and expression.

In *Overcoming Indecisiveness* I listed some major personal

assets to use as a source of self-confidence. This list and a few extra words make for a good summary of the assets described and provide a few others that have relevance for us. Of course, knowing these assets as assets in ourselves and our children increases our confidence in ourselves and in them. Even the unconscious message they receive from us in this regard enhances self-esteem. To the extent that we can enhance these assets, help them to make use of, and to own them is even more important in our effort here.

—Good physical health, strength, and an abundance of energy.

—Having a family, siblings, and friends—not to be taken for granted.

—Having had caring and responsible parents—as per the discussions in this book, ample security is provided so that energy may be devoted to self-realization rather than to survival. Children who spend their lives warding off danger and laboring to survive have little opportunity for creative development. Of course, we are interested in *special* care that is particularly nourishing to self-realization and that is the basis for discussion in section 4.

—Having had parents who provided a model of mutual love. Invaluable security is provided here.

—Coming from a life-affirming family that had a capacity for joy. This one feeds self-esteem and is I believe a great source of spontaneity and creativity.

—Coming from a family whose members cooperated with each other. The example and exercising of cooperative relating makes it so much easier to actualize this part of emotional development.

—A family background that permitted free expression of emotions.

—Strong gender identification (knowing and feeling like a male or a female). Much here depends on parental acceptance of a boy or girl and liking masculine or feminine characteristics.

—Having sexual feelings.

—A history of productive functioning. This is on any level at any time, including helping in the kitchen, the garden, the family business, etc.

—A pleasant appearance, good looks, or unusual attractiveness.

—A sense of humor.

—Good intellectual endowment. Remember, most of us have more than enough and most of us don't use what we have nearly enough.

—Imagination and creativity. This link here is obvious but will be weak and useless if the child's imagination is treated as a liability rather than as an asset and even a gift.

—Aesthetic appreciation. This wonderful asset flourishes when parents appreciate their child's appreciation of beautiful things. Some very young children have an unusual innate capacity for discerning the most subtle differences between sounds and sights. Some have an uncanny ability for fine movement and demonstrate unusual manual dexterity. All of these flourish when recognized and nourished (through encouragement).

Early evidence of appreciation of beauty, the ability to discern nuances in sound combined with manual dexterity and the free flow of emotionale make for the possibility of becoming a skilled violinist, pianist, etc. Some of these children I believe have an early history of a highly developed sense of touch. Some as babies can't stand to be touched too strongly. There are those of us whose skins are more sensitive than others and who *feel more* through touch and express more through touching. All of us have much more in common than we have apart but we are different in some ways also.

—An early respect for individuality and differences. Nonparental respect of our differences feeds self-rejection. Sensitivity to and appreciation of our individuality feeds self-esteem and self-acceptance.

—Being articulate.

—Stick-to-itiveness and flexibility and accommodation ability.

—Education. This is all-inclusive on any level from learning to ride a bike, to read, to listen to music, etc.

—Homemaking skills.

—Earning power—gold stars, pennies, dollars.

—Good judgment—an umbrella for so much else.

—Teaching ability—often linked to articulateness plus the motivation to help others (to understand and to know) and this is also a form of self-assertion.

—A capacity for new interests. This one is linked to curiosity.

—Strong feelings.

—A capacity for involvement with people, activities, and causes.

—Generosity. The ability to give, to exchange, and to receive graciously applies to toys, to services, and to ideas and advice. This asset is obviously enriching in all of its ramifications.

—Any kind of charm or charisma. Hopefully this is used well and not in the service of getting narcissistic supplies or in mischievous manipulation of people.

—Any talent or special skills.

—Liking people.

—A history of emotional exchange and sexual exchange at an appropriate age.

—Frustration tolerance.

—Anxiety tolerance.

—The ability to be alone.

—Healthy desires and ambitions. These are the antithesis of compulsive drivenness in which one is ruthless to one's self and others and which leads to workaholism and a constricted existence. Healthy desire and ambition help to appropriately apply one's proclivities and assets to the self-realizing process on all levels—intellectual, emotional, creative, and occupational—without sacrificing one for the other—in short, living a full life.

—Occupational fulfillment.

—Being able to discern reality from fiction.

Liabilities, or Destructive Forces

We all have them.

Aside from congenital defects, they are all acquired. We are not born with them. To the extent that they are not fed by the damaging forces we will discuss in the next section we are fortunate indeed. To the extent that they are neutralized we are so much better off. Damaging forces breed and nourish them. Enablers, described in the last section, neutralize and destroy them.

The liabilities destroy assets and block intellectual, emotional, and creative development. Indeed, they often destroy constructive forces before any blossoming takes place at all—killed in the cradle, so to speak.

It is obviously of value to recognize the enemy and so this list describes some of this malevolent army's principal soldiers. As with constructive forces, destructive forces tend to overlap and to feed each other. In many cases they are derivative of each other or give birth to each other. For example, morbid dependency leads to inappropriate claims on the person depended on. When these claims are not fulfilled, bitterness—another liability—is born.

It is extremely important as adults to recognize these forces in ourselves if we are to help our children in this regard. Recognizing them and even changing them prevents visiting liabilities on our children. But recognition must not lead to self-hate, which is always destructive. We need compassion for ourselves and others even as we recognize human liabilities and limitations. Denial of these qualities insures their propagation. Acceptance humanizes us and increases humility and compassion, laying the groundwork for constructive change.

As I've indicated, I do not believe liabilities are inborn. I believe that they are always the result of feelings of depletion, impoverishment, vulnerability, inadequacy, fragility, and all the characteristics we commonly regard as part of the neurotic process. I believe liabilities are reactions to destructive influences found in the immediate environment, especially in the family. I believe they are also imitative and picked up in imitation of relatives from an early age. There are some subcultures in which entire groups have made a societal norm of some of the most destructive forces like aggression and paranoia.

But since these characteristics are acquired and destructive, they can be prevented and can be changed. I believe people veer toward health. Neurosis in any form takes enormous input to sustain a position away from health. For example, it is more natural and easier for us to love than to hate. Hatred takes much input. Believe it or not, malevolent forces require near total dedication. When this is not forthcoming, they can be dislodged because their presence is not natural to begin with and therefore does not have solid footing.

But recognition is mandatory as is motivation. Prevention—very much part of this book—is as in other illnesses invaluable. Habits, however unnatural, are hard to break. To the extent that habits have no time to form, constructive work in this as in other areas is so much easier. Here then are some of the most destructive and most prevalent liabilities:

• *Poor self-esteem.* This one as indicated earlier is fed by all destructive forces and is a crushing and metastatic liability. It spreads all over and feeds all other liabilities as it deprives its victim of the possibility of fulfillment on all scores.

• *Self-hate.* Another malignant force always linked to poor self-esteem but a more active process. I wrote about self-hate and its great neutralizer compassion in the book *Compassion and Self-Hate,* in which I detailed the various forms and effects of both. I recommend that book to adults and teenagers in connection with the work we are doing here.

Poor self-esteem and concomitant anxiety feed the fabrication of compensatory self-idealization, or as Karen Horney put it, start the individual on a search for glory. Falls from self-glorification positions produce self-hate, pushing the individual to further attempts to self-idealize or glorify. Self-hate blocks all assets and is especially destructive to spontaneity and reality about self and others. Exorbitant expectations lead to continuous disappointment, hopelessness, and resignation.

• *Hopelessness.* This liability is acute to start with—strong and short-lived. But if repeated a number of times it soon becomes chronic and very difficult to dislodge. Hopelessness— the feeling that various aspects of self can never be brought together; that satisfaction in any kind of function will never be forthcoming; that parents can never be satisfied; that there is no use in believing in or doing anything; that good feelings about self can never be restored—if they ever existed at all ("I can't remember ever feeling good")—is much more prevalent in children than any of us knew just a few years ago. Hopelessness always detracts from function in all areas and if severe enough can result in complete intellectual and emotional paralysis. When hopelessness results and is part of severe depression, suicide is possible.

This highly destructive liability often starts out on an unconscious level, its first signs being a gradual withdrawal from previous interests and involvements. Even when it is highly in evidence, its causes often remain unconscious. While it is fed by larger, seemingly insoluble world problems and helplessness in these areas—the possibility of nuclear destruction, acid rain, air pollution, etc.—serious hopelessness is almost always due to poor self-esteem—in short, one's destructive relationship with one's self vis-à-vis the world. Unfortunately, children can feel hopeless for years without parental intervention. This is often due to parents who practice denial and can't tolerate the possibility of serious problems existing in their children because of the guilt they would feel with recognition.

Many so-called lazy children are suffering from hopelessness and some of the "laziest" are seriously and dangerously depressed.

• Resignation. This liability is accompanied by at least some degree of hopelessness. This is not an inborn characteristic but it may seem that way. This is so because it can often be traced to early childhood and because it permeates the personality and one's way of relating so thoroughly.

Giving up may not be at once apparent because hopelessness and depression are often not in evidence. Having given up, the individual has protected himself in a "sour grape in advance" manner from symptoms related to anxiety. In effect the victim using this powerful defense against pain says, "Since I don't care anyway, nothing can hurt me." Of course, these people are hurt because self-realization cannot take place without full involvement and commitment.

Resigned people stay away from involvement and commitment because these would be evidence of caring, and caring makes one vulnerable to "failure," "loss," and conflict. To allow one's self to be in conflict is also evidence of caring. One of the purposes of resignation is to prevent the pain of all conflicts (Should I make this choice or that? Should I work toward people liking me or toward mastering them?) by removing one's self. This is done by sustaining the illusion that one can be above it all and having the belief that freedom is more important than anything else. Freedom is the motivating force of what becomes a way of life. Freedom here means freedom from caring, from involvement, from commitment. This kind of chronic surrender makes it virtually impossible to participate sufficiently for real development or satisfaction in any aspect of living to take place.

What the individual is really committed to here is the status quo. Resigned people are almost immovable. They fight to remain in fixed positions and are famous for rigidity. This is not because they feel strongly or highly principled about the stands they've taken. Largely they have not taken stands at all but are in positions (being single, being married, working in a particular job, etc.) because they've drifted into them or have backed into them. Moves are extremely difficult because to move would indicate too much caring. Emotional expression also demonstrates too much caring.

This end-point of "detachment," as Karen Horney called it, is extremely common. We all have it at least to some degree. Those of us who have made it a way of life are extremely sensitive to anything that looks or feels even slightly coercive—internally or externally. These include feelings, interests, advice, ideas, our own or other people's, etc. These "coercive forces" are usually ignored or neutralized by making light or nothing of them.

This defense, like all major character trends (which largely determine how we relate to ourselves and to others), when it is "morbid" (a way of life) can be traced to early childhood. It is, we must remember, a defensive maneuver to avoid emotional pain. Therefore, it is not surprising that resigned people have had a difficult background that motivated them to give up. This is also fed imitatively by a parent or parents who also demonstrated considerable resignation.

Independence is very valuable. But severe detachment* must be thought of as malignant independence that only gives the illusion of independence since it always results in a blow to one's adequacy, thus in actuality making the victim more dependent. The height of resignation is the reclusive person who can't stand anybody's presence. Paradoxically, these people need other people's care and help and are totally dependent.

• *Undue self-effacement, morbid dependency, compliance.* Karen Horney described this character trend in all of her works. I say *this character trend* because these forces always exist together. There are those of us in whom self-effacement is our major way of living. This in itself needn't be destructive. In the case of detachment, reserved people are not sick and often have a great ability to be alone and often demonstrate more than usual integrity. Self-effacing people can be unusually empathic, sympathetic, tuned in, and compassionate. *But* just as detachment gone wild can produce paralyzing resignation, self-effacement in exaggerated form is a major liability. It is also a common one and also starts out as a defense against what are felt as threatening forces in the immediate environment.

In this liability the individual overinvests—*love* as the solution

---

*I would like to point out that our society also promotes detachment. "Don't get invclved." "Every man for himself." "Mind your own business," etc. But society alone cannot account for this manifestation.

to all problems. These people tend to efface themselves and through *love* see the possibility of melding with a stronger self on whom they can depend for directions in all things.

The feeling here is that if they conform and comply with everyone around them, if they are loved by everyone and never make waves, they will be safe. Unfortunately, this effacing or *erasing* of self, as I called it in another book, results in a feeling of weakness and inadequacy. Hence the search for someone to love and to be loved by and to be cared for—morbid dependency.

The inability to say "No!" often gets them into all kinds of complicated difficulties.

The destructive possibilities here abound. The self on all levels (intellectual, emotional, creative) must suffer the consequence of this utter conformity and compliance.

The passivity that ensues guarantees lack of development of emotional expression. Feelings are repressed and are either expressed in surreptitious, devious ways or are, on occasion, explosive and destructive. Anger is frightening because its expression leads to the fear of being "too noticed" as well as possibly incurring the loss of love. The claims on love as the panacea to all problems make for repeated disappointments and still more anger and repression. Martyrdom and feelings of not being appreciated for uncalled-for self-sacrifice and feelings of abuse abound. This guarantees disturbed relating and more emotional difficulty. The self-effacing person tends to be sneakily aggressive (passive-aggressive) because the overt show of anger would jeopardize the need to be loved at all costs. Passive aggression is insidious and hard to strike back at and creates frustration, which is a prime relationship destroyer. Of course, dependent people are great guilt producers and very possessive (I'll talk about this liability a little later on) and these are highly destructive to relationships.

Of course, spontaneity is lost since conformity in order to be liked destroys interest in one's own values and feelings. "Whatever you want to do is all right with me." Compulsive conformity and compliance sometimes lead to compulsive rebelliousness, but this, too, is the antithesis of using one's own feelings, thoughts, and values in issues. Since self-assertion is taboo because it may be at variance with someone who will withdraw love, creativity, which is a self-assertive process, is neglected and often destroyed. To be loved by everyone is the impossible goal here. Popularity is the name of the game. Too often, this is fed by both parents (and media), who also believe that this paves the way for safety. In actuality, this is a killer of individuality and produces the equally destructive self-illusion of helplessness.

In any case, it would be correct to see this extremely prevalent and important liability—liking, loving, and desire to be loved—turned into an exaggerated and malignant need and concept about love. Likewise, normal interdependency (we all depend on each other and trade skills and services) is converted into morbid dependency.

• *Malignant expansiveness.* This again is one of Karen Horney's principal character trends gone wild. She describes these aspects of character types brilliantly in her theoretical books. This one may be viewed as exaggerated self-assertion. The victim here as in the above (the self-effacer rationalizes his/her effacement as a generous caring about others) sees him/herself as a benevolent enabler. Actually, he/she is at best a benevolent despot.

Self-aggrandizement and mastery is the name of the game here and mastery is seen as the way to be safe and to attain glory (the opposite of the self-effacer, though of course all three trends exist in all of us to some degree—to the extent that we are conflicted between self-effacement and expansiveness we may be so anxious as to unconsciously choose resignation as a way out).

Exaggerated mastery also brings with it some strange bedfellows, all liabilities, such as a high degree of narcissism, perfectionism, arrogance, vindictiveness, and a highly exaggerated notion of one's ability, sometimes to the point of delusions of grandeur. This is the antithesis of the false modesty of the effacer. Admiration and respect are more important here than love.

The victim here sees life only in broad sweeps and therefore has a hard time with detail and steps between goals and development. These people often take on more than they can handle and are unable to complete projects because too many are started. It is difficult for them to develop, let alone to actualize even good ideas. Grandiose impatience is destructive to development on all scores and particularly to disciplines requiring much training. These people can be exploitive and directly pressuring, manipulating, and inundating, and this makes for disturbed relationships. "How come they don't appreciate my help?" often follows an attempt to bomb the other individual into the submissive "right" path.

Expansiveness often accompanies macho confusion and may be related to familial (parental) and cultural role models. Sometimes it is a reaction to self-effacement and is used to cover up strong urges toward dependency.

Exaggerated expansiveness often leads to severe falls from exaggerated versions of self and these produce intense self-hate and depression. Many normally expansive children are "encouraged" by parents toward even more self-assertion—actually, aggression and self-illusion. This makes for poor development of resources and fragility. Real strength rests on reality and real development and not on bogus versions of self and coverups, however fast-talking and convincing an individual may be. Deep down none of us fool ourselves.

• *Hostility.* I am using this term in a special way. By *hostility* I mean anger that is chronically repressed so that the individual is almost always angry whether he/she is conscious of it or not.

In *The Angry Book* I described the many ways that anger is repressed, expressed, and the results. But here I only want to say a few things.

(1) I believe that this liability often comes from an early background of parents who feared anger and who promoted its suppression or from an early background of self-effacement.

(2) Anger will out, and if not expressed appropriately, will be expressed perversely—malicious gossip, psychosomatic disturbances, rage reactions, duplicitous sabotage (telling the person the "truth" about himself at a time of high vulnerability), etc.

(3) When anger is repressed, relationships suffer because messages between people become confused and duplicitous.

(4) The repression of anger always involves the repression

of other emotions, too, especially feelings of love and aliveness—the sensation of "being glad to be alive."

(5) Repressed anger contributes to cynicism and bitterness
and alienation, which I will discuss later.

• *Bitterness and cynicism.* These liabilities occur in all of
us but are especially prevalent early on in repressed and constricted children. They are propagated by cynical parents and
relatively joyless households.

These liabilities rob the individual of richness of experience.
They put drastic limits on what can be potentially accrued
from experiences that are enriching to other people.

These result in an aberrated view of self, other people, and
the world, and have a general impoverishing effect—one important result of which is pessimism.

• *Pessimism.* This liability in analysis is often traceable to
early childhood and a tragic and sustained belief in inevitable
failure. This is often connected to what is felt as an early paucity
of success of any kind. Parents, especially overprotective ones,
often unwittingly promote pessimism as an extension of "keeping them safe." "Nothing ventured, nothing lost"—no risk, but
no success either or the feeling of being in touch, let alone
owning one's assets and abilities.

This treacherous liability has an inhibiting and often paralyzing effect. Believing that the outcome of any would-be enterprise will inevitably be tragic destroys attempts of any kind
and provides a life full of "what could have beens." The effect
of lack of *attempts* guarantees failure even as it robs its victim
of experiences necessary for the developmental exercise of intellect, emotionale, and creative skills.

This liability feeds hopelessness and resignation and contributes to reverberating vicious cycles. Combined with cynicism
and pessimism, relationships are disturbed. Many of these dour
people are simply avoided because their effect is felt to be
unpleasant and sometimes even demoralizing. The combined
destructive effect on the capacity to experience joy can be
crushing to this most valuable asset (joy) as well as to self-
esteem.

• *The need to score vindictive triumphs.* This liability often
accompanies arrogance. To have to "get even," or better than

even, is a way of restoring one's sick pride or putting one's self back to a supposed position of superiority. Much energy is used in these enterprises since the chronic hostility sustained by vindictive people becomes an ever-present preoccupying force.

Vindictive triumph is an excellent distraction from self-development and invariably has a destructive effect on self and on relationships with others. This liability I believe starts very early and very often comes from a highly judgmental household replete with confusions about strength and weakness and failure and success and manliness.

"Don't let anyone ever get away with anything" is the guiding principle, but what is often implicit, too, is "even if it costs you your life." Sometimes a life is literally lost in a vindictive foray or in a pride fight (over a parking space). *But* even where literal death does not take place, the center of gravity of our lives is not within ourselves. It is out there in the hands of the person we must score over. This is so because his action commands our responsive action rather than our behavior coming from an ever-developing value system of our own.

• *Invidiousness.* This liability is a chronic form of vindictive triumph. By invidiousness, I mean *the need to get other people to envy us.* Each time this is accomplished we feel we have scored over the other person. Not until the other person or persons "drop dead from envy" do we feel that what we have attained (possession, accomplishment, position, prestige, marriage, child, etc.) is worthwhile. The other person's envy motivates us here and as such our destiny is again in someone else's hands. This modus operandi is very common and often dictates an entire style of life, utterly removed from real personal development. The condition is often traced to a household of adversaries who were constantly jockeying for superior positions and competing with each other—hardly a setting for constructive creative development.

This liability and the need for triumph are often present with extreme materialism and shallow narcissistic living. It is easy to see how a child in our culture, bombarded by stimuli to possess "things," sees "things" as the easiest route to attain superior positions over friends.

Here, too, the saddest part of this liability is the distraction from development of self and personal values. Cunning becomes a substitute for values and real intellectual and emotional development. Relationships are superficial, adversarial, and antagonistic since other people are seen either as competitors, stepping stones, or ornaments to produce envy. Real caring and emotional investment are scarce in an atmosphere devoted to scoring.

Again, these liabilities, like all other human characteristics, exist in different degrees with different people. To the extent that they exist at all, they are destructive and it does not matter that its victim is or isn't fully conscious of these motivating forces.

Often, where these liabilities utterly dictate lifestyle and behavior, one finds a childhood pattern of deprivation and abuse—supposed or real. In these cases I have been able to trace back to fantasies of vindictive triumph and "making everyone envious and sorry" to very early ages—six or even younger. "Jack, I'm coming back in my convertible Cadillac and then you will be sorry," or "I'm going back to my class reunion and when they see me, my wife, my car (and my bank account) they will drop dead!" The last fantasy combines vindictive triumph and its blood brother, invidiousness.

In extreme cases, life, values, and real priorities take second seat to pride restoration and the need to triumph. These are people who die for their principle, whose only principle is "never let other people take advantage or get ahead." Unfortunately, this kind of self-depleting, self-deadening, self-shrinking process is often too subtle to be picked up easily. But it is extremely prevalent. I have found it especially so in chronic workaholics who were largely unconsciously still "getting even" and "proving themselves" for childhood wrongdoings and deprivations.

In treatment, one of the first evidences of improvement is the relief felt when the patient can let the other guy get ahead and can even be taken advantage of now and then without feeling like a wimp. As health is restored and life itself becomes valuable, "scoring over the next guy" gives way to one's own real priorities and values. This often happens for the first time in adulthood, rather than as part of a continuum from birth, as experienced in healthier households.

• *Projection or externalization.* This liability is often in evidence along with vindictiveness. In this one the child early on develops the habit of seeing his/her own unwanted characteristics in other people. In this way it is always "the other guy" who is to blame, as responsibility for who one is and what one does is abandoned. Here, too, the center of gravity for one's existence so necessary for stability and development is shifted to other people.

Externalization, actually a broader view of projection, is also fed by the inordinate need to be liked (self-effacers) and the compulsive need to be admired and respected (expansive narcissists). What the other person feels and thinks becomes more important than one's own ideas. This is obviously destructive to the serious evaluation of one's own productions. It's *them*— the amorphous, *them* or in some cases actual persons—who become the reason and often are felt as the cause of the outcome of one's life.

• *Paranoia.* This massive liability is an extreme form of projection. It often starts in households that are felt to be very dangerous, hostile, volatile, and unpredictable to the developing child. It can be as mild as undue suspiciousness or as severe as delusional thinking involving beliefs of being hated and of fear of potential attack and of persecution. These are fed by feelings of intense self-hate projected to the would-be attacker who is usually utterly innocent. While we are all at times mildly paranoid, it is fortunate that true paranoia is not that common.

• *Jealousy and envy.* In jealousy, the individual is threatened by the possibility of someone or something being taken away from him/her. In envy there is a desire to have what someone else has and usually the persistent belief that everyone else has more than what the envious person has.

These poisons are intimately connected, come from common roots, and feed each other. The envious person feels that other people are like him and therefore wants what he has, even though he feels severely impoverished. This feeds his jealousy. The jealous person feels a chronic sense of loss, believing in advance that everything he owns will surely be taken from him, thus he envies people who seem to have more than he does.

Jealousy is not related to love. Love rests on mutual trust.

Envy is not based on ambition and healthy desire. Both are born of feelings of inadequacy, fragility, low self-esteem, self-hate, feelings of being undeserving, and on cynicism and bitterness. In many cases they can be traced to households replete with much sibling rivalry, competition, suspicion, pitting children against each other, and favoritism.

Jealousy and envy are extremely destructive to relationships and corrosive to self. These are externalizing devices that divert from central autonomy even as they make for distorted perceptions of self, others, and the world. The enormous energy and time required by these poisons are extremely deleterious to development on any level and in all areas. Both jealousy and envy contribute enormously to feelings of depletion, inadequacy, fragility, and distrust, which sustain the belief that the immediate world is an ever-dangerous, threatening place in which to live. These increase cynicism and hopelessness, making for vicious cycles, which if not interrupted make for continuous disquietude and unhappiness.

Reassurance never works, here or with other such liabilities. Sources of these miseries must be exposed and dealt with. Early childhood prevention is most effective. Later on therapy is necessary, but for this to take place these liabilities must be recognized as being the highly destructive forces they really are.

• *Rigidity, stubborness, and the need always to be right.* This liability—and I classify them as one because they are always together—is often coupled with perfectionism and arrogance.

The effect on development is disastrous because learning here is most difficult. Learning requires openness, flexibility, and humility enough to know there is always much we don't know.

Learning requires the ability and willingness to be wrong and to profit from mistakes as well as other people's experience and expertise—all the antithesis of this serious liability. Of course, relationships suffer from this liability in large measure. Perfectionism and the need always to be right often produce fear of any undertaking in which one may be wrong. The same is true of the need for perfect results. The combination makes for a constricted life, devoid of experiences and wisdom, which makes one's stubborn claims to be right especially inappropriate. This is a disaster to relationships on all levels.

Not surprisingly, this one, too, is derivative of profound feelings of inadequacy and is a response and reaction to basically poor self-esteem.

• *Stinginess.* This liability is often traceable to early feelings of insecurity, inadequacy, and sometimes to actual deprivation—material and emotional. Unfortunately, this liability usually involves emotions as well as money. The victim is tight with feelings and pleasures and often deprives him/herself as well as others. The deleterious effects on development, emotionally and creatively, are abundant and relationships to self and to others suffer.

• *Egocentricity.* Narcissism—self-centeredness—ranges from mild to severe and all of us have at least a little of it. But when narcissism is more than mildly present it is extremely destructive. It leads to grandiosity, sometimes of megalomanic proportions, to isolation, ruthlessness, vast distortions in perception of people and the world, shallowness and superficiality, and always stunts development. This is inevitable when one is robbed of the experience of caring about other people and having normal give-and-take experiences with them.

Narcissism is the result of damage in childhood, a distorted view of self and the world early on, and a dearth of self-esteem. It is never to be confused with real self-interest, which is healthy and never excludes caring about other people.

Selfishness and greed exclude the feelings and needs of others and rob the victim of development in all areas since this can only happen through genuine exchange with other people. Indeed, the most destructive aspect of self-centeredness or selfishness is its isolating effect.

Healthy exchange with other people is the most enriching human process that exists. In "giving" emotionally, intellectually, and creatively we tap, use, and develop our resources in the most constructive and satisfying way. Extreme narcissists are isolated from this experience and are deflected from it by a constant need for a one-way flow of narcissistic supplies. I am reminded of one woman I know who is not narcissistic to the point of autism or psychosis but nevertheless is very self-centered. Her quest for admiration has been endless. Her entire focus has been to get people to tell her she is beautiful. She confuses flattery and admiration with love. Her development, despite much innate intelligence and talent, is stunted because other than this quest for admiration, all else has been blotted out. Her relationships are short-lived because she terminates them as quickly as people lose interest in expressing admiration for her. Actually, she is beautiful, but sadly she does not believe it. No reassurance helps because it doesn't alter her deep-down poor self-esteem, feelings of emptiness (further fed by her superficiality and lack of interest in anything beyond her looks), and her considerable self-hate fed by a sense of isolation. How can she feel other than isolated when real emotional involvement derived from mutual caring is utterly lacking?

• *Paucity of interests.* There are children whose early life is full of interests, including collecting all kinds of things, animals, sports, books, clubs, etc. But some have a history of extreme impoverishment in this area. This often continues into adulthood and is evidence of either very poor environmental opportunity—lack of a rich environment or early evidence of hopelessness, resignation, or even depression. I believe all children have natural curiosity and even the slightest nourishment produces interests. When this is lacking, damage of one or another kind is taking place.

• *Lack of history of:* friendships, cooperative exchanges, sexual feelings, strong feelings, etc. These, as the above indicate, damage. We all suffer some damage. Degree is very important. A history of lack of sexual feelings is often evidence of serious emotional difficulty. A reliable history of absolute lack of masturbation in boys is very often evidence of serious emotional damage often associated with severe repression and deadening of feelings.

• *Addiction.* Included in this liability are substance addictions: food, drugs, alcohol, tobacco, as well as work addiction, sexual addiction, and undue compulsivity in any regard (religious, health preoccupation, etc.). These are destructive in all areas and invariably have both a constricting and depleting effect. More and more, addictions are recognized as often starting at relatively early ages. They are often the result of feelings of inadequacy, repressed anger, and undue anxiety coupled with conformity and compliance. They offer anesthesia as well as diversion from problems that are felt to be hopelessly insoluble. This is true of many psychiatric manifestations (anxiety attacks, phobias, hypochondria, hysteria, etc.), which are largely the result of inability to face facts about one's self and to accept reality. Unfortunately, the addiction, as with other symptoms, presents larger problems than the ones the individual attempts to escape from.

• *Unusual shyness—This is not a "cute" characteristic!* The shy child often grows up to a shy adult and is unhappy, however much the shyness may be rationalized. It is often rationalized as healthy reserve and independence, etc. It is no such thing! It is a manifestation of discomfort in the presence of other people and of fear of awkwardness and a belief in not knowing how to behave. It is usually accompanied by severe self-consciousness born of a sense of uncertainty and low self-esteem rather than grandiosity. The shy person knows he/she is not the center of attention. They are not usually narcissistic. But any attention to them at all is felt painfully even as they want it as much as anyone else and easily feel rejected.

Some people currently believe that shyness is an inborn, genetic, constitutional characteristic. I believe that some children are more sensitive than others from birth. They feel more, perceive more, and react more. But I don't yet feel there is sufficient proof that shyness is inherited.

I have known and worked with a number of shy people and have found the following to be true:

(1) They did not, for whatever reason, feel they were as good as other people. This feeling of inferiority started in very early life and was not treated seriously at the time.

(2) They compensated by withdrawal, much living in the imagination, and becoming *loners* in some cases.

(3) They were angry. Sometimes they were conscious of their anger, sometimes they weren't. They all felt cheated and usually envied other kids and adults who seemed so easy around other people, especially the opposite sex.

(4) They often had exorbitant expectations of themselves. Sometimes they came from families who were essentially asocial and falsely prided themselves as not needing other people and ordinary participations.

(5) They often felt as outsiders and some had a history of much moving from home to home in early life and from school to school.

(6) Some were intellectually gifted and these gifts were not only unappreciated but also served to exclude them from a milieu where "eggheads" were shunned and looked upon as "nerds."

(7) Some never learned or exercised basic activities indulged in by young peers—dancing, bowling, and dating at appropriate ages.

(8) Many felt hopeless and resigned. Shyness is highly destructive as it results in a paucity of experiential enrichment that comes of free exchange with people. Of course, some very shy people have been creatively productive but unhappy nevertheless.

• *Sullenness.* Having what is commonly referred to as a "sour disposition" is, as far as I am concerned, never genetic. Sullenness and reserve have absolutely nothing to do with one another. People who demand gregarious behavior may view less than bubbling-over people as sullen, but this is not the case.

Sullenness is acquired and is the result of unhappiness. Chronic sullenness is often the result of deep unhappiness and combined inability to tap and use one's inner resources as well as frustration in dealing with other people.

A sour disposition signals unhappiness in children as well as adults. Unfortunately, it usually is repulsive as most people view it as potentially contagious. In repelling people it complicates difficulties already present. While popularity is a highly questionable and overrated commodity, we do need people to relate with in order to grow.

• *Possessiveness.* This liability may not overtly appear so but is a form of morbid dependency in which the individual must establish ownership of the other individual in order to feel secure. The possessive person never feels secure. No amount of ownership proof helps because the basic problems of feelings of inadequacy, fragility, and impoverishment must be addressed directly for growth to take place.

Possession usually takes place through the attempt to take over the other individual's life, to give constant direction, to invade privacy constantly, to want to know about every move, thought, feeling of the other person, to live vicariously through the other person, etc. The effect on relationships as well as on one's own mature, independent emotional evolution is disastrous.

Possessiveness not unexpectedly is often seen in tandem with envy and jealousy. As with the other two, possessiveness is never a function of love. It is always the result of emotional stunting, infantilism—lack of adult development and extreme emotional dependency (often a carry-over from the truly dependent child who never made a complete break into being a separate, whole person)—and often the result of severe overprotection, which I will discuss in section 3.

• *Undue ambivalence.* We all have mixed, confused, and conflicting feelings. This is characteristic of the human condition. Indeed, richness of different feelings often leads to creative decisions of great value. *But* undue ambivalence, being chronically torn apart by diametrically opposed internal emotional forces, can be extremely destructive to functions in all areas of life.

Undue ambivalence often leads to unrelenting anxiety and concomitant depression. The individual becomes hopeless, feeling that there is no aspect of her/his life that can be requited or ever completed satisfactorily. The victim feels constantly torn apart, at loose ends, "scattered," and unable to bring integrated forces to focus sufficiently for fruitful function. Inhibition and paralysis to the point of complete indecisiveness leading to avoidance of participation in all areas of self-use is not unusual. This condition, if severe enough, produces resignation, hopelessness, and often eventually leads to a deadening of feelings and even to a paucity of intellectual activity. This self-deadening is a defense mechanism against feeling torn apart. In becoming "issue-free," confronting nothing at all, the victim anesthesizes him/herself against feeling pulled apart.

I believe this kind of liability, existing in various degrees in many of us, can be traced to early childhood. It is, I feel, often the result of ambivalent parents, perfectionistic parents, and exploitive parents. Overinvestment in all issues can often be traced to hysterical parents who invested inappropriate emotion in even the smallest issues. Expectations of perfectionistic, exploitive parents often deliver the message to the child that acceptance and eventually self-acceptance is only possible if all aspects of an issue are satisfied. This makes relinquishing of options in choices that have to be made virtually impossible. The ambivalent child erroneously comes to believe that he/she can have it all and if all cannot be had or achieved, self-rejection follows, as does self-hate. Decisions rest on the ability to surrender options and discarding them in favor of the choice option which becomes the decision. Inability to accept the truth, that prices must be paid, results in indecisiveness, repeated failures, and eventually inability to function on any level commensurate with innate abilities.

The parent who promotes double-bind situations is perhaps the generator of ambivalence par excellence. Given a choice between two or more mutually exclusive options, the parent indicates that only satisfaction of both or more of the options is acceptable. Since this is impossible, the child remains in limbo and tends to inflict this same sadistic maneuver on himself throughout his life.

For example: The parent says, "It would be nice if you stay home but if you do you are acting like a homebody infant. It would be nice if you got out but if you do I will feel that you don't really care about me."

This kind of no-win—damned if you do, damned if you don't—bind is usually a subtly conveyed message that is repeatedly delivered to the child throughout his/her early life. Some parents don't know they do it. But their doing it, as a result of desiring all of their options vis-à-vis the child satisfied, produces disastrous results.

Chronic excessive ambivalence may vary from mild to severe but it is always a serious liability. In severe cases, it accompanies serious emotional disturbances, requiring professional help.

• *Constriction—lack of imagination.* This liability is usually expressed as a lack of vision and too often a lack of insight as well. It is often linked to a liability described earlier—paucity of interests. As with the latter, origin may be traced to an environment lacking in stimulation. But overprotection, fear, clinging to convention, and an overriding need to be liked often play a role. This liability is obviously the antithesis of the goals we are striving for, especially in the area of creativity. Unfortunately, this liability is also an indication of deadened feelings—the result of childhood anxiety related to fear of spontaneity. This may well have as a basis a fear the child has of living in a very insecure and even dangerous environment.

• *Aggressiveness and arrogance are not assets!* Why do I state this emphatically? I do so because in our competitive society aggression and arrogance are often confused with self-assertion and encouraged as desirable virtues in children.

In *self-assertion*, recognition of one's needs and acting accordingly does not occur at other people's expense or detriment. Status is not determined relative to hierarchical standard. This means, I don't feel good because I do better than someone else—usually a so-called friend. My well-being, in self-assertion, does not rest on and receives no nourishment from putting someone else down. In fact, much of the action in self-assertion relative to other people is to use my resources in a positive and constructive way in cooperative tandem with other people rather than against them.

I've already mentioned this liability in discussing malignant expansiveness. In arrogance, idealizing characteristics and qualities are ascribed to one's self (arrogate to one's self) that have little or no basis in fact. Affectations and actions relative to other (lesser) people are assumed accordingly. Arrogance demands special status treatment even though no special status is evident. It is destructive in at least several ways.

(1) It blocks learning and growing because the struggle to grow is felt as a demeaning and unnecessary process to an individual who believes he/she already knows everything.

(2) In making for a distorted view of self it also distorts perception of the world and other people relative to self.

(3) It makes for abrasive behavior and as in narcissism it

is destructive to the sensibilities of other people. The obnoxious behavior that is characteristic produces disturbed relationships.

(4) The distortion of opinions regarding self leads to destructive decisions often based on expertise and strengths that are highly exaggerated or simply not there.

(5) Even as arrogance grows, self-confidence is eroded and self-hate is increased because disastrous consequences of arrogance demoralize the victim as arrogance fails to take the place of real ability and real self-esteem.

Arrogance can often be traced to one or more of the following:

(1) Imitation of an arrogant parent—often of the same gender.

(2) Exaggerated opinions of nonexistent talents and status of the child by parents.

(3) Profound feelings of inadequacy, often the result of overprotection or neglect, leading to severe lack of real self-esteem.

This disastrous liability is always a cover-up of underlying fear—fear of fragility and vulnerability and fear of being found out—that one is lacking in all the areas held important by the victim. This fear is often connected to confused feelings of lack of masculinity in men and femininity in women.

Help for arrogance that has become firmly entrenched past childhood usually is possible only after the victim has "failed" and been disappointed enough times to become depressed. This reaction to "failure" (in business, in marriage, in exams, etc.) disturbs the idealized image of self enough to bring on intense self-hate that cannot be neutralized by further arrogance. The individual is then open to examine and to change the underlying feelings about him/herself.

• *Guilt* is the antithesis of responsibility. Guilt is usually associated with failure to achieve one's idealized, glorified version of one's self. It is destructive to all concerned—parents and children—and especially harmful when used as a manipulative tool. It almost always has an enervating, depleting, paralyzing effect, leading to little or no constructive change.

Taking responsibility for actions and for changes that may be necessary is a mature and constructive dynamic, leading to necessary remedy. Taking responsibility is usually a reality-oriented process and provides a focal point from which necessary action can be taken, using inner resources to facilitate goals that are within human possibility.

• *Untoward or neurotic pride.* We all share this liability, at least to some extent. Pride is used to cover up and to compensate for feelings of fragility. It is used to promote a false picture of ourselves to ourselves and to promote further belief in idealized versions of ourselves. Thus, pride is invested in different aspects of ourselves: pride in mastery (pride in never being helpless or dependent); pride in sexual ability; pride invested in being intellectually superior; in always being loved and loving; in being understanding and supertolerant; in being attractive— universally; in being absolutely honest, etc. The list is as long as all attributes of the human condition as well as some imaginary ones thrown in, too. Pride invested this way is always involved with gross exaggerations and extremes. This means not just being independent but totally independent; totally understanding; totally loving, etc. This obviously leads to great vulnerability since reality will repeatedly confront us with limitations inherent in the human condition.

Thus, pride is constantly hurt and falls from pride leave us feeling self-hating and confused. We often project this self-hate to others, making for destructive relationships. There is further destruction to relationships through arrogance that almost always accompanies sick pride to a lesser or greater extent. I shall discuss this aspect further in section 4 in the chapter on keeping the lines of communication open and breaking pride deadlocks.

But I do want to say here that undue pride puts us in a fragile situation in which we are constantly in danger of being knocked off our perches. It also makes us expend great energy to prove the impossible about ourselves, thus wasting much time and effort otherwise available for real self-growth in a futile quest for self-glorification. It also precludes growth and extension of real self, especially in the areas in which pride is invested. If we are already the smartest, then why educate ourselves further?

In this way pride makes for great resistance to real insight, change, and growth and reduces constructive flexibility and the ability to adapt and accommodate. Pride is further characterized by compulsive behavior in which one must operate within parameters that never threaten pride positions. Thus, new challenges become inappropriately frightening despite delusions of strength and nonexistent flexibility. When big moves away from positions of familiarity are taken, they are often done with destructive impulsivity—foolishly—because this is the only way the prideful person can break out of pride entrapments.

The rigidity and self-delusion accompanying unusual pride destroy humility, which is the source of great strength as well as the nurturer of openness to self-illumination and real growth.

I remember a statement made by Alexander Reid Martin, a late wonderful colleague—"You can't fall far when you are standing on the ground." Humility, the antithesis of pride, permits real exploration because the truth with humility does not hurt—it illuminates.

Unfortunately, we live in a society that constantly tells us to be proud and to be superior. Coupled with a household that does likewise and in which pride-oriented people reign supreme as well as contribute in myriad ways to poor self-esteem, the possibility for exaggerated pride is enormous.

To the extent that a household is healthy and damages—discussed in section 3—are minimal, pride will be minimal also.

• *Lack of conscience.* This is a very serious liability to whatever extent it is present. It can vary in degree from a relative inability to identify with other people and to empathize with them, to not knowing the difference between right and wrong. At its worst, this liability results in sociopathic antisocial behavior without regard for consequences.

Obviously, this liability makes for very disturbed relationships with people and grossly impairs motivation and ability to learn or to develop. Compassion is always lacking in people with this liability—compassion for self and others. This is also true for response to compassion or to any kind of insight or understanding given, which may have small effect or no effect at all.

This liability may be connected to vast overindulgence and overpermissiveness, with no establishment of limits of any kind, as well as upbringing in a highly ruthless, dangerous environment of severe emotional and material deprivation coupled with a high degree of hopelessness and cynicism (all obvious severe liabilities themselves and cripplers of human feelings). Some people feel that lack of conscience can be traced to repression of and reaction to a buried, severely castigating conscience. Other workers feel that sociopathy may have genetic roots and connection to subtle but serious kinds of organic brain damage.

In any case, I believe this is a particular area in which professional expertise must be applied as soon as the condition is revealed. I consider this condition to be even more serious in its consequences to its victims and to the victim's potential victims than frank psychosis—obvious mental illness—which, of course, is itself a blatant severe liability.

Later on in section 4 I discuss my feelings about reward and punishment verus discussion and the imparting of insight. This is the one liability that almost always requires reward-punishment treatment for any kind of inroads to be made. Where this liability exists, setting absolute, immovable limits constitutes the most compassionate treatment for all concerned. Love here means being tough! In this connection I suggest reading the book *Tough Love: How Parents Can Deal with Drug Abuse* by Pauline Neff. But I hasten to add that I do not believe in the book's application—the tough love approach where this liability doesn't exist. Also, tough love must never be used as a rationalization for sadistic or cruel punishment or behavior of any kind.

• *Castigating conscience.* This liability is often linked to perfectionism, chronic guilt feelings, overscrupulous behavior and worries, and an inability to have fun or to experience joy.

This liability can obviously be very damaging in all areas of life. It produces severe inhibition and even paralysis in one's ability to think and often to feel. The individual is often beset by severe compulsive ritualistic behavior, broken only by an occasional impulsive acting out—both of which are highly damaging, leaving no energy or time for what is worthwhile.

This liability is sometimes traceable to severely restrictive, constricted home environments and perfectionistic parents, but it also occurs in children who were given no guidelines at all—severe neglect. These children set up their own internalized guidelines that have become malignantly exaggerated and have

taken over the child completely, leaving little or no freedom
of movement.

In these cases one can often find enormous fear of loss of
impulse control. These people are terrified of "something bad"
in themselves "coming out and taking over." *Bad,* on investigation, usually means angry feelings, and there is often confusion
here about anger and its exaggerated potential for damage. *Bad*
also is often connected to normal sexual feelings as well as
pleasurable feelings. Any feeling of spontaneity is often suppressed out of fear of what might emerge that would destroy
a terribly unrealistic, inhuman, puristic, saintlike version of
one's self.

Where this liability exists, psychotherapy of an analytic kind
can be highly relieving.

• *Overwhelming materialism.* I see this one as a liability because the concentration on things and money to buy more things
often deflects from development in more important areas. The
addiction to having more and more things to show off heightens
narcissism and makes for shallow living. This means that intellectual, emotional, and creative possibilities become secondary
to acquisitiveness. People badly caught in this liability do not
develop well in the area of emotional investment. Things are
more important than either people, ideas, or art. When art
is bought, it is for money value and to show off, rather than
for aesthetic appreciation.

This damage can usually be linked to an environment replete
with materialistic, shallow living and often an immediate community caught in the same bind—children of which recapitulate
it with high fidelity. This liability is especially prevalent in highly
adversarial homes, which I describe in the last chapter of the
next section on "Damages."

In supermaterialism, anything that doesn't immediately connect with money—music, art, beauty, feelings, people, ideas,
etc.—is depreciated and really felt as purposeless, wasteful,
and distracting from the all-important goal of material gain.

Recognition and high motivation and struggle can help, especially if instituted early.

• *Alienation.* As I said elsewhere, alienation from one's feelings or losing touch with one's feelings—deadening one's self—

is the big umbrella liability. All the other liabilities I've described have a deadening effect on us, put us out of touch with our spontaneous selves and assets.

The damaging processes described in the next section always have the effect of blunting our feelings and making feelings and resources less available to ourselves. Let me remind the reader that a big show of feelings, in hysterical outbursts or in families that are chronically overreacting so that anything quickly reaches crisis proportions, is not being in touch with real feelings. Actually, this can be a diversionary escape from feelings and represents much froth with little connection to substance.

Children often start to deaden themselves inadvertently as a response to emotional pain. This removal from feelings is an attempt to avoid the suffering that ensues in the presence of damage.

Alienation, in making our inner resources unavailable or even less available, has deleterious effects on all areas of our lives, intellectually, emotionally, and creatively. It has serious repercussions in the area of relationships.

But the formation of alienation is avoidable and also reversible! As we understand and avoid the growth of liabilities through preventing damages, we avoid the proliferation of alienation. As we apply the practices described in section 4 under "Enablers," we set up a bulwark against the possibility of developing serious alienation.

III
Damages

In this section I want to describe some of the major damaging actions inflicted on children of all ages.

These damages are sometimes blatant and easy to recognize. They are often subtle and parents may not be aware of their existence at all, let alone their destructive effects. In fact, children who suffer as a result of some of these actions may be unable to trace the sources of their difficulties without psychoanalysis years later. Obviously much denial (on the part of parents) and repression (on the part of children) take place. To the extent that parents are not in touch or can't cope with their own liabilities, they tend to foist them on their children.

Damage is often indirect, through an assault on self-esteem and the enhancement of self-hate. Sometimes it is direct in its attack on intellectual, emotional, and creative processes and development. The net effect in either case is the same—generation, growth, and enhancement of liabilities and stunting and diminution of assets and inner resources. The process produces inhibition and paralysis of development.

Unfortunately, damages can be easily learned. This means we tend to pass them on from one generation to the next. It is not unusual for battered children to batter their children. All of us to at least some extent are victims of victims. This is why it is extremely important to recognize these enemies for what they are. Recognition is vital to prevention.

Most of the examples described here are not subtle but that is why I use these so as to make these attacks easier to recognize and to understand. The examples I cite come from real people. Patients and other people have described various damages to me over the years. Some of them come from my own personal history. I don't believe they are unusual. My patients were themselves a good example of the general population in terms of mental health. In describing their lives, there are always some distortions. I'm sure parents could at times effectively explain or even deny some of their actions. But I feel certain that these are mostly accurate. More important, the feelings

90

are valid. This is how the person perceived his life as a child to be and if he felt emotionally battered, the general effect was that of battering, regardless of accuracy of detail.

None of us are exempt. We've all experienced some of them. We've all inflicted some of them. I believe we can all identify with most of them. However subtle, they are damaging. However limited, they will produce limited damage. Of course, much depends on other conditions, too. Dilution by enablers, described in the next section, is crucial. Where beneficial conditions are completely missing, damages become that much more potent in their destructive effect.

To sum up simply—*these are the do-nots!* They can't be avoided all of the time. We are, after all, subject to our own psychologies and problems and act accordingly. *But* with motivation and recognition there are a considerable number of pitfalls we can avoid.

Not surprisingly, it is not unusual to find multiple damages working together and existing in the same household. I have described them separately for the sake of clarification.

Silence

ANABELLE: I did not know how quiet my house was until I began to visit other people's houses—friends you know—when I was maybe seven, eight years old. Maybe older—before I began to really notice. Looking back now, I realize how much I was drawn to other people's houses. Things were so lively. I had a girlfriend, Claire—we were in the eighth grade. She never wanted to come to my house. Now I know why. My parents were nice enough to her. But in her house people talked. Sometimes they argued. My house was quiet. Sometimes I'd wish my parents would have a fight. If they did, I never saw or heard it.

You ask how they felt. I don't know. I think that when they got angry they said even less. Not exactly the silent treatment— but then again maybe it was that way—strong feelings equaled more silence.

Yes, there was some kind of talk in the house. Guess if there had not been I never would have learned how to talk, except I heard my share in other kid's houses like Claire's— where sometimes I spoke, too, but not a lot. In my house the talk was strictly utilitarian. "Pass the salt." "Buy some milk on the way home"—that was the kind of talk. I don't remember any real conversations about important subjects. I guess everyone pretty much kept whatever was on their minds to themselves.

COMMENT: Interestingly, when she started treatment Anabelle

had very little to say and difficulty making associations and expressing feelings, with one exception. She had the fullest reaction and response to the question of communication in her home during her childhood and adolescence. She expressed more feelings and talked more about the lack of expression of feelings, the silence in her childhood, than about anything else.

It became apparent that as an adult she still felt very strongly about the dearth of *feeling talk* in her home and had as a child missed it and craved it very much. She says that she wasn't aware until she visited other people's homes. But I think the vacuum in her house impressed her and certainly affected her long before that. I think that the unconscious effect became crystallized and verbalized when she noted the contrast of her silent home and the speaking and emotionally richer homes of her friends. The hunger was there but what it was she hungered for became apparent later on. When I say emotionally richer, I mean Claire's home was one in which feelings were exchanged. I do not know how strong or weak feelings were in Anabelle's house—no one told.

Anabelle needed treatment. She felt that "much was missing." She needed to find expression for herself as an adult, and eventually she did. Considering the paucity of verbal, emotional expression and exchange in her home, Anabelle did quite well, attesting to the valuable force of alive inner resources. It was her high motivation for self-exploration and growth that brought her to me. Eventually she became a successful editor—dealing in words.

But this particular damage, to whatever extent it exists, is highly destructive. It gives the child no start at all in exercising intellectual and emotional facilities. It makes for awkwardness in this important activity later on. It can be critically stunting and lead to much inner frustration and a deep, chronic sense of deprivation. It delays and often cripples the realization of full potential in the critical areas of emotionale and its expression as well as intellectual function stimulated by communication.

"Silent Treatment" Manipulations

AARON: Do you know what the "silent treatment" is like, especially to a little kid? That's what she used to do. Believe me, my infractions were so minor—what can I say? I mean, how much could a three-, four-year-old kid do that was so damned wrong? But that was her way. She'd stop talking, just like that—all of a sudden—mute. Oh, she took care of my needs—but no words. Would have traded for getting hit, scolded—anything. But this was her way. Reminded her of it recently. She hardly remembered. Denial? I don't think so because she says now, "What was so terrible?" She thinks if she didn't hit out— physically like some other mothers—how bad a thing could she be doing?

I'll tell you—I used to go around in a state of apprehension. Never knew when the sword would fall, when I'd be isolated, cut off by the silent storm. That's how I felt, cut off! When I was a little older, maybe eight or nine, I tried to plead my case. Sometimes I never did find out what I did wrong—so I never got the chance to get it out—clear the air. She just shut down and out and could stay that way a day or two and not say a word. He, my father, hardly said much anyway. So I went around in the dark and even when I had been punished enough (to fill her crazy need), she still did not explain herself or explain how I wronged her. She just went on like nothing at all happened. Pretty damn cruel. I'd never do it to anyone.

How I felt? Terrible! Alone! Abandoned! Scared! I could cry now. I felt cast out—like I was nothing—just worthless

95

garbage. I guess this sounds kind of melodramatic but it was rough and even now—she's an old lady—I find it hard to forgive her.

COMMENT: Aaron describes a sadistic ploy par excellence which is expertly designed to inflict punishment as it contributes to profound feelings of insecurity and worthlessness. Remember, an attack on self-esteem is an attack on intellectual, emotional, and creative potential.

Aaron was a man suffering from a combination of irrational fears or phobias largely fed by a sense of isolation and fragility. These were traceable to the "silent treatment," which was a concretized form and symbolic of a household where communication at best was very poor.

The treatment he describes demonstrates the enormous frustration involved and pain inflicted when a child is not told "what is wrong," much less given an opportunity to express his feelings in the matter. Cutting off *give-and-take*, especially with a child who is still highly dependent, is cruelly stultifying and inflicts incredible pain and damage. The feeling of being "garbage" is easy to understand because it is appropriate to the reality of being emotionally cut off, cast out, and being made into feeling as being nonexistent.

Direct Assault on Self-Esteem: Verbal Abuse

BILL: "You were never any good. You are no good and you will never be any good!" He didn't say it all the time, but he said it enough so that I'm sure I believed it. I still feel that way. Well, not quite like then. But it hasn't gone away completely either. We had any arguments at all and—bang—those same words. I don't know if he really believed it. But he said it and it hurt. I think somewhere along the line he convinced me. In my last two years of high school I kind of gave up. I felt, what was the use? Nothing I did would be any good anyway. How could it be if I wasn't any good? How would it ever be good if I would never be good?

How could you say that to a person—to a kid—to your own kid? How can you feel that you have any right to say something like that? I could kill him now for it—that's how angry I am at him. And at her, too—she used to listen to this and never say a word. Know she was scared. But I find it hard to forgive them—either of them. Yet, my feeling of "what's the use" must have come from more than that—because I can't tell you how hopeless I felt as a kid. Never knew when he would have a fit and hit me with those words. But I went on and here I am. And I'll tell you, I suppose I do forgive them. Still love her. He's gone and I miss him. There were good times, too, and he could be loving. What a temper he had!—and I guess there were hard times. He yelled at her, too. But I was the one he called no good.

COMMENT: Bill is telling it all:

The awful effect of verbal abuse—actually a form of emotional battering—"hit me with those words."

The anxiety generated by the uncertainty of arrival of the next attack.

The anxiety and guilt (even if not mentioned or fully conscious of) generated by conflicting feelings.

Suspiciousness and doubts about good feelings expressed.

Self-corrosive rage generated by feelings of disloyalty expressed by the other parent's (his mother) nonintervention. Concomitant ambivalent feelings leading to repression of anger as well as other feelings.

Resignation and hopelessness generated.

Feelings of worthlessness.

Long-term self-hating effects of being a nonperson, the same as Aaron felt through his mother's silent period attacks.

Bill went on to describe fantasies of vindictive triumphs that he had from childhood and how he was driven to workaholism (and consequent impoverished and disturbed relationships) in a fruitless effort to prove self-worth.

Bill had one advantage. At least this kind of direct assault is readily visible and palpable. Being conscious of it makes some kind of rational defense easier than when attacks are subtle and out of awareness. Later on in treatment it is easier to recall, to relive, to reassess, and sometimes to forgive.

The most valuable aspect of reassessment is to put the assault into proper perspective. This means that Bill knows now that his father was wrong! His own evaluation of himself, based on reality rather than on his father's projected self-hate, is the antithesis of his father's. Damage was done. The clock cannot be turned back. But it is possible to make the present and future better. This is especially true for Bill's children, who will not have to suffer from their father's unresolved conflicts as Bill did when he was a child. This breaking of generational passing on of destructive behavior is of immense constructive consequence to all concerned.

Vicarious Living and Manipulation

BETTY: I was Trilby. He was and still tries to be Svengali. He was the puppeteer, the ventriloquist. You know who I was— the dummy, of course. Funny, hadn't thought about it in years— wonder if there's a connection? When I was very young I loved all kinds of marionettes—these little hand puppets that little kids play with. He manipulated me. I manipulated them.

Anyway, that was the way it was. Privacy was an unknown thing. He had to know everything I did. Mom was interested, too. But him—I think he would have gone out on dates with me if he could. Oh, he was loving and kind but he used this a lot as a kind of tool—in which, because of his goodness— and he was good—he was entitled to have full reports on everything I did—or thought. Always wanted to know what I was thinking, doing, planning.

Used to get such a kick out of any of my accomplishments. When I was admitted to Arista (high-school academic honor society), he bragged about it as if he had done it himself. He was a poor student, you see—a good guy—but he didn't do all that much with his life. I think I was the chosen one— you know, the one who would make it all up and worthwhile— like he really did it himself. Hell of a burden to put on someone. If what I did wasn't so great, I could see his disappointment. Made me feel bad. Was a good father. I think my mother resented it—and me—I think she still does—but she doesn't say anything. Wish he gave her the attention instead of me. Or my kid brother. I think he feels neglected. God—he doesn't know how lucky he's been. He could do his own thing and not feel that someone else was trying to get into his skin.

COMMENT: Vicarious living—living through another person—and manipulation are common forms of sadism. We think of sadism as cruel behavior—the infliction of pain—and indeed this is a form of sadism. But vicarious living is just as destructive and has exactly the same roots as its more obvious brother (or sister?). Both are motivated by feelings of inner deadness and both are attempts to feel—through other people's pain or activities.

Enjoying a child's accomplishments is a healthy and appropriate response and constructive to both child and parent. This kind of response is encouraging to the child and is a way of demonstrating caring. But Betty describes something of a different quality and degree. She describes a virtual takeover—an exploitation for the purpose of extending one's self through domination and direction. This kind of sadism ignores the victim's own needs, development, and desires. It runs roughshod over the victim's own proclivities as it seeks to satisfy the exploiter's appetites. Betty describes a blatant and somewhat extreme case (I've known even more extreme ones going on with couples who live—or are they dying?—together), but to whatever extent vicarious living takes place, it is destructive.

I believe it is worth mentioning here any number of young boys who are exploited by fathers who feel they fave failed as athletes in their own youths. These children are exploited by their fathers' attempts to have them, through athletic accomplishment, restore the family pride in macho status. "Failures" are often brutally assaulted and embarrassed as self-doubt is generated by disappointed and sexually confused fathers. Quite often the enjoyment of sport and games is destroyed for a lifetime. I have had any number of successful men in treatment who feel self-doubt because they were not outstanding in sports.

This is blatant exploitation and sadism, practiced entirely too often in a population of confused men who do not understand that qualities are human rather than male or female. We hear about the character built on the playing fields and in competitive games. I have seen much damage to self-esteem, ignoring of sensibilities and self-hate generated in perfectly masculine but sensitive boys where illusions about glory were generated on the playing fields.

Not surprisingly, in adult life Betty felt unfulfilled and undefined—"Sometimes I feel I don't know who I am."

Also—no surprise—her relationships with men suffered. Interestingly, she was attracted to men she perceived as "strong" but who were actually manipulative and much like her father except that they were overtly cruel. These relationships were destructive and almost always ended with her suffering from depression.

Betty suffered from considerable detachment and resignation but this was not as serious as her removal from feelings and her chronic identity crisis. These were direct offshoots of her not having any chance at all as a child of "being my own person." She not only lacked privacy and the chance to feel ownership of her self, she also lacked the experience of exercising her own abilities without direction, dilution, and interference from her father, "the puppeteer."

Her detachment is perhaps her powerful reaction to being treated as a possession and extension of her father. Detachment seemingly could guarantee not falling into another puppeteer's hands. But attraction to the familiar position of puppet continued, as evidenced by attraction to other puppeteers.

Analytic work revealed these dynamics to Betty as well as the information that all men are not sadists. It also helped her to find and use her considerable feelings, assets, and talents in her very own behalf. Her struggle, growth, and self-realization continue.

Stolen Childhood

CHARLENE: My parents were kids—literally and emotionally—and they never did grow up. I think this is one of the dangers when teenagers marry. Even if the marriage stays together, they never grow up. My parents never did. From the beginning we were all brothers and sisters and I think they were the youngest of the family. There was never any question who was the oldest. Me! From the second I was born. Those were the words I heard from the beginning. "How grown-up Charlene is." "How reasonable." How I never cried. "How responsible." "A real little lady." All that crap!

Truth is, I never knew how to play with the other kids. As a matter of fact, I never knew how to play. Nobody ever noticed I was unhappy. I didn't want the job. But like they say, "Someone had to do it." I'll tell you, I went from adulthood to adulthood—never knew childhood existed.

They were the ones that went on having fun. You see, they could go out dancing and all because they had me to count on. Unlike other kids, I could stay home alone when I must have been two, three years old. A short time later I was baby-sitting. I did the shopping. I cooked. I balanced bankbooks. Later on I had them on a budget. Oh, they bragged about me, all right. Why shouldn't they? I was the greatest little manager. Believe me, be impossible to hire someone as good.

I got my escape finally, when I made up my mind to go to college. Of course, they never did—never got past high school. No college admits four-year-olds and besides, their ambitions were very limited. How can I describe them? They were—they are adolescents. They and my two brothers and sister are still the same way—trying to rank each other, smart-assing back and forth—real kid stuff.

They had plenty of fights. Of course, you know who the mediator was. My mother used to get hysterical. My father would get scared and sulk. I'd calm her down like a three-year-old having a tantrum and I'd get him to start talking.

Of course, I never got away completely. They still call. I still manage things for them, I suppose. Look—maybe it's my fault, too. Maybe I should let them swim or sink. The other kids made out. I hardly see the boys or my sister. My parents— sometimes they're lovable.

I guess I'm still on the hook. Still can't have fun. Don't know how. They just can't make decisions at all. Who else is going to look out for them? You can't imagine their childish-ness. I think they have normal intelligence—maybe even bright—but they're really so simplistic—innocents, but I resent my missing it all—you know—the being a kid. Have to add something else. I never felt safe. How could we feel safe? Who would look after us—protect us? Other kids? It still lingers on. I still don't feel safe.

COMMENT: The big danger here is a powerful reaction to stolen childhood in infantilizing one's own child and extending his/her own childhood well into adulthood. This produces a child who is exactly like his childish grandparents. The other danger is vicariously living out one's missed childhood through one's own child, thus robbing one's child of both adulthood and self. These are some of my major concerns in treating people with Char-lene's background.

Of course, a good part of Charlene's behavior is fed by her early fear that her parents could not take care of her or them-selves and therefore she had to take over. There is no question, though, of her abilities to take over. Unfortunately, these abili-ties were used to exploit her and to deprive her of the important growing-up phases of life so important to human development.

Use of a child as a mediator is a very destructive form of exploitation. Charlene, feeling very grown-up and dealing with her parents as children, did not suffer from this mediator form of destruction as much as children who feel less grown-up do. Destruction here is largely due to feeling pulled apart, to guilt engendered, and to fear of abandonment by the parent not sided with. It also contributes to duplicity and self-effacement in an effort to please everyone and to have peace at any cost.

Being in charge is all right and useful, especially for a person as competent and experienced as Charlene. But this *good thing* is malignant in her case. Her sense of responsibility is overwhelming as well as her great fear of helplessness. How can it be otherwise? She could not trust her parents to be in charge and now it is difficult for her to trust anyone else. Indeed, delegating even the smallest authority to other people is fraught with difficulty.

Though she made a partial escape through going away to college, she still remains tied to her infantile parents and feels guilty when she strays too far.

Inability to trust, the need for superclose parental ties, and the need to control have made for disturbed relationships. Remedy and change are possible here.

But joy, humor, playfulness, "feeling safe," as she puts it, imagination, and letting go are much more difficult to attain and this terribly exploited woman will never attain full potential in these areas. As a consequence, I feel that self-realization in terms of emotionale and especially in creativity have been damaged irreparably. But again, the prognosis for her own child (her marriage is stormy but she has a child) is much better as she gains increasing insight as regards her problems.

Charlene never learned to relate to peers and to have a good time. At the time of this writing, joy and abandon are still emotions that require much struggle for her.

Overprotection—Infantilization

CHARLES: It's not as if I was an only child. Angela is six years older than I am. But I think we were both worried about to the same degree. Maybe not. Maybe me more. Being the youngest—a boy. Understand they were dying to have a boy. We were made to feel like we were made out of glass. Touch us and we'd break. Look at me—six-foot-three—two hundred sixty pounds. I was always big and strong. They didn't know it. I didn't know it.

Apprehension was the theme song. Where the two of us were concerned—Angela and me—they were apprehensive about everything. She was twenty before she ever dated and when she finally married it couldn't have been to a worse, more uncaring guy.

Okay, back to me. I was their major target area. What I mean is that they must have felt they were living in a war zone and and I was ground zero. I was the one who would be most vulnerable to catastrophes of some kind and had to be protected at all cost. That's how it was—a catastrophe-oriented society. But none of us had any idea about this. I mean, it all came under the heading of "sensible care." We were getting "sensible care," only I was getting an awful lot of it. I always had a weight problem and part of the care program was stuffing me with good food. Probably was good but too much of anything is pretty bad. They had the notion that eating would stave off disease. They also came to believe that I was prone to sinus trouble, sore throats, flu, stomach disorders—

you name it—more than any other kid in a thousand-mile range. Therefore, I couldn't go out if it was too cold or it rained or with anyone who sneezed more than once or, for that matter, anyone who looked like he could get into any kind of trouble. "Safety" was the most important word in their vocabulary—but not with themselves—only Angela and me—mostly me!

What I couldn't do? Let me make a list.

Couldn't see movies that might scare or confuse me.

Couldn't sell magazines like the other kids. This one really hurt. I really wanted to do it. Of course, they saw it as dangerous.

Couldn't watch "silly" TV or listen to "silly" music.

Couldn't eat hot dogs or pizza or sweets, etc., or anything too cold or too hot. Ice cream, okay, if it was at home. God, how I craved these things!

Could play ball but only "safe kinds"—tennis, handball.

Could not go in friends' parents' cars—never knew how safe they drove.

Couldn't cross streets alone until about five years later than any other kids.

Kids went fishing. Not me. Might get a hook in my eye. Truth is, I was the most careful kid in the world and perfectly well coordinated. Guess they just couldn't believe that anyone who came from them could be capable in anything.

Of course, the slightest thing and I was right there in the doctor's office for the day. I remember not telling them when I really felt sick. Of course, my mother went over my homework six different ways, too. God, how embarrassed I was, her still taking me to school for years after the other kids came and went alone. They were always reading about kidnappings and worrying. Who the hell would want me anyway? Anyway, small wonder I see so little of them now.

COMMENT: Overprotection is infantilization and in a way the reverse side of stolen childhood. But it is even more destructive. Charles describes a severe case; however, we must remember that overprotection in any form always has deleterious effects. Sometimes parents who are highly motivated in giving good care err on the side of overprotection rather than to be negligent.

It is easier to rationalize overprotection and to avoid guilt. But overprotection is even more destructive than negligence or overpermissiveness. I should point out that very anxious parents often convey a state of apprehension and lack of confidence in children without resorting to any of the censoring steps taken by Charles's parents. This, too, is deleterious to child development and to the conversion of innate assets into usable inner resources.

Overprotection has, of course, little or nothing to do with the child intrinsically. It is a disease of the parent fostered on the child. Charles puts it well: "They just couldn't believe that anything that came from them could be capable in anything." Severe overprotection may be the result of one parent's direct problem and the other's negligence—not interfering or a folie à deux in which both parents augment each other's irrationalities and displace them to the child.

Of course, these parents are extremely insecure, lacking in confidence, and sometimes even paranoid. Their view of the world is distorted and cynical, and as Charles points out, they are catastrophe-oriented. Some know they are overprotective, some deny it, some don't know at all. Some are perfectionistic and more concerned with their self-image of parenthood than what is actually good parenting. Many in later years cannot understand children's bitterness since they had spent so much time and energy on their children.

Many severely overprotecting parents actually feel intense repressed hostility toward their children because ordinary responsibility has been converted into a monstrous burden and the cause of unrelenting fear of impending catastrophe. In actuality, the child becomes the repository of the parent's self-hate. This is not understood or accepted by the parent, who rationalizes this irrational behavior as a function of deep love. Franklin Delano Roosevelt's and General Douglas MacArthur's mothers moving to houses near their son's colleges to live were not acts of love. They were neurotic, compulsive moves and served to infantilize their sons, who became adequate people despite them.

Another insidious and hidden function of overprotection is the need to stay young oneself. Some parents unconsciously do not want their children to grow up or to leave. They want everyone to retain the status quo so that they, too, will remain young relative to the child and in control.

Charles exhibited many of the complications of overprotection. He felt fragile, lacking in confidence, easily frightened, fearful of growing up, vulnerable, unduly anxious, lacking in self-affirming experiences, hypochondriacal, and suffered from many anxiety attacks. These turned out to be connected to the rage he felt at his parents that he attempted to repress. Despite his anger he wanted still (in his thirties) to be a "good boy" and each time his anger surfaced, it was converted to acute anxiety.

Charles came to me mainly because of his obesity. He was sixty pounds overweight. He had been down from two-ninety to two hundred and had gained back sixty pounds and felt he was out of control. I felt that his obesity was connected to (1) the habit of overeating established by parental stuffing, (2) rebelliousness due to the prohibition of certain foods that he ate in plenitude once he left home, (3) anger (followed by guilt for being angry and for going against childhood food prohibitions) that resulted in eating binges that were equivalent rage reactions or temper tantrums, and (4) eating sweets to make up for lack of sweetness in his life. His relationships were disturbed and confused. He wanted and hated feminine attention at the same time. Most important of all was (5) his feeling of insubstantiality. Overeating was an attempt to compensate by taking in food and adding substance to himself.

But the more damaging results here and in other cases were more subtle. Overprotection destroys the possibility of full development of self on all levels. It is inundating, constricting, and stifling. It blocks normal exercise of assets, preventing their development into usable inner resources. It extends one's infancy and dependency way beyond the borders of necessity, resulting in atrophy of self on an intellectual, emotional, and creative level. It makes for confused and complex relationships. The victim craves mothering and independence at the same time and can be painfully overpossessive and hateful. Just as the crippled person needs and hates his crutch, which is a reminder of his infirmity, the dependent person hates his bene-factor, who connects him to his infirmity.

Mostly it provides a lifetime of poor self-esteem. If the parent has no confidence in the child as a separate, whole person, how can the child have confidence? In this regard, perhaps the greatest of damage done to the child is, namely, lack of a sense of being a self, a person, a whole, capable person; instead the child feels like a parasitic appendage. Charles in fairly typical fashion looked for a woman who would mother him much as his mother did, but each time he found one, he'd hate her for being "just like my mother." He obviously suffered from great inner conflict between morbid dependency and being the good boy and detachment—being the free boy.

From my point of view, overprotection is perhaps the greatest robber of them all. It is *the* big exploiter. The child is used as a means of the parent coping with his/her own fragility and fear. In that usage, the very substance of the child is consumed.

Early on, Charles and I both came to realize that his obesity is a serious symptom but that it is a symptom of deeper problems connected to his early life. Charles is a very talented man in many areas. As he's become more interested in the ways he relates to himself and others and makes connections to patterns established in the past, he becomes less interested in weight loss but loses weight. More important, the reclamation of his self has begun and he is beginning to have the courage to use his talent and to establish his own priorities and style in life.

In cases of severe untreated overprotection we sometimes see generations of fragile-feeling people continuing the process to and through their children. But we also see reactions to their own early lives in which great detachment from their children takes place, resulting in overpermissiveness and even ne-glect. Some much-victimized people don't want children at all. They feel too cynical and bitter and weak to take on the burden and they feel it is a burden since they were such burdens as kids. They also do not want children to "suffer the way I did." Charles felt that way. But he is changing his mind.

Guilt-producing Manipulation— Passive Aggression

DAVE: My mother has always been the martyr par excellence. "I live only for you—for the family. You are my whole life." None of us could stand up to it and that includes my father, poor guy. Sometimes in exasperation he'd call her a "joy kill"— really meant "killjoy," but then she had him feel guilty for calling her that. That was the way she got us to do or not to do whatever it is she had in mind.

Amazing—the power of this little, passive-looking lady. To the outsider it looked like he was the head of the family. This couldn't be further from the truth. I guess her aggression wasn't always so passive. She was a classical passive-aggressive person—still is. Remember her letting me have some kids over for my birthday party who she didn't like. I was eleven. She always overfed people—very generous with food. But when those kids came to the party, she just about starved them and somehow forgot to buy ice cream. My mother, by the way, is famous for never fogetting anything.

Awful thing is how guilty I felt if I did anything at all for myself. I would always feel that maybe I was being selfish, uncaring. I mean, who could compare to her martyrdom and self-deprivation? I don't remember her ever taking a choice cut or even a full portion at the dinner table. Tell you something—I still have a hell of a problem buying anything for myself. I just have to make sure that Helen and the kids have the

110

same or its equivalent before I can get it for myself. And I know damned well this isn't generosity on my part. I don't need analysis to know this is a hangover from her influence.

I mean, how does a kid fight back? Really can't. My father, who was quite an aggressive guy in the outside world, couldn't. Helen is not a martyr—thank God. But she says that I manipulate with false modesty and crap, and I know she's right.

Self-assertion isn't my strongest point. I know very well I never made the kind of money I should have considering my abilities. I never had the position either. Have to listen to Helen more. Do you think this all comes from early on?—probably does—doesn't everything? But my mother really was and is something else. She personified that woman who supposedly said, "Go ahead, go out, have a good time—don't worry about me. So what if I fall down the steps and break a hip while you're gone." I worried about her plenty. Still do, I guess—when I'm in danger of having a good time, Helen says.

COMMENT: Manipulation through production of guilt is often attributed to Jewish mothers. Neither Jews nor mothers have a monopoly on this particular poison. Every psychotherapist will attest to that. Perhaps one of the reasons this damaging action is so prevalent is because it is easy to do—especially when the child is most vulnerable at an early age and is most dependent on parental goodwill. It is also very effective! Indeed, this form of passive aggression produces desired results (compliance with hidden demands) even as it disarms the victim. To fight back produces inordinate supplies of more and more guilt. How can one fight a parent who says, "I live only for you— you are my whole life"? To bear the burden of being someone's whole life is dreadful enough, but to add guilt to that burden is unbearable. And the guilt added is inevitable when one fights the person who has sacrificed all for you.

Passive aggression is that way. The passive manipulator poses to him/herself as being absolutely free of ulterior motives, let alone aggressive or hostile intent. Their need to be loved and the claims they make based on their martyrdom must maintain the illusion of self-sacrifice both to self and to others, no matter what.

It is interesting how entire families are so bamboozled by these manipulations that they, too, do everything they can to sustain the myth of "the wonderful parent." But the hostility that is engendered but seldom expressed by the martyr's victims is destructive to all concerned. Other feelings also remain stunted. The victim often sustains the same behavior. Relationships are dishonest and disturbed—no one telling how they really feel. Sometimes explosive rages take place that can even result in patricide or matricide—"She was such a wonderful person—just don't know how he could have done it."

I have one patient whose passive aggression and martyred manipulation resulted in the estrangement of her husband and four children. She is just beginning to understand that she always wants to be the perfectly wonderful, self-sacrificing nice guy while she always wants to have her way. The people in her life eventually could no longer tolerate her duplicity. She realizes that she is not that nice. She can't always have her way. She must stop fooling herself and others.

Perhaps the most poignant thing Dave says as far as I'm concerned is the joy-killing aspect of this process. The child actually learns to feel guilty about being happy and must find increasingly difficult stratagems to circumvent this problem. Dave makes sure everyone else has something before he can get it. Guilt about joy is particularly destructive to self-realization. If we get anxious and feel guilty and evil and believe we are doing something bad to a parent when we do something for ourselves, how can we do intellectually, emotionally, or creatively satisfying things? Creativity is, after all, a self-assertive activity and it brings great self-satisfaction and joy.

Small wonder inhibition in this area has, unconsciously for years, kept Dave safe from the possibility of too much professional and economic success.

But Dave is fortunate. He has Helen for a wife and she is the antithesis of his mother. Helen stands up to his mother very effectively, despite Dave's protestations, which are becoming less frequent. Interestingly, his mother has more respect for Helen than for any other member of the family.

Dave came to me because of unhappiness with his lack of work satisfaction. His own memories and free associations are very effective in showing him where it all started and the counterproductivity involved in all areas of his life. Both he and the woman I mentioned whose passive aggression resulted in familial estrangement are struggling and making significant progress. Of course, none of this would have been necessary if their early lives had been different—but we are the victims of victims. I believe Helen and David's children will not suffer from the inhibitions and frustrations, let alone lack of joy, characteristic of so much of their father's life.

Inapropriate Fighting

A few weeks ago I was in a restaurant and at a table next to mine a young couple and their nine- or ten-year-old daughter were having dinner.

A discussion about trivia between father and daughter deteriorated into a fight. The mother never said anything. After a few minutes of disagreement the little girl only said, "I'm sorry—I didn't mean anything," repeatedly. The father was loud enough and so enraged that everyone within five or six tables could hear it all.

What had started out as a light discussion about a trivial, meaningless subject was soon converted into a vindictive harangue on the part of the father. His obvious real concerns were (1) his being right, (2) any questioning of his expertise on any subject, (3) his authority—over his daughter.

It was obvious the little girl was right in her opinions as regarded the subject of the discussion. He knew it. She knew it and I knew it. Obviously suffering from considerable fragility, arbitrary rightness (the need to be right, especially with one's own children), and insufferable pride, he used his authoritative position as a parent to put the child down. He used phony logic in an attempt to confuse her, he used bombast, questions about her questioning his authority, threatening gestures and voice, and finally threats themselves to put her down.

The child was obviously the object of much displaced rage on his part (perhaps how he felt about his own parents or bosses) and suffered the consequences of a totally inappropriate

114

and unfair fight. It was not really a fight at all since a fight consists of some kind of match and this was more like an execution. From the little girl's terror and responses—she cowered into the corner, automatically repeating apologies—and from her mother's mute, white-faced stance, it was obvious this was a many-times-repeated performance. It was also obvious from his threats and the child's physical curling up and terror that she had been physically abused in the past. Fortunately, this was a restaurant.

Obviously the no-fight fight had quickly deteriorated from a discussion of subject matter to a pride-oriented onslaught designed to vilify a helpless victim. I must say that I and several other people at my table and others were sorely tempted to smash this bully or at least have him thrown out of the place— this despite obvious evidence of his own fragility and pain. But I also knew that any action that would cause him further embarrassment or pain would result in dangerous displacement to the child and probably her mother—who looked as if she was already beaten into submission.

The child, at first, before being bullied into submissive apologies, sounded very intelligent. I'm sure she wondered how she had once again stumbled into this lunatic hornet's nest. I am also sure she was on the road to becoming as mute as her mother.

It is obvious what this kind of thing does to self-esteem and self-expression and the kind of rage it generates in the victim, who must suffer repression and its consequences to other emotions. It is also obvious what this does to girls, their trust of boys and men, and their relationships generally. Patients I have had who had been subjected to this kind of sadism unconsciously confused these kinds of men with strength and masculinity. They therefore were attracted to them, formed relationships with them, and hated them and themselves. Some had children and became as mute as the woman in the restaurant when their children were blasted—completing the cycle once again.

The unfair or bad fight or the inappropriate fight, which is really no fight at all, is characterized usually by two conditions: (1) The opponents are often of grossly unequal strengths. This is always true in the case of parent and child. Therefore, this condition (lack of equality) must always be taken into consideration and much noblesse oblige must be practiced by the parent if the fight is to be a "good" or constructive fight. (2) The bad fight has nothing at all to do with subject matter. At best it is a contest of wills, authority, and pride. At worst it is an action designed for vilification and vindictive triumph. Its purpose is to put down the supposed opponent—to victimize him/her, to "make him crawl," as one of my patients described it—to subjugate and to destroy and in so doing to elevate one's self.

Of course, the results are destructive, as I've already described. Chronically applied, real communication becomes impossible. As in all cases of sadism, everyone is demeaned and weakened by the process. Even if there is some kind of perverted macho satisfaction produced, this rapidly disintegrates and leaves a residue of self-hate that cannot be eradicated by rationalization or righteous indignation.

Double-Binding

DANA: First she would urge me to go out with friends, that I was too much of a homebody. Then she would sulk because I was hardly home. She seemed pleased that I was doing so well in school and the next day she would say that I was studying too much. I always had the encouragement from her to get as much schooling as I could but always had the feeling she resented my having more education than she did. She wanted me to get ahead of her and stay behind her at the same time. Damned if you do, damned if you don't. She always did have trouble making up her mind. Thank God Dad wasn't that way. He encouraged me to just go on and do my own thing—no shilly-shallying, up and back, indecisive insanity.

COMMENT: Double-binding parents produce destructive ambivalence, described in the last section as a serious liability. It also produces inhibition, paralysis, indecisiveness, confusion, and guilt. These impede development in all areas. Dana was lucky indeed to enjoy the constructive mitigating force of her father. Some people believe that the enormous ambivalence created by chronic double-binding pressures may contribute to schizophrenia in children. These children feel pulled in two directions at the same time and cannot find which way to go for acceptance and inner peace. This influence applied to feelings of all kinds

117

creates internal divisiveness and splits, preventing integration of self on all levels.

I would like to mention here another very common double-bind effect produced by chronically disagreeing parents. One parent pulls in one direction, the other in another. One says, "You can go to the movies," the other says, "You can't." The child can only please one at a time and is chronically in the wrong, at least with one parent, as he/she is emotionally pulled apart.

I believe that these kinds of double-binding parents suffer from intense ambivalence themselves. They are unwilling to pay a price and want to satisfy all aspects of all issues all of the time. For example, Dana's mother does want Dana to surpass her but does not want to be surpassed. Her double standards and double messages result from springing from one position to the other in the attempt to satisfy both needs, which are mutually exclusive. She does not want to pay the price— namely, sacrificing one satisfaction in order to have the other one. Much of this ambivalence comes from the parents' own inability to resolve inner conflicts as well as gross immaturity and inability to surrender personal desires for the greater good of the child. This springs from considerable narcissism as well as feelings of gross inadequacy.

The goal here, as elsewhere, is to help the victim of this influence to realize that prices must be paid and that hierarchies of priorities must be established for movement to take place. This aids the dilution of ambivalence and the resolution of chronic conflicts fed by the immature and irrational need for total satisfaction of all desires.

Hopefully, as health is restored and paralysis is relieved, greater integration and use of assets can be used to attain self-realization and goals. This kind of progress results in greater satisfaction in all areas of life and less chance of inflicting one's own children with double-bind maneuvers.

Favoritism

ELLEN: There was no question who was the favorite in my family. Me! This is not some kind of distortion or ego trip or wishful thinking of any kind. I certainly wish it was otherwise. Everyone knew it, though my mother sometimes tried to kid herself out of it or even to act otherwise. But she couldn't and still can't.

Hasn't a damn thing to do with my being superior to my brother or sister in any way or to my being the firstborn. It's really quite simple and I think I figured it out when I was about six. I look like her, think and act like her, and I've heard her say this a million times since infancy. So, since she is very self-centered, who should she center on but a facsimile of herself who she sees as *me?* My father dotes on her, too, so he extends his adoration of her to the extension of her—me. And they aren't even subtle. They really say this in a thousand ways. "Ellen this, Ellen that, Ellen the wonderful." And I live up to it. I don't mean I'm wonderful. I mean I have always gone around—Miss Lightfoot—terrified of any kind of misstep.

Of course, my broher and sister can't stand me. They love me—I really believe that. God knows, I love them. Why shouldn't I? They may not resemble my mother as much as I do and they may be lucky in that regard. But I'll tell you— they really are wonderful people. They are even wonderful to my parents, whose favor they keep uselessly seeking. But of course they are angry at my parents and me. How could it be otherwise? In a room full of people my mother still goes

119

on bragging about my wonderful childhood pranks and accomplishments. Never says a word about them. It's boring as hell, embarrassing as hell, and does not do any good to family cohesiveness.

My dad is not a big talker. But would you believe that in between head nodding to indicate agreement with my mother, he throws in a few words about Ellen the prodigy, too? Let me tell you, I was not extraordinary in any way and still am not. But I look like her. Coloring and all. I'm sure that in part I like it—the attention and all—but wish it had been otherwise. Pretty damned sick, and outside my family no one knew I was specially anointed and, as you know, this wasn't easy.

Oh, yes, I told her—gently, you see—had to be careful not to hurt her—or my reputation. But she never listened. To this day I am the love of her life and his, too, I'm afraid. It really is disgusting!

I know it sounds like a strange point of view—I mean, me, the favorite, complaining. Can you imagine the complaints my brother and sister have? It's not that they are not loved. They are. I think in certain ways my father has gone out of his way to make it up to them—sometimes foolishly, even inappropriately, indulgent. But how can you make this kind of thing up? Everyone gets hurt.

Not my mother. I don't even think she feels guilty. I've never noticed any evidence of it. Yet I have to say, we are good friends. We do enjoy each other's company—speak on the phone at least every day. I tell her to call Rob and Jane, too. But her heart really isn't in it. Funny mixed-up business. Guess she can't help herself. But I'm going to help myself.

I'm going to go out of my way to make sure that I don't do this to my kids. I know that nobody, including parents and their children, can or should feel the same way about everyone. After all my psych courses I know that every relationship is different. But that's no reason for favoritism.

I don't think it will happen in my family because, first, I just won't let it and, second, I really don't think I'm as egocentric as Mom. I wonder if she sees me as an individual at all or in loving me she's really loving herself.

COMMENT: Ellen tells it the way it is. Let me summarize a few important points:

(1) Favoritism is not a genetic or natural phenomenon.

(2) I believe favoritism is often due to arrested (adolescent) development in which the best friend exaggeration and fixation is displaced to a child. Displacements of feelings from other relationships—toward Mom, Pop, etc.—may contribute. It may also be a hangover from early childhood days when the child can only handle one friend relationship at a time. Ellen has an excellent point and it may well be due to narcissism and seeing a designated child as most like and an extension of one's self.

(3) Favoritism is destructive to all of the people involved—especially to the favorite, who must live up to the required image. Self-hate and constriction on all levels, especially to individuality, are always in evidence. Parents who practice favoritism are often inadvertently possessive and overprotective. There is usually great hostility, repression, and its consequences by the favorite and lesser siblings, one for being burdened, the others for being neglected and emotionally denied. Resignation and hopelessness are not unusual in the less-favored siblings.

(4) Favoritism contributes to destructive sibling rivalry. I'll have more to say about this in discussing adversarial households.

(5) The favorite may have a very difficult time in nonfamilial relationships where being special no longer pertains. This leads to feeling abused, rejected, and disappointed.

(6) Intimate relationships may suffer deeply as claims are made on the basis of parental idealizations which have no basis in fact (a so-called spoiled child reaction).

(7) Sexual difficulties and confusions may ensue as a result of unresolved feelings toward a parent who in favoring a child was also unwittingly seductive.

(8) Self-esteem suffers as well as a sense of identity due to unrealistic expectations of self and disappointments. The self-esteem of the nonfavored suffers for obvious reasons.

(9) Favoritism is a breeder of jealousy and envy.

Rejection

EDWARD: My mother took care of me. She still does the obligatory things. Calls when I'm sick, comes to graduations, guess she would come to my funeral, too. I know I sound bitter and melodramatic, maybe paranoid, too. But I'm not exaggerating when I tell you the simple truth is she never did and doesn't love me. She is a responsible person and so she does what mothers are required to do. Makes the right motions. But she does not and never did make the right sounds. Would be the strangest thing to hear her say some of the things she has told my sisters, like "I love you."I never heard it from her. I never got a genuine hug from her and praise that I get from her is absolutely wooden and mechanical. I know damned well she never wanted me, never knew what to do with me, and has emotionally rejected me as much as she could and still live with herself.

Sure I've given her a hard time. Yes, she says I'm arrogant and that I put people off and make myself unlovable and all that kind of crap. But it is mostly with her and a response to her. The fact is, I get along okay. I'm twenty-seven. I'm a graduate engineer. I have a good job. I have a girlfriend. Thank God my sisters and my father don't have my mother's problem. I think she has a hard time with men. She and my father have almost nothing to do with each other. And I think her feelings or nonfeelings about me have nothing to do with me on a personal basis, though, God knows, I feel them personally. She must have had a problem long before I came along

122

and it all became focused on me. Would have been great for her if she had only girls.

You see, that hurts too. She's great pals with my sisters. She genuinely loves them and shows it to them in every way possible. I don't think it's because she believes boys shouldn't have affection or any crap like that. She's too smart for that. I think she just doesn't like boys or men. I understand she was very popular. She is very beautiful and very smart. But I don't think she knows how to be a friend to a man.

Do I love her? Yes, I guess I do. I should hate her. Look! I'm not talking about who is the favorite or anything like that. She doesn't like me. She doesn't like my father. If she never saw us again, she wouldn't miss us. In fact, she'd be a lot happier.

My sisters? No, I don't hate them! I guess I envy them. But I don't hate them. In fact, I love them. I think my father loves me. But he's kind of—you know—kind of distant, reserved, keeps to himself, doesn't show his feelings. I think he feels plenty hurt, too. She feels plenty and shows it and can be plenty warm and affectionate. But none of it for us— only for my sisters. Guess I'm lucky. You see, my sisters make up for it. They've always loved me. At least with them I'm someone. More than someone. I'm important. They genuinely love me. Sometimes we have given each other a hard time but not for long. I'm really one of their favorites. This has made me feel good.

I know I can be pretty cool with her. More than cool. I say some pretty mean things. Lately I just have as little to do with her as I can. Believe me, I tried. In a lot of ways I was a superachiever. Small as I am, I made all the teams. I was a great student. I tried and she hardly even noticed. She was never really cruel to me and yet her rejection was and is one hell of a cruelty. She saved her enthusiasm for the girls. The slightest thing on their part was a call for hugs and kisses.

I hear about the affection given to the baby of the family. Not me. From my sisters—yes. From her I am just an afterthought.

COMMENT: Rejection is intimately connected to favoritism but can be considered a more severe form. It is also a form of mutism—chronic emotional mutism in which nothing seems to be received, given, or exchanged and as in mutism reducing its victim to a nonentity status. In this connection, regardless of origin, the effect is always sadistic and its consequences are the same as for those of other victims of sadistic ploys.

Through peculiar circumstances I interviewed Edward's mother and she did in fact reject him, largely due to animosity of complex origin toward men. But he was the unfortunate and blatant victim of her difficulties and responded accordingly. In most cases rejection is not this blatant and may be unconscious to all concerned. But it is destructive. Edward is indeed fortunate that he did (and his mother confirmed this) have his sisters' love and his father's as well. But rejection by either parent is destructive and by both without ameliorative intervening forces is catastrophic.

Edward was in fact very short (short and short-changed) but evidenced many assets, including unusual intelligence and mechanical ability. I wondered about his shortness. The other members of the family were considerably taller than Ed. I wonder still if his short stature is not the result of his mother's rejection. Undue and serious lack of growth has been noted by pediatricians in children who suffered from maternal rejection. These doctors feel that hormonal response is lacking when emotional deprivation takes place early in life. Some describe vast improvement when the child is placed in the hands of an accepting foster mother.

But what about emotional growth? Emotional growth always suffers when any aspect of one's intrinsic self is rejected, especially from infancy on. Edward was fortunate—his father was neutral but at least somewhat accepting, even if not enthusiastically. He seemed to lack enthusiasm in all areas and seems like a resigned person. But Edward's sisters, while they couldn't fulfill the role as well as a caring adult, did at least provide some of the aspects of surrogate maternal acceptance. Additionally, Edward's mother, while being rejecting, at least was not otherwise abusively cruel and did provide the material necessities of life.

Of course, Edward also has the advantage of being born with considerable intellectual potential and talents. But he did and does suffer and, just as he will never attain his full physical stature, damage to his emotional and creative life will never be eradicated. Pitifully, despite attempts to give up the quest, much time and energy are expended in his frustrating, fruitless attempt to show his mother his worth and to get her love. Of course, the only possibility of success in this area would be change and growth in his mother. This requires from her high motivation and years of analytic work.

Let me at this point list some of the damaging aspects of parental rejection on any level, of any aspect of one's self, let alone of one's total rejection.

(1) Rejection of one's self—feeling that something is terribly wrong with one's self and never knowing quite what.

(2) Self-hate and all of its complicating ramifications.

(3) Wasted time and energy in an attempt to live a life that would after all get parental approval.

(4) Search for vindictive triumphs and the self-corrosive effects to compensate for rejection.

(5) Having to fight terrible odds in order to devote energy and time to development of real self and one's own real values.

(6) Disturbed relationships as a result of displacements from past hurts and inability to trust.

(7) Where other constructive forces are missing, there is a good possibility of developing resignation, chronic hopelessness, and severe depression.

(8) In an unconscious effort to embark on an alternative to the above, the child may resort to acting out and antisocial behavior.

(9) Lifelong rage and frustration, making self-realization and happiness impossible.

(10) Rejected children are particularly susceptible to peer pressures. They will often do exceedingly dangerous and self-damaging things in order to be accepted at truly any cost. Carried on into adulthood, they are often the victims of sadists who sense their vulnerability. Compulsive promiscuity is often due to the fear of rejection unless sexual favors are granted, having nothing at all to do with desire or fulfillment.

Incommunicado, or "No One to Talk with or To"

FANNY: I think everyone was busy with their own thing. They acted like they listened but they never heard anything I said. They were, each of them, in their own worlds—she with her friends—he in his business things and sports. I practically told them I was going to do it—kill myself—and I don't think they even heard me. They seemed so shocked when they visited me in the hospital, but even then I think they got into some kind of fight and didn't hear me. I tried to find someone who would really listen. I had one teacher. She got scared and sent me to my guidance counselor. None of it worked. I needed my folks but they were too busy, each going their separate ways or fighting when they were together.

Then after we moved the last time, I really felt hopeless. I kind of gave up. I think they moved as a way of solving their problems with each other. They couldn't understand why I wasn't happy—such a big beautiful room, gorgeous house, and all that. They couldn't understand how I hated going to a new school—how I had to make friends all over again. I had no one at all. I was a total outsider—with the other kids, with teachers, and mostly with them, my parents.

When he walked out, that did it. I didn't know if he would come back. I felt, What's the use, anyway? I wanted out. I couldn't stand it any more. I honest to God felt there was nothing to live for. There was no more fun left in the world—

at least not for me. I was shut out of it all—cut off. Boy, could I have used someone to really let it all out to.

I feel better these days. I stopped pills to feel better. I know I have to depend on me. We talk more and I have some good friends. Besides, the group has helped a lot. We are all outsiders together so I guess we're insiders. We understand each other. We are not cut off. Know something? There were a number of times I tried to tell them how I felt. They didn't listen. They joked me away. They changed the subject. They just did something else. It was no use.

COMMENT: Unlike out-and-out rejection, as with Edward, or favoritism, as with Ellen, the overt elements may not be apparent. Fanny's parents may actually be unconscious of and will deny any but loving feelings. They may even demonstrate evidence of care. But this is a form of rejection—more subtle than that of Edward but more difficult to pinpoint and to fight and clearly more insidious.

Favoritism here is of a peculiar variety in which the parents, due to their own childishness, favor themselves over the child. Unlike Charlene's experience, these parents do not have peer experiences with their child. Therefore, unlike Charlene (where she was one of the kids along with her parents), Fanny is a child apart and isolated from the other children—her parents.

Damage here is obvious. Lack of practice in emotional exchange and verbal use are damaging in themselves. As in silence and rejection, and as I indicated, this is a form of both—poor self-esteem, self-hate, excessive vulnerability, and severe fragility abound. Stunting in all areas takes place.

Sometimes pride is invested in being the outsider. The victim feels that being an equal participant among any peer group is an impossibility. Therefore, he/she "chooses" to be a proud and superior outsider, fooling him/herself into believing in false individuality and superiority. This, of course, is a compensatory mechanism for feeling cut off and rejected. It is counterproductive in that it makes for further isolation, severe loneliness, repressed anger (at the others to whom camaraderie seems to come so easily), chronic feelings of being abused, and lack of satisfaction born of group participation.

Fanny, in addition to having no one with whom to talk, also had the misfortune of having moved at a crucial time in her life and losing what supportive connections she may have had. She was also the victim of immature, narcissistic parents who couldn't hear her because their concentration on themselves permitted no intrusion. Their fighting with each other and even separating at times created further feelings of lack of central focus and connection so desperately needed by this girl.

When attempts to communicate suffering are thwarted, this is usually due to an inability of the parents to accept problems in their children and responsibility for their existence or solution. This is often connected to guilt on the part of the parent as well as an inability to tolerate the anxiety generated by full awareness of the problem. For years these parents often practice denial that the problem exists and are then shocked by its "sudden" emergence.

Fanny perfectly describes the terrible hopelessness characteristic of suicide attempts in young people. Attempts for relief through drugs and alcohol, thwarted attempts to talk to someone, parents who are "too busy," fighting, moving to an unfamiliar neighborhood and school when one is already depressed—these are all commonplace in young people who feel isolated, joyless, and hopeless.

I feel that having someone to talk with—*seriously*—who really *listens* and *cares* is lifesaving. Fanny's group and individual therapy is helping enormously. She is finding out what a worthwhile person she really is—someone worth listening to and talking with.

Incommunicado is not only dangerous—it is always terribly stultifying, even in small doses. In the section on "Enablers" we will discuss the importance of real talk.

Parental Chauvinism

FRANK: Listen, my family had faults, I suppose, but it wasn't all that bad. Actually it was pretty good. My brother was a brilliant student. I was not. But my parents had high hopes for us and supported us all the way. He's doing great as a urologist and I'm finally on my way with this new job.

Without Pop's push I never would have gone to law school. At first I resented it. Wanted to be free, you know—do what I want. But I came to realize that there really wasn't much to do with my freedom if I didn't have interesting work to do. But Lenny—my brother—and my folks kept after me. Not really pushing but discussing my future a lot. They were really quite supportive. Getting into law school was not easy. My father, God bless him, really went to bat for me.

My sisters? One is going with a guy. The other is still dating a lot. They'll both get married—have kids. What's so bad? Look at Mom. I think my mother is happy. She wants the same for the girls. They both went to college. Good students. Actually better than us. The women often are. My father says their passivity makes them better students. I think he's right. What's the point of all that training for them? It's costly and wasteful. They really want a house in the suburbs, anyway. I'll tell you, guys aren't attracted to women who are professionals. Who needs all that conflict? I go out with a woman— I don't want to talk about her professional life. My sisters— I think they're happy. Maybe not. But would being a doctor or a lawyer help? All they really want is a guy—the right guy, of course—someone like Pop, I suppose. Isn't that the way it usually is?

Talk about? I don't know—current things, I suppose—my work—hers, too, but I'll be honest with you—I like a woman to be a good listener. I suppose I sound like a male chauvinist but I'm not different than most. Women's movement and all. Let's be honest. Women want to get married. That's the way it still is. My sisters would feel a lot better if they get good guys. That's what it is all about.

Yes, they get depressed, but it's related to men. Let me tell you, they were always treated real well—clothes, good schools. They will be okay. Anyway, Lenny is doing great and I'm on the right track, too.

COMMENT: Chauvinism, as with all kinds of prejudice—bigotry, and self-inflation—is a form of exploitation and projected self-hate. The chauvinist projects his/her own shortcomings to the *lesser human being* while he extols his own rights and virtues.

The effect is always that of constriction, stunting, and self-delusion.

Male chauvinism, especially derived from a familial prejudice, is particularly damaging. It invariably leads to rejection of all aspects of self seen as feminine or less than masculine. These include feelings and their expression, cooperation rather than competition, creative effort especially in the arts, peace, fellowship, etc. This means cutting off large aspects of self, preventing their development and satisfaction therein derived.

The male chauvinist also cuts off real knowledge of adult reality and relating to women on a fruitful level. His illness pushes him in the direction of sadomasochistic relationships and his view of both women and men is largely distorted. This distortion and confusion is usually transmitted behaviorally from one generation to the next, with consequent damage to all concerned.

I was unable to get a clear picture of Lenny's psychosexual life but I feel certain it is disturbed. Frank turned out to have very poor relationships with women, whom he largely treated with contempt and distrust. I believe his distrust largely comes from the deep-down feeling that male superiority is really a lie and will be found out. This, as in all prejudice, makes for paranoia, which comes from the feeling that the one prejudiced against will find out the truth and will rebel. Predictably, Frank's relationships are short-lived. Women with even minimal self-esteem do not tolerate his arrogance.

Frank's sisters are victims. They have no real vehicles for self-expression. They have been relegated to third-class citizenship and no one has been interested in their real potential on any level. They have been brainwashed into believing that their only prestige can come through a man with whom they must form a dependency relationship. They are used and exploited to sustain their father's mythical belief in male superiority. They are asked to sustain their parent's belief and now Frank's, too, that the best relationship is that between a passive, intellectually, and creatively undeveloped woman and an aggressive, worldly (moneymaking, professionally competent) male.

Everyone in this household is caught in this terribly sadistic, destructive ploy. Everyone is constricted and wasted. The intellectual assets of the women represent a particularly tragic waste.

Frank was not interested in treatment. He came because a girl he liked rejected him, but he was unwilling to view his role in her wise decision. He concluded with, "Maybe I need an Oriental woman or maybe I don't have to settle down for quite some time. Marriage isn't for everyone." My thought was, I hoped if he did marry and have children—boys or girls—he would somehow become depressed enough to acquire motivation to sustain psychotherapy before they were born.

Damned by Faint Praise and Discouraged

When my father read *Jordi,* the first book I wrote, his comment was, "It's all right, but why couldn't it be longer?" This is faint praise indeed, and to a young child it can be devastatingly discouraging. It wasn't to me. I was over thirty. The book had excellent responses. I was in analytic treatment and I was more than just a little aware of my father's responses, their effects, and his motivation, too. I went on to write many more books. But it could have worked out differently. My good fortune lay in the many enabling characteristics of my early family background that neutralized the maladaptive ones.

My father was a chronic faint-praiser. Enthusiasm for projects contemplated or completed was never overwhelming. "It's all right" was relatively high praise. A silent grunt was often the comment. On the other hand, we did have rich discussions about subjects that in no way involved creative effort on my part.

Through analytic treatment I finally gave up the idea of ever really pleasing him. I stopped trying. Pleasing my mother was nice, my sister, too, my wife, other people, and fortunately I learned the great value of pleasing myself. Many small children often don't learn this and can't, because their interpretation of something missing from their accomplishments results in profound discouragement and resignation. They desperately need strong parental approval in order to approve of their own accomplishments. Some, in lieu of becoming resigned, become chronic workaholics, still trying to please and still feeling that something is missing.

What possibly motivated him? What motivates other parents to be so stingy in the praise they hand out? Let me list several possibilities and I believe that they are not mutually exclusive and usually go on unconsciously.

(1) Fear of a child's ascendancy, which will make the parent feel old or less than successful or "all washed-up" or unneeded.

(2) Fear of giving the child a "big head," making him grandiose and arrogant.

(3) Fear of giving the child too big expectations, which may incur disappointment.

(4) Parental cynicism, pessimism, and disappointment in self and the world displaced to the child.

(5) Notions of false modesty and how to promote it.

(6) Fear of angering the gods. This one really belonged to my father and is characteristic of many Jews of my father's generation. Italians call it "warding off the evil eye." If you call too much notice to a good thing, it will be taken from you. Therefore, the less notice the better.

Gender Confusion Exploitation: A Stolen Life

GEORGE: Boss? There was never any question about it in my family. My mother was the boss of all bosses. Not really true, she was the *only* boss! My father mostly wasn't there—a very simple man—a nice guy, I suppose, but I never really got to know him. Worked hard to make a living. When he was home he faded into the background. Don't think I ever heard him raise his voice or, for that matter, I never heard him give an opinion. He was like a boarder in the house, ate his meals, went to bed, went to work.

They never went out together—not ever. At home, when she had friends over—she played cards a lot—he was never included. I don't think I even knew as a kid that couples did things together.

I think she was embarrassed by him—maybe more—ashamed, you know. Thought she married beneath her. Never said it but you could tell. She kept him hidden in the background.

Yes, she was smart. Still is. A very bright lady. Always knew how to run things. Really a good manager. They were married in Europe before they came here. An arranged marriage and I am the result of that arrangement. When he died no one seemed to notice. The insurance money replaced him.

Me? I was, am the apple of her eye. Dressed me in Little Lord Fauntleroy suits. Had a handkerchief pinned to my shirt like a girl. I was the cleanest, neatest, best-dressed, and best-behaved, and probably the most hated and scared kid in the school. But if I came home with a spot on my shirt or tie, she'd have a fit. Never hit me, but boy, she could let you have it with her voice and she never let up. She always had incredible energy.

I was the proverbial sissy of the school. Not my fault. Never occurred to me to play ball or anything like that. If I got dirty or scraped a knee, I'd never hear the end of it.

You know, she could hardly read or write. I did it for her. I did everything for her. She managed and I did it. I was her cook, her maid, her escort, her decorator. And everyone else's, too. She didn't mind lending me out. She traded my work for people's favors, though in all fairness I have to say she was generous with her time and money, too. She was always the first to visit anyone who was sick, to take care of their needs, and so on. But not for my father. She hardly gave him the time of day.

My services? I hung curtains for her friends, picked colors for them. Would you believe it! Even as a kid I had a marvelous color sense and I was always very skillful with my hands. Used to arrange flowers. Go with them—her friends—to buy furniture. Later on, of course, when I started to learn hairdressing, I practiced on them. They got a good deal. A cut that I now get seventy-five dollars for—have to say I am the best—I gave them free. Not because I needed practice. I was a natural at it right from the start. Made her an awful big shot with everyone. Her George who could do anything. Would you believe that I was a gourmet cook? She used to lend me out for that, too. Since I was maybe twelve years old—I could make the most fantastic meals.

No, her friends didn't think of it as strange. Why would they? They all loved me. Still do. Why not? I was always there to do things for them.

No, I never played with their kids. I wasn't like a kid at all. Guess I was strange. Who had time? I was an A student—she'd kill me if I wasn't. Had to study. Really wasn't all that smart. Except in languages. Good at them. More than good. Thought of being a translator but didn't go on to college. When he died, even with the insurance, needed money—cost of living and all that. And right off I made a lot of money. I was so good at it—cutting hair—need an aesthetic sense and I've got it. And the women adore me. I've had plenty of practice with them.

I was always busy. Went everywhere with her. I was her escort—movies, shows, restaurants, even parties at her friends' houses. Then later on we got a car. I drove. She couldn't. She was a big shot with everyone but she needed me. She couldn't be alone. I was the prince consort. Everyone took it for granted. We were a pair.

COMMENT: Fortunately, this degree of exploitation and usurping a life—and this is truly a case of a stolen life—is relatively rare. But it happens, and lesser degrees of this kind of use of a child are not so rare.

George's mother combines high frustration, self-aggrandizement, considerable narcissism, and morbid dependency. She cannot be or do things alone. She needs a usable, malleable partner, and her son is the victim. George's father was too self-effacing, detached, and resigned and probably hopeless and depressed to have any constructive effect. George, of course, was inundated, taken over, and trained for his particular job as surrogate husband and tool for his mother's use.

Our culture is confused and confuses us about so-called male and female characteristics. This often results in a negation and stunting of many aspects of self—in women, self-assertion, expression of anger, use of logic (ridiculously seen as male), athletic talent, aspirations in medicine, law, architecture, engineering; in men, passivity, feelings, such as love, warmth, poetry, art, music, weeping, etc. These are all human characteristics and are only gender-oriented by untoward influences.

George's mother went beyond the cultural pressures. She (1) destroyed the possibility of development of male-oriented characteristics or aspirations, and (2) she destroyed the possibility of development of free individuality. George's background— a seductive, exploitive mother who uses her son as surrogate husband and the presence of a father who is not substantial enough to provide a male model to identify with—is very common in the early history of homosexuals.

George had both homosexual and heterosexual experiences. He was very unhappy with homosexuality, and depression and anxiety connected with confusion and repressed rage at his mother brought him into treatment. He also suffered from all the repercussions of severe overprotection that I discussed in a previous chapter. Of course, George's *life with mother* is an example of sadomasochism in which extreme manipulation and exploitation are the principal sadistic elements.

In treatment, George made considerable progress and at present leads a totally heterosexual life. He is much more self-accepting and enjoys life to a greater extent.

George is a highly talented man and is very successful in his field. Of late he has taken up painting and shows considerable talent as an artist.

With different influences I wonder what his life would have been like. He came to see me when he was thirty-five years old and was still very much in thralldom to his mother. Breaking the insidious connection took about four years. At that time he said he felt reborn but had enormous catching up to do as a separate person whom he knew very little about.

Ignoring Creative Proclivities:
A Stolen Life

GIL: Everyone in my family is gifted—creative, you know. Not just my immediate family—cousins, aunts, uncles—all of them. Sounds grandiose, me saying it right out like that, but it's true. Mostly it's music. We all play musical instruments and most of us have played since childhood. My brother composed music—good stuff—from the age of five. I've played the piano since I can remember. I have two cousins who are gifted writers. My sister is quite an artist.

But there is the family business. You've heard about it. It's a household word. Everyone knows and uses our products. Wasn't always that way. My grandfather and uncles started it. They were immigrants but they had tremendous drive and they had business smarts, too.

You see—we're still a middle-class family. The money didn't change anything. Security—making a living and, for the girls, getting married—these are the things that really count. At least, that's how we've all lived.

The simple fact is that the business has swallowed all of us and I mean all of us, including the husbands of each and every woman in the family, without exception. The business is successful! We all have money! We are all miserable failures!

How? Why? None of us are happy! That's really a laugh. Truth is, we vary from miserable to unhappy. We have a great share of broken marriages, alcoholism, problems—serious

138

ones—with kids, a few suicide attempts—thank God none of us have succeeded—and obviously a fair share of nervous breakdowns. But most of all, it's frustration—frustration and yearning.

Yearning I guess for what could have been. For who we really are. You see, we all know about the talent we had. Most of us took serious lessons, in music mostly and art, too. A few even went to special schools—you know—for gifted children. I took every music course I could. Was a kind of family pride thing that we all shared. But that made it all the more frustrating. Because we knew from the beginning that the big monster was waiting there to get us.

Even as we did creative things and the family bragged about them, the idea of really doing them seriously was ridiculed. "Can't make a living playing music—besides, who is going to carry on the family business?" How many times I heard that in one or another ways.

And, of course, we were spoiled. We all always had more money than any kid should have. How could we chance giving any of it up? We were—are still—middle-class people, after all. The material things are all-important.

Personal progress was never measured by talent or creative possibilities. It was measured by position and salary in the company.

And we all signed on. The devil's pact. For the so-called good life, we gave away our souls. We were too young to know about the price until it was too late. The price—emptiness and yearning and a sense of the really essential things in life missing.

I guess I sound like a spoiled brat. But the sense I have is that I'm living a life that was designed for me instead of its being my own. I don't know what my so-called own would have been like but I know this is not it.

Midlife crisis? Fifty is past midlife—who lives to one hundred? Maybe I mean a midlife crisis or maybe more of an identity crisis. But I'm not happy. You know—it may sound crazy but I'm thinking of leaving the company. Taking piano lessons again makes me happy. But it's a bit too late to concertize.

You are right, of course. It's easier to leave than to have

a place to go. A Gauguin I'm not. I'm not about to rough
it. Have gotten too used to creature comforts and we do live
better than just comfortable. Guess that's how we got into it
all in the first place. Do you know how seductive it is to a
kid? We started with a low salary but by the end of the year
we were somehow already up to fifty thousand a year. And,
of course, the applause in the background—never for music—
always for position, power, and money in the company.

COMMENT: Interesting, how good fortune and great ability can
be perverted and used counterproductively. How wonderful
if the family company could have been used as a patron of
creative aspirations, effort, and life-style. But in Gil's case his
real aspirations, proclivities, desires, and potential development
were set aside and left to wither. This, too, then represents
a form of exploitation as well as a stolen life. Here is a life
stolen by a family colossus that preordained priorities and values
that overrode and crushed individual needs and desires. How
often does this happen in a smaller way, on a more subtle
level? How many of us trade our lives and our real feelings
and desires for the quest for success and glory, as defined con-
ventionally by a culture driven by material needs?

I believe that artists are misplaced and live as displaced persons when they do not live an artistic life-style. Creative proclivities or drives or talents flourish with difficulty in a subculture
devoted to conventional, material gain, and competitive victory.
Imposition and inundation by a value system imposed from
infancy on destroys the possibility of any flowering at all. Creative assets, untended, uninspired, discouraged, and ignored,
do not go away. They become corrosive and burn vast, deep
holes in the emotional well-being of the victim. They leave
active residues of unrequited desires that cannot be fulfilled
by any substitute whatsoever.

Gil may not go on to concertize. But at the time of this
writing I report that his renewed interest in music and music
making has increased his aliveness and satisfaction in life more
than anything else since childhood. This happens despite lack
of living the life of the artist—among other artists and with
the relationships between artwork and viewer, listeners, etc.

It happens because music for Gil is the real thing and even in light doses is more effective than any substitute, synthetic satisfactions.

Interestingly, the entire family prided itself on its artistic abilities but relegated these to a minor position in the scope of things. Here was a family that built a valuable and successful economic machine but the machine—the business—became the leader as well as the servant. As a leader it had a dehumanizing effect and trampled on sensitivities and creative needs. This resulted in feelings of emptiness, loss of self, self-hate, depression, hopelessness, and suicide attempts.

I am pleased that Gil is insistent that his children do not enter the family business. One is interested in medicine and one in being a philosophy professor. Neither seems musically inclined. Gil is one of the few members of his family blessed with a constructive marriage. The others were largely directed by business, financial, and political pressures and did not do well. His wife was highly supportive in his seeking treatment and freedom as well as their children's course away from the "monster."

The Family Myth

HELENE: You once said that reality is sanity's best friend. If that is the case, everyone in my family ought to be in a lunatic asylum.

We were brought up to believe that we were special. I don't mean special in a healthy way—uniquely individual, that kind of thing. We were brought up to feel that we were a kind of royalty. We were snobs, proud of it, and thought—and I still haven't dislodged the feeling—that it was justified. How, I really don't know. Because I can tell you—we were quite ordinary. Maybe even a bit less than ordinary.

The truth is, we lived on the wrong side of the tracks. Our house was pretty messy. Money was always scarce. Dad drove a really old jalopy.

I remember being embarrassed about bringing anyone home. So what did we feel so high and mighty about? It's not that we were gifted in any way or that we sat around listening to great music or discussing important events of the day or were particularly well-read. But we always heard about this-here special thing—my mother—her girls, and so on.

I'll tell you what it did. To this day we have very few friends. To this day no one—especially no man—was ever good enough for me or my sisters. We are all married to very decent guys and we all treat them as if they are much less than we somehow deserved because we are some kind of royalty that married commoners.

My mother is still at it—still turning up her nose. It's crazy—

insane—but being here I feel I ought to tell you about the craziest part of me and my family.

COMMENT: Every family, I believe, establishes an image of itself that more or less conforms with or deviates from reality.

This image I feel profoundly affects the outcome of how a child feels about him/herself and how he/she relates to other people.

To the extent that the image is reality-oriented, especially in terms of real values—family warmth, devotion and caring, mutual cooperation—the individuals are that much better off.

Affectations, exaggerations, and gross misrepresentations invariably have destructive effects. They make for self-identity confusions, false expectations, disappointments and feelings of abuse and lack of appreciation, disturbed and confused relationships, and isolation.

Helene describes her early situation and the established myth and her subsequent lack of marriage satisfaction as well. Her family snobbism and mythology seem to have been a reaction and an effort to erase feelings of social inferiority. Her mother invested pride in being special, superior, and outstanding to compensate for the feeling of being "on the wrong side of the tracks" and as a means of warding off the pain of possible social rejection.

Helene has the possibility of struggling against all the false notions of social superiority and of becoming less of a victim of superconciousness of hierarchical social standing. This makes self-acceptance and acceptance of others—including intimate others (her husband)—a real possibility. It also contributes to a sense of reality and to feelings of substantiality. As affectation is removed, a sense of real self can emerge. This aids the development of real priorities, values, and feelings. These would ordinarily evolve from childhood but were submerged by the deviation of time and energy into substantiating and sustaining the family myth.

I might point out that the myth, in this case widely deviant from reality, contributed to resignation and stagnation on all levels. As long as the family ascribed to their status of royalty, they negated the possibility of struggling to improve their economic conditions, superconsciousness of which made for the myth in the first place.

At this time Helene's mother continues to live life in virtual isolation, especially since she became a widow a few years ago.

Helene, though still a "snob," enjoys being with people more than ever. She entertains at home. She likes her house. Though she continues to be hypercritical of her husband, she knows that he has been a positive force in her life.

Disaster Orientation: Gloom and Doom

HILLY: Take a chance? In my family nobody ever took a chance on anything or anyone. It wasn't exactly pessimism. It was the belief in disaster. Maybe it was because they had, in fact, been in so many disasters before they came to this country. I don't really know. How can I describe how it was?

You know, it was a kind of Addams' family look. Even the furniture was heavy and dark. To this day I can't get enough light. First thing I look at when I go for an apartment is light and everything in it has to be light and bright, too. God, we were always so heavy. We were like a family of moles. No one ever told us to come out of hiding when there was no longer any reason to hide. It was like that.

But it was more than that! There was always a state of apprehension. It was as if we were waiting for some kind of disaster that never happened. We didn't live to go out and get things—have fun—take the usual risks people take. We lived to avoid danger. You know, we never took a plane ride—any of us—until I went to work in publishing. My father invested only in Treasury bonds and government-insured bank accounts, and he still waited for the banks to close and the government to reneg on the insurance. Reminds me of some of the people in publishing who are much more concerned and oriented to not having remainders than to actually selling books.

Amazing that my folks did as well as they did. Captain Caution, but they did very well—financially, that is—though not nearly as well as they might have done. He's really a very gifted man and made out despite himself. But the fun department is something else. They really don't know how. Joy has really escaped them. I don't think they'd be capable of more than just existing, no matter what they'd done.

Of course, they always discouraged me in every way.

No. I wouldn't call it overprotective exactly. I got out in the world fairly early. Thank God.

For example, I could have gone to Music and Art High School. They insisted on a regular academic high school. Later on when I wanted to go to Swarthmore, they pushed for an Ivy League school—Barnard—and they won. When I bought my co-op—which is worth five times now what I paid for it then—they worried about if I lost my job, how I would make mortgage payments.

But I'll tell you something. I fought it. I went my way. You know, I got into treatment on my own and I've done all right. But to this day, when things go well or when I'm having fun, I feel anxious, apprehensive. My sister and brother have not done as well. They're more dependent people. They are subdued, Caspar Milquetoast people. Frankly, I believe they are chronically depressed. But they never got into treatment. They work for Dad.

COMMENT: Hilly is a tribute to human hope and the natural quest for self-realization and joy. She made her way despite the many vicissitudes she suffered—some of which were not unlike those of Charles, who describes the ravages of overprotection. Unfortunately, her brother and sister apparently fell by the wayside. No child is subject to the same environment. Parents change and the presence of other children also changes family emotional dynamics. Of course, genetic attributes are also different for each child.

I suspect that Hilly had an irrepressible vitality as well as many inner assets and much support from her parents, despite their desperately gloomy outlook.

Of course, she still suffers from more than usual anxiety

and apprehension, but she moves toward light and struggles for joy.

We are the victims of victims, and Hilly's parents, who came from persecution in Europe, were traumatized beyond the possibility of total repair. But I must say, I have known of a number of gloom-and-doom households without this history. They are often the result of the union of depressed people who then go on to train children to live the same way. This unfortunately may be true for Hilly's brother and sister, but how wonderful that Hilly broke this disastrous chain. I feel certain that her children will not be subject to joyless apprehensiveness.

From my point of view, joy is what life is all about. I devoted a chapter to the subject in *Compassion and Self-Hate*. Hilly's childhood was spent in a killjoy household par excellence. Additionally, it was disaster-oriented. This kind of atmosphere is usually terribly crippling in all areas and severely inhibiting, preventing experiences necessary for full development.

Hilly's parents are fortunate in that their unusual abilities have made it possible to transcend their enormous handicaps in terms of economic gain and even some self-realization. Sadly, their "success" is a failure in terms of adding to any sense of inner security or experiencing joy.

Doom-and-gloom households are very often resigned households, too—where the belief prevails that nothing can change and that the unhappy status quo is fixed forever.

This resignation and hopelessness is pervasive and contagious and can have a chronic, demoralizing effect on susceptible children.

Getting Attention
the Perverse Way

INNA: I hated being sick but I loved being sick. I hated being in trouble and I loved it. I used to be sorry—I mean when the pain was over. I'd prolong it as long as possible. Still feel that way.

No—wasn't masochism. Never enjoyed pain for pain's sake—not that crazy. But obviously crazy enough.

Remember tearing the ligaments in my leg when I was a kid. I got sympathy. I got hugs. I got kisses. Used a cane for six weeks. Made me special—maybe even heroic.

No! Was not a question of not having to do things—nothing like that. It was the attention—the feeling of being someone. I hated to give up that cane.

Indifferent. That's the word that describes it best. They were indifferent. But when someone was sick, it was like a firecracker went off. They came out of their sleep. They woke up. Not hysterical. Nothing melodramatic, but caring. When anyone they knew went to the hospital, they never failed to visit, bring things. They became tuned in, you see—but it took trouble to do it.

Oh yes, it wasn't just sickness. When I had trouble in school they were concerned, talked to me, wanted to look at the work I was doing—all that. When I got depressed, splitting with a guy I was seeing, same thing—they were all ears, attention, support, caring.

148

When things went well and I gave them no pain, they didn't know I was alive. Don't get the wrong idea—they weren't exactly tuned-in types, but in their kind of cold, removed way, they were and are good people otherwise. Truth is, we never really wanted for anything—except it would have been nice to get nonemergency attention, you see.

COMMENT: When attention and relatedness through good verbal communication is missing, for whatever reason (detachment or preoccupation with occupations, etc.), the child will often make use of and misuse anything on hand that seems "to work."

Inna learned early on that sickness, injury, depression, school problems, and any situation requiring help "worked." These became manipulative tools and to this day she finds it difficult to give them up. She immediately brings to mind several extremely obese patients I have seen over the years who in part could not give up their obesity for the same reason.

Their obesity made them a center of attention, gave them special family status, and however perverse and destructive the mechanism, they could not surrender it. In some of these cases, being "the family fat center of attention" and having certain "privileges" as a result remained largely unconscious. These people were exempt from ordinary chores and responsibilities, as well as from certain social expectations. *But,* of course, the price paid in terms of physical and emotional health was very high indeed.

Inna used sickness and "trouble" as a manipulative tool much as one uses sullenness, conveying a sense of being abused, martyrdom, and the engendering of guilt. They are all destructive!

Concentration on "being sick," making problems, and sustaining problems, blocks and detracts from healthy development and use of self as an adequate, independent person.

Inna found, too, that her manipulation does not work in the business or social world. Other people did not respond like her parents. They did not view her helplessness, real or imagined, as rationale for special privileges. They found Inna to be cloying and annoying and her claims for attention unfounded and even irrational, as so often is the case with children caught in this kind of bind (and this is not an uncommon damage). Inna retaliated through passive-aggressive attacks—coming late, forgetting reports, manipulating boyfriends through being tired or sick, etc. Passive aggression permits hostile retaliatory action without jeopardizing sick, helpless status as self-assertion and overt aggression would.

Inna, interestingly, realized she needed help, when a young man who was quite involved with her said that her never feeling well, her moodiness, her work difficulties, etc., were felt by him as attacks on him and as very sharp, painful weapons. First she cried and called him insensitive and uncaring. After he "split," and he was one of many who did leave despite her considerable physical beauty and intelligence, she thought it over and concluded that something was "very wrong"—and it wasn't with her boyfriends. Prior to this she thought that she just hadn't found the right man or the right job and that people were uncaring.

Inna had to learn that people care. But they care most when positive, constructive, optimistic, giving, cooperative, responsible, adult, helpful, understanding moves are made in their direction.

There is a perversion here. Constructive activity has been perverted. The delusion has been established that constructive development and activity lead to "being taken for granted," "neglect," "feeling like a nobody." Sickness, helplessness, problems, difficulties, and hopelessness have been elevated in the delusion that these ought to be nourished and sustained in order to get attention, prestige, love and status (at work). This perversion and its delusions destroy much of the possibility of full development in all areas, leading to joy through self-realization as well as through fruitful relating with other people.

Inna's recognition on a fully conscious level of what has been happening is extremely helpful. She is struggling to "turn things around." This is not easy and involves much in feeling different about one's self and "taking chances" that other people do, in fact, reacting differently than her parents do.

Of course, in healthier homes, parents are fully conscious

relative to their children much of the time. Children don't have the need to alarm their parents out of inattentive lethargy. Sickness and problems bring appropriate concern and attention. Concern and caring are ever-present and healthy pursuits bring involvement and joyful attention.

Television

Television can be constructive as a recreational, educational, and inspirational instrument. What a wonderful way to convey information and to interest young people in enriching cultural activities—music, dance, drama, the arts, current events, politics, science, behavioral science, and literature, medicine, math—just about all aspects of the human condition. Much of this goes on, too.

But the media can be very destructive, too, and I feel that it is appropriate to list the damages from this source in this context.

(1) Television is extremely addictive and easily replaces other interests and involvements, often nullifying them altogether. This is especially true when very young children are placed in front of TV repeatedly, largely as a means of distracting them.

(2) Television used as a baby-sitter removes the human element and contact and has a deadening effect, much as does a sleeping pill. It disturbs natural responses and rhythms relative to sleep and appetite. Some people cannot sleep without TV. Some children would rather watch TV than eat.

(3) Television, overused, tends to overstimulate as well as hypnotize. This produces stimulation or adrenalin addiction as well as television tranquilizer addiction. Eventually children feel out of sorts if they have not had their usual input of TV time.

(4) Television addicts to increasing levels of stimulation needs,

thus producing an increased appetite for the exotic, the horrible, the violent, the melodramatic.

(5) Television distorts and demeans reality and everyday life through its soap-opera dramatizations as well as its talk-show elitism. The guests on these shows promote a world of Shangrila comfort and pleasure that transcends all earthly problems and that doesn't exist.

(6) Through the talk shows and interest extended to the lives of the "stars," notoriety and celebrity are promoted as being more important than substance or genuine expertise.

(7) Television destroys active imagination and generation of one's own fantasies and creative efforts as well as healthy struggle by passively spoon-feeding manufactured fantasies.

(8) Television destroys the will to struggle and mesmerizes with fantasy, producing a waste of time and energy and devitalizing the entire energy-producing mechanism.

(9) Television supplants familial communal life and exchange so that substance conversation ceases to take place.

(10) Television largely establishes a value system based on plastic mediocrity as it supplants books, music, etc., that give substance to development but require healthy struggle.

(11) Television produces an endless appetite for things and status through advertisement and self-promotion of pseudo-experts. This, combined with deprivations of a cultural nature already described and the desire for notoriety over substance, contributes to a high degree of materialism, shallowness, and superficiality.

(12) Television in large part, certainly through ads especially directed at girls and their looks as well as through "stars," promotes narcissism, detachment, and alienation. This, combined with addiction to increasing stimulation, destroys sensibilities, sensitivities, empathy, and aliveness. Without conscious awareness, a deadening process takes place. Entire households are mesmerized by the media. They awaken with it, talk about the characters on it as if they are family members, and go to sleep with it, even as they are separated and isolated by it.

(13) Television can be crippling to constructive values and concepts, promoting macho, sexist, tough-guy confusions; de-

structive, violent heroes and phony ideas about courage, strength, and ruthlessness, and putting down intellectual interest and development as being eggheaded and nerd producing.

Children of high TV exposure know a lot of little things but know very little in depth and subtleties escape them. Intellectual damage has taken place.

I do not believe that television should be used as part of a reward-punishment strategy. That makes it that much more enticing.

But very young children must be shielded from it! *Only* appropriate programs must be allowed and only limited time must be permitted for it. Because it is in the house and readily available is no reason it must not be treated with at least the care exerted in the choice of theater or movies children are taken to. It is strong medicine and must be treated as all other strong medicines.

It must not be permitted to supplant conversation, books, music, art, active thinking, feeling, fantasizing. Indeed, it is best that these are well ingrained before the child is exposed to television at all.

The Unlivable House—
Perfectionism

IDA: Funny you should ask—about my house, that is—the physical house. Funny I should say that—"physical house"—because it was that way psychologically, too.

How shall I describe it? I was brought up in a museum. A very small museum but a museum nevertheless. A very boring, constricted museum.

You know, I have several cousins. They used to come up to the front door and then they'd get frozen. My aunt couldn't get them to go inside. It was the perfection that would paralyze them. Everything was perfect and perfectly in place. A museum looks lived in and casual by comparison.

My mother was an absolute perfectionist. It wasn't just a clean house. It was superclean. Immaculate and sterile. She kept me that way, too, and my father—why he went along with it I don't know. To keep peace, I guess. To keep her from going to pieces. Now that I'm a psychology student I think I realize that my mother was an obsessive-compulsive lunatic—absolutely rigid.

We were museum pieces—like everything else in that morgue of a house. I wasn't just the neatest kid—I always—always—looked like I stepped out of the window of a department store. My father, too. You should have seen our drawers and closets and refrigerator and the way we ate. We are surely the only family in America that ate bread without crumbs. She must have bought crumb-free bread. I wonder if there is such a thing.

155

And routines—we had exact routines. My life as a child was the life of a railroad train—so much time to study, play, talk, sleep, etc. Spontaneity didn't exist. Really a wonder I'm not a catatonic or don't in some way reflect this absolute rigidity. Every October we bought our spring clothes. Every April our winter clothes—exact numbers of each item for each outfit.

Clothes didn't help my mother. She had them and never went into the street dressed less than perfectly. But she still looked like a scrubwoman because that's what she really was. It's a credit to my genes or basic health that I've come this far because my childhood was spent as a model, as a doll, and not as a living creature at all. And I was an only child—no one else for my mother to visit her perfectionistic rigidity on.

When I started school she set up a little corner of my room as a study place. She was more interested in how neat and clean I kept it than anything else. Though she was a perfectionist about my grades, too. I had to do perfectly in school and I just about did. I was, still am, number one in every school I went to. I'm sorry to say that in that regard I'm still as compulsive and rigid as she was. Can't think of getting less than an A. Pretty crazy.

Yes, I had friends. I used to love to go to their houses— on schedule, of course—allotted time and not one minute longer.

Like my cousins—they hated to come to my house. Kids know a prison when they see it—no matter how gilded it is. They know a warden when they see one, too. One of them said my house made him feel stifled. I knew exactly what he meant.

My friends? I liked the ones who were the most easygoing. More than that—the ones who seemed carefree, even sloppy— which they all seemed, compared to me. But my mother— especially when I was very small—chose them for me. Yes, you can guess—they were chosen on the basis of how they looked and dressed. Neatness was everything. When I started to date she applied the same criteria to boys. God! She really was a constricted, superficial ass—never saw anything beneath the surface. Maybe that was what attracted me to psychology.

My father was helpless! He must have known she'd collapse if he tried to loosen things up. I suspect he had a separate life. I'd sometimes have fantasies that he had a nice, sloppy wife and kids somewhere else and how I'd have loved to be one of those kids.

He did save me, though. He stood up to her when it came time for me to go to secondary school. He insisted I go to a school away from home and I did. Maybe it relieved her anxieties, too. For me it was wonderful. I stepped out of the museum into the real world. The fairy princess—Sleeping Beauty—came alive. When I came home we had fights. I wouldn't take her bullying, neat crap any more. But despite myself, I'm still a bug on cleanliness myself and here I am working on a doctorate and I love the subject and I still have to be the perfect A student.

Do you think that my mother, deep down, was terrified of her own "dirty" impulses—sexual, rage, etc.—and that she was very controlled and her perfectionism was a way to keep everything under control? Did she really want to fling everything around and roll in the gutter—figuratively and literally, too? Was that poor little obsessed scrubwoman really a raging, wild woman underneath—who lost her way—and kept herself intact with a museum life?

COMMENT: Perhaps Ida's theory about her mother's terror of underlying impulses and fear of loss of control is correct. In any case, this kind of perfectionism makes for rigidity, constriction, and loss of spontaneity. Ida is still and probably always will be perfectionistic herself. Thankfully, she is not as sick in this area as her mother. Ida was very fortunate. Questioning revealed that there was a good deal of intellectual and emotional exchange between herself and her father. He viewed her as a real person.

In households like the one described by Ida there is very often both an intellectual and emotional vacuum. Time and energy are usually spent on superficial and shallow niceties (keeping it all neat), leaving little for more important human pursuits.

Going away to school certainly helped, as did her rebellion— something her father could not do.

Here is a classic case of a family whose way of life is determined by its sickest member. The implications of damage sustained by this kind of parental perfectionism are obvious: lack of self-esteem engendered by human imperfections; lack of feeling human as a consequence of being treated as a nonliving object (a doll); rigidity; constriction; more perfectionism; lack of social experience and enrichment (Ida could not play in any game or with anyone who was "dirty"), etc.

In some cases, children who are victims of this kind of household run away, act out, and in their rebellion become extremely self-damaging. This is a way of attempting to save themselves—their alive selves—but sometimes the attempt itself kills them—fast cars, drugs, etc.—any and all symbols that are confused with freedom.

Interestingly, the symptom for which Ida seeks treatment was sexual dysfunction. Despite knowing otherwise, she felt sex was "dirty" and she couldn't "let go." This symptom was a residual of the enslavement she suffered from and much confusion about intimacy and cleanliness. Her mother preferred social distance for her to preserve her physical cleanliness and unconsciously probably her emotional cleanliness, too. She did not want Ida, her prized possession, to be sullied or adulterated in any way. Ida complied with this dictum unconsciously in adult life until she understood it.

As for "letting go"—this is very difficult for perfectionistic people with little real self-esteem who need absolute control for security. Ida said, "I feel if I let go, when I come back I may not be there."

She's beginning to know who she is on a gut level and that she is much more than her mother's museum doll. As this happens, she is taking more chances with letting go. Hopefully, one of these days she will score a grade of B or even a C in a course or at least on a paper—despite the fact that she is a brilliant student. This may be evidence of greater flexibility and self-acceptance.

Reality Twisting—Duplicity

JOE: My mother's middle name should have been "Duplicity." That's what she was really good at—being duplicitous and turning reality around to suit her needs. How my father stood it I don't know. He was a straight guy. Matter of fact, I do know. He paid no attention. But, of course, that didn't help us— the kids. My mother could convince you black was white and white was black and she could have your head spinning.

I remember her telling friends of hers that her daughters never had to help around the house—you know, with cleaning or dishes and things like that. She was into her rich lady-bountiful pose. Mind you, she told this in front of my sisters. Brazen as you please, because, you see, it was a complete fabrication. Who knows, maybe she believed it herself—at least for the moment. The fact is, my sisters always took care of the house so that my mother could go out and do what she wanted. This kind of thing went on in a hundred different ways.

She always implied—more than implied—*said* that we were special: a myth based on absolutely nothing. She could be simplicity itself one minute and full of affectation the next. She must have lived in a dreamworld most of the time. Look— the real truth is that we were a very ordinary family—less than ordinary. God knows there was always a money shortage. She put on an act—had us believe we were some kind of ideal bunch. One day I asked myself—based on what? And I knew that it was all nonsense—a dream.

She once promised to take me to the circus when my birthday

came up. This was a big plan, you see. She told me this months ahead of time. Couldn't wait. Looked forward to it. Can still taste the whole thing now, twenty-five years later.

We never went. She changed her mind. Just didn't feel like it. Saying that would have been bad enough—not keeping a promise to a kid. But what she did was much worse. She said I was sick. Put the onus on me. I wasn't sick at all. Took my temperature. Put me to bed. Kept me there a couple of days. What a liar. What duplicity. What a distorter—of the truth—of reality! There were lots of things like that. What a manipulator. She never fooled me. Don't think she fooled herself either.

COMMENT: This kind of damage produces vast insecurity and cynicism. It contributes to distrust and difficulty in being open even with the most benevolent loved ones. If severe enough it contributes to chronic suspiciousness and paranoia. It makes for distortions of reality in terms of one's own identity vis-à-vis the world. Distortions about the family and illusions about familial nonexistent special status contribute to arrogance, abrasive behavior, and disturbed relationships. This often takes the form of claims made on other people for special treatment that when not forthcoming leads to self-pity, feeling misunderstood, and abused.

Joe's early recognition of his mother's duplicity and family mythology helped him considerably—"to retain my sanity," as he once put it. But he was nevertheless cynical and hurt and had a difficult time trusting women. He came to understand that his mother's behavior was not a reflection on other women and his relationships improved significantly. He still has trouble with cynicism, which he struggles against, and is absolutely intolerant of affectation.

His greatest admiration is for integrity and he despises affectation. He tends to be overscrupulous in delivering "straight" messages to people and in keeping his word.

Family-Designated Roles

JANE: I was *the smart one*. My brother Jack was *the bad one*. Sam was *the dumb one*. May was *the good one*. Iris was the artist—*the creative one*. That's how it was in my family. Everyone had a role assignment and we acted accordingly.

Of course, no one ever said in so many words, "You will be this or that," but it must have been decided and conveyed to us very early because I remember the assignments being there from the start—all of the time. And when anyone outside the family was around, my parents used to describe each of us that way and don't think we didn't hear it and live up to it, too. A self-fulfilling prophecy.

I remember how surprised they were when my brother Sam published his first book. He turned out to be creative and smart, too. Iris is artistic but she never did anything with it—maybe too frightened about what she thought was expected of her— what she had to live up to. Sam did not self-destruct, largely because he got very depressed in his teens and got help.

I hated my role but having to live up to it, I was a real grind. I got all A's, not because I was so smart—we were all okay in the IQ department. It was because I couldn't go against their version of me. I still resent it.

COMMENT: This kind of expectation through role assignment is invariably inappropriate and destructive. I shall discuss appropriate expectations as enablers in section 4. It is often coercive and completely neglectful of the child's real proclivities

161

and appropriate only to the parents' vicarious needs rather than the child's assets, inclinations, and desires.

This damage is a form of child exploitation and often a form of family self-idealization—giving the parents the illusion of having an interesting, multifaceted family. It is also related to favoritism and contains most of the destructive elements found in that damage.

This kind of externalizing compartmentalization is usually an extension of parental internal compartments. Various aspects of self are felt separately and then projected to various children to play them out vicariously.

This damage makes for enormous prejudice and bias—people can't escape their roles; alienation from feelings and assets that would dilute the role assigned—for example, anger is a threat to the role of the good one; constriction—an inability to experience one's self in "other roles"—that is, other aspects of self. It also makes for much repressed rage for being pressured into a role and for being cheated of other possibilities. It also contributes to confusion, anxiety, self-hate, and depression—as aspects of self come up that shouldn't be there because the child has been convinced that he/she is someone who doesn't have those feelings.

Jane came to me because of depression and the feeling that she was tired of being an overachiever. She wanted "to relax and to enjoy life." The above damage was one of several that occurred in childhood but it was an important one.

In time she realized that no one could force her into playing any role she didn't want. As she took over responsibility for her own life and goals, spontaneity returned, and considerable liberation and the ability to experience joy were born.

Overpermissiveness, Neglect, and Overindulgence

These destructive devices can be found separately but they are usually found together.

JESSE: The kids—I mean the ones outside our family—all envied us. We were the ones who could do anything. No one ever told us when to come home, how late to stay out—what to eat, not eat—we could do, go, anything, anywhere. Of course, we did pretty poorly in school. I don't think they—my parents, that is—looked at homework even once past the fourth or fifth grade or so.

We were on our own. And we got into trouble, too—my brothers wrecked several cars—drugs—I had a couple of abortions. They seemed to care then but not for long. I think, I know, I did things to shock them periodically—I got a job as a go-go dancer but their attention never lasted beyond the shock. It's a wonder I didn't wind up really bad. My youngest brother has been in and out of drying-out places and my oldest is always in serious trouble, with lawyers and all.

Other kids also envied the things they'd get us. Anything we wanted—clothes, cars, money. Truth is, I burned out years ago—stopped wanting anything.

I know I must sound like an ingrate—overindulged, spoiled—and I suppose I was. But aren't parents supposed to care—I mean really care—beyond giving you anything you want just

163

to shut you up? We were ships without rudders—no direction at all. I'll tell you, here I am—twenty-seven—I don't know who I am or where I'm going and I guess that's what I'd like to find out.

COMMENT: Obviously, material gifts in no way compensate for emotional and intellectual neglect. Without guidance—limits, communication, response—inner feelings of self are missing. Expectations of self are virtually nil and the message conveyed is that the child is not worth caring about. Overindulgence further leads to stimulation addiction and to acting out in self-destructive, dangerous ways, both as a means of getting attention and to enhance feelings of aliveness to compensate for inner impoverishment and feelings of deadness.

If acting out destructivley takes an antisocial turn, it is often necessary to set absolute limits on what is and isn't acceptable (read the book *Tough Love*—I mention it elsewhere, too). Being able to say NO and even closing the door on a child can in these cases be compassionately lifesaving. Much in this case depends on the "crowd the child runs with," especially if the child is compliant and conforming and the crowd is wild. In essence, the crowd—peers—takes the role of the absent parents and provides "values."

But overpermissiveness sometimes produces a child who reacts sharply the reverse way in order to attempt to establish inner limits. He/she will become superconventional, overscrupulous, overreligious, and prisoner of a rigid, compulsive inner tyranny but also impoverished in terms of feelings of real self.

I referred Jesse to a very benevolent, nourishing, but firm woman psychoanalyst. I felt she needed to work with a special parent surrogate in order to really grow up and to be the self she doesn't know.

But what makes parents behave in this way—to inflict this damage? Here are a few possibilities.

(1) Parents who never really wanted children but had them because "it was the thing to do," and in effect negate their existence by largely ignoring them.

(2) Parents who are highly narcissistic and too self-indulgent

to give time and energy elsewhere and "do not want to be bothered."

(3) Severely self-effacing parents who are terrified of any self-assertion at all.

(4) Parents who are extremely infantile themselves, with limited emotional development despite financial success.

(5) Chronically hostile parents who hate themselves and each other and their offspring.

(6) Thoroughly confused, misinformed parents who think complete permissiveness equals good upbringing and a chance for the child to be uniquely his/herself without dilution of anyone else's influence.

(7) Sociopathic parents with very limited conscience or the ability to empathize or to identify with and who have very poor limits themselves.

(8) Parents who are overreacting to their own extremely rigid and strict upbringing.

The Adversarial Household— Sibling Rivalry

We all come from homes that are adversarial to at least some extent. Degree matters very much and damage can be measured to the extent that adversarial or even worse—antagonistic—conditions and influences prevail. Adversarial households are replete with the damages described in this section.

As I explained in *One to One,* adversarial relationships are largely relationships between friendly competitors. Adversaries in this special sense compete but maintain limited and tenuous cooperation as long as each party feels he/she is getting his/her fair share. Indeed, fair share and making sure that no one else gets ahead supercede cooperation and common good as well as familial considerations. "Me first" and "me most" take precedence here and not in terms of individual development but rather as functions of making sure no one gets ahead of me or more than I.

In antagonistic relationships there is no longer even tenuous cooperation or mutual acceptance on any basis. In this (again my own application and definition) kind of relating, the prime force is rejection. People are no longer *friends* on any basis. They may live together for years but the underlying current is mutual hatred—utter lack of support or exchange of support on even a competitive level and mutual deprecation and rejection. As we go downhill from cooperative to adversarial to severely adversarial to antagonistic households, we go from

166

us to *me and you* to *me, too,* to *me only and the hell with you.*

It is not surprising that most families are at least somewhat adversarial. Our entire society is adversarial—with rare cooperative, compassionate, altruistic dilution—which often seems almost intrusive in an ambience in which competition is the hallmark. The world "out there" is a highly competitive world, largely based on the "get ahead of the next guy" motive and "I'll do for you—but only if you do for me" dictum. "I'll do for you— without regard either for what you do for me and without any get-ahead motive but only because I accept you and your needs and enjoy my contribution to your self-realization" is relatively rare. It exists to a greater extent in the inside or family world and I'll describe this kind of cooperative family relating in the section on "Enablers," but adversarial, competitive invasions from the outside to the family are inevitable.

The family and its members all operate in the outside world through school, work, media, and all aspects of their lives. No family is exempt from cultural, that is, societal influences and pressures. I include immediate influences of neighbors and neighborhood as well as the world at large. To the extent that the family and its members are healthy, they continue to relate on a cooperative basis and to neutralize and dilute adversarial pressures. But the fact remains that many households are largely adversarial. In those that are severely and mainly adversarial— where competition and the need to guard one's own interests are of prime importance—we usually find many of the damages already described.

Adversarial and antagonistic households may be viewed as negative enablers—that is, they enable so many of the other damages to flourish and to multiply. Now let us examine some of the characteristics and serious damages specifically generated and sustained by adversarial relating. Most of these are present together and overlap. Question of degree is very important.

—Sibling rivalry is generated, sustained, and exaggerated. I believe that sibling rivalry is for the most part an acquired characteristic rather than an instinctual one. In any case—acquired or instinctual—it is sustained, emphasized, and becomes an exaggerated destructive force in an adversarial household. In severely adversarial households we often find everyone in the family acting as sibling rivals. In effect this means that the fear of not getting one's "fair share" generates enough anxiety so that differences in age as well as developmental status are virtually blotted out. This means that parents act more like rival brothers and sisters than parents and that older siblings do not recognize the special limits and dependency needs of much younger brothers and sisters. Of course, this is the stuff of abdication of responsibility and the perfect germinating ground for neglect and abuse—much of it blatant.

—Rather than communicating, often characteristic here is "smart talk," "ranking," and everyone giving the smartest answer possible to outwit and outshow family rivals. Performance and response are more important than communicating real information. Thus, there is little opportunity for the help that would come of mutual exchange.

—Accomplishment by family members is often perceived as threatening to hierarchical order ("who will be on top now?") and often produces envy and jealousy.

—There is a competition for parental admiration and approval as well as for narcissistic supplies.

—Family members tend to idealize themselves and their families despite lack of healthy family identification and often see the family as a besieged fortress. In effect, they extend their vision of the family jungle to the outside world, where it becomes exaggerated and threatening, increasing insecurity and the ability to try new ventures.

—"We are like a theater play or ball game where every player is on his own and playing against each other, not knowing he is on the same team or in the same play." This, of course, deprives the members of mutual aid and the achievement of common goals. This patient distinctly remembered, "My parents used to put us up against each other and then couldn't understand why we couldn't cooperate."

—The concentration on "not being taken advantage of" and "getting my fair share" is enormous and deflects an inordinate amount of energy from real self-development.

—A disturbed family identification ensues due to family disharmony. This hurts self-esteem, feeling for one's roots, and cuts off supplies of emotional nourishment. This makes for feelings of fragility and vulnerability, increasing suspiciousness and hurting the possibility of fruitful relating.

—Feeling good about one's self is too often connected with feeling superior to other members of the family and eventually to other people with whom one relates rather than through self-realization. This in effect puts one's well-being in someone else's hands. This externalizing of the aspect of competition—"the other guy determines where I have to go"—removes the center of gravity of one's self from inside to outside. This is highly destructive to real self-autonomy.

—Sibling rivalry and adversarial relating are often carried over into marriage and competition with one's spouse and children, compounding the difficulty.

—Alienation from feelings is commonplace here because feelings have not been exercised sufficiently and tend to be blunted. Love is doled out in limited supply as it is often interpreted as "giving in," "weakness," and "setting yourself up"—making one's self vulnerable.

—In this household there is little or no real, nonconditional, mutual enhancement. The lack of cooperative interchange leaves everyone impoverished.

IV
The Enablers

These are the enablers.

In this section I want to describe some of the most important things we can do to aid self-realization.

The enablers block liabilities and damages as they help to develop assets and to tap inner resources. Of course, any time we recognize and actively block a damage we are enabling. In describing damages in the last section we are in effect describing enablers, too, in simply reversing the action or process involved in damage. But in this section I want to discuss the active, direct enabling we can do, which represents contributions additional to blocking or doing the reverse of damaging.

We can't do them all and we can't do any of them perfectly. We still are subject to our own emotional limitations. To the extent that parents are in touch with and use their own assets, they help their children to own theirs and to develop them into usable inner resources. Enablers are genuine. Therefore, they must come from our own genuine selves. Contrivances and empty gestures are not enablers and only add to confusion and frustration. Therefore, it is more than a little helpful when we ourselves are in a state of active and constructive change and growth. Exercising the enablers does that. In doing "good things" for our children we improve our own selves, helping us to do more good things for our children. This in effect establishes constructive cycles characteristics of cooperative and creative relating.

To the extent that we become enablers (participants in other people's and our own emotional, intellectual, and creative fruition) we break the victim-of-victim's chain. By this chain, I mean the destructive forces that are passed on from generation to generation through habitually feeding liability formation through damaging behavior. But we do more than that. We also awaken constructive forces and possibilities, putting families on the road to creative satisfaction that may have been lost for generations.

Lack of self-realization is not genetic: it is a function of serious environmental hopelessness and resignation. We can do something about it. This section deals with direct applications to the problem and its solution. Doing these things may not be easy at first and may even be difficult. New ways can be hard. But there is little in life that will bring greater satisfaction than participation in other persons', especially our own children's self-realization.

The struggle does get easier because we are, after all, making adaptations to natural human behavior rather than to bizarre formulations. We are not going off the track. We are getting back on. Spontaneity can be restored. Enabling can become a natural way of life. As it does, life becomes easier and richer for all concerned. Results are never perfect. But to whatever extent we apply enablers, I am convinced we will have results.

Stability

We've already talked about the enormous importance of self-esteem in the process of self-enhancement.

Stability is a great enhancer of self-esteem. It permits the developing individual to feel himself as belonging and as counting—the antithesis of being an outcast or as having no roots, so to speak. Energy and time are spent in valuable exploration—inner and outer—as assets are brought into focus and develop into accessible inner resources. Time and energy are not spent in worry, apprehension, anticipation of disaster, and in warding off threats—real or imagined. This is not unlike a beleaguered nation that dissipates its resources in endless defense projects.

We can readily see that security is more than an enabler of self-esteem. It also provides a fairly safe and livable environment in which self-development can take place—where real living supplants the fight for survival.

Stability is not to be confused with rigid and resigned clinging to a status quo, however much that status quo may actually be constricting and even destructive. This is not stability! This is a reaction to profound feelings of insecurity and an attempt to ward off anxiety. It is surrender to the belief that one is incapable of change, adaptation, or confrontation with the unfamiliar. It is born of poor self-esteem and is a form of paralysis.

Stability is related to genuine feelings of enjoying conditions of living. It does not preclude flexibility or change.

What enhances a child's feeling of stability and provides this ambience where roots can take hold so that growth can take place?

175

When I was a child we moved a great deal. Times were very hard and *making a living* was top priority. I went to eight elementary schools. This is not the stuff of security. Having to make adjustments and adaptations—to new place, new schools, rules, and curriculums when we are too young to do it—is not constructive. For every person who says, "It did me good," there are a hundred who suffer considerable damage to inner security, which really makes all kinds of moves later in life so much harder.

So I obviously feel that *consistency of place* (geography) and school (work and social life) is an important enabler in early life in its contribution to security.

But what if this is not possible? In my case it wasn't. My feelings of security could have been better. But they weren't completely destroyed. I did okay, after all. How come? Because I did enjoy the comfort of much greater enablers of security!

Being taken appropriately care of! I knew that no matter where we lived I would be taken care of. That no matter which school I went to or whatever happened there I would be taken care of. I knew my parents cared and that my care was assured. This was conveyed to me in their actions and verbally as well— especially when we moved. I was lucky because I also knew we would stay together until I grew up. Neighborhoods might change but our family and relationships would remain intact. Actions do speak louder than words but the words are extremely valuable and potent, especially to the frightened child. The words, accompanied by hugs and kisses, convey the message even as the real stuff is delivered through real care.

A family intact is then still another great enabler of emotional security. Obviously this isn't always possible. *But* it is possible for living adults to convey to the child that even in divorce (or death of a living relative in which others survive) the child's care will be assured. It is also possible and necessary that the child knows that surviving parents will continue to be highly emotionally invested and involved with the child, regardless of their status with each other. This verbal commitment only has value if real quality time and energy are spent on the child.

In practice, I have seen acrimonious battles for custody or visitation rights followed by disinterest and detachment and the child appropriately feeling rejected as his world and security evaporate. In divorce it is important to indicate to the child that he/she is not responsible for the breakup. I have had any number of adult patients (especially women) who felt otherwise for a lifetime ever since their parents broke up when they were very young. Some people feel this is partly due to the child's real wish for this to happen, as part of oedipal yearnings for one or another parent. I believe it is due to feeling severely punished, for in some way not feeling as being "good enough."

Harmony between adult family members has great value. *Peace* is always an enormous enabler. But this is not to be confused with *silence* described in the last section or deadness or enforced tyranny of any kind. Harmony and peace allow for disagreement and fights but mean that good and caring feelings about each other always eventually transcend all else and underlie all else, including temporary turbulence.

But what if *disharmonious* messages are constantly conveyed? What if parents simply don't get along but stay together? Then again, it is very valuable to "not take it out on the kids" and to indicate to them that (1) they are not responsible; (2) they will be taken care of and loved, no matter what! (3) that parent-child relationships will continue, no matter what is said or done; (4) that at least some time and energy are reserved for spending time with the children. It is of value to spend time with each child alone, giving him or her full attention, not diluted by siblings. If parents can't refrain from sniping at each other, then it is valuable for each parent to spend time with the children separately; (5) try to fight in privacy—no kids around. Good (nonvindictive) fights are all right for children to witness, but where parents have become antagonists, vindictive, arrogant, mutual debasement is destructive to children; (6) of course, do not use children as coteam members or as mediators.

Talk

Talk! Talk with them—that is, when they are wide-awake, not half-asleep. Talk to them!

I can't stress enough the incredible value of talk—verbal communication—especially talk of substance.

Substance talk goes way past utilitarian "take out the garbage," "buy some milk" talk.

Substance talks gives and invites. It opens up rather than closes. It is dialogue—conversation—rather than manifestos, commands, speeches, or tutorial sessions.

In *"giving talk"* we tell of feelings, ideas, thoughts, opinions, concepts, desires, values—what is and isn't important to us. We tell where we stand on issues of the day, on current and historical events—familial, personal, and otherwise. In short—we tell who we are.

In *"inviting talk"* we do the same in reverse by listening and indicating that we want to know and to exchange. We listen without moralizing and without judgment and we do so with great patience. It takes time and effort for young children to express themselves and to learn to articulate. But we listen to what they have to say and we hear the music as well as the words—the tone, the mood, the feelings, what is unsaid as well as what is said.

"Parallel talk" is not constructive. It is usually self-serving and not a dialogue at all, but lecturing. Parallel talk means that both persons talk independently of each other, each only involved in saying his/her piece.

"Responsive talk" is real dialogue. This takes place when each person in a conversation responds with his/her thoughts to the other person's thoughts, thus ongoing give and take—responsivity—takes place.

Parents can teach this to children by example, through their own responses to the child—the antithesis of ignoring what the child has to say.

When we have associations to the other person's associations to a topic in question, we dignify each other's productions as we enrich each other. This is the effective way that two or more people collaborate in a joint creative effort ("brainstorming"), which is more enriching than each saying his separate piece without response to one another's verbalizations.

But this is the way they learn: by imitation through perceiving; by listening and through exercising the process and the practice of talking.

Your support is of enormous consequence in this area and can only come to full measure by total involvement with the child in the talking process. This is the way he/she also knows that you care—infinitely better than applause following a performance. It is through mutual serious substance talks that the child derives the satisfaction of getting better and better able to describe what he/she feels. This motivates further talking.

Through talk, information—crucial information, some too subtle to be consciously perceived regarding the human condition—is conveyed.

Through talk and increased ability to articulate, clear thinking becomes possible.

Through talk, a mutually supportive bond is established between parent and child.

Through talk, emotions are expressed, amplified, and grow.

Through talk and the process of verbal associations, creative ideas come up which will come to fruition in the future.

But talking must take place for this to happen, and this means talk that invites openness and intimacy.

Openness and intimacy, so much the ingredients of love, do not happen when a loved partner is found at last. They are rather the result of early experience, largely a function of serious familial talking, in which real revelation took place through serious talking.

Can children catch up who have not benefited from real talk early on? Perhaps. But if they do, it is with great difficulty.

The head-start and continuing motivation to feel, to have opinions, to think, to grow, to express, to exchange with— which enormously motivate relating on all levels, born of familial talk—are unparalleled anywhere or by anything else. Of course, the attention paid in the process—the relating that takes place; the accrued skill of being able to verbalize—increases self-esteem enormously. This is especially true when this happens early in life while the child is still forming a concept of his/her self.

The process is easy and natural for the child. Whatever his/her age, healthy children love the closeness and challenge that talk brings. This occurs relative to profound books or to goo-goo sounds relating to rattles and dolls.

In this talking it is good to remember that a kind of play therapy is taking place. The parent need not be a trained therapist to perceive feelings like anger, frustration, and happiness about certain items which come out during talking about things that otherwise may not be revealed. Encouraging the child to talk out feelings is highly therapeutic. It teaches him/her not to repress; it shows that you take feelings seriously; it gets him/her to take his/her feelings seriously.

Is the child ever too young to start?

No! I do not believe the child benefits by reading to it in utero, though it may be a good rehearsal for parents.

But the child can start and really does start from the moment he/she is born. Baby talk is a serious start and does convey meaning to the tuned-in parent. Response—verbal response— by the parent is appreciated by the child, who is stimulated and responds accordingly. This already establishes communicating bonds.

Parental talk must be appropriate to the child's age and, more important, to the level of maturity. This precludes talking above their heads or down to them. Patronizing children is not constructive substance talking!

When a child questions, answer so that he/she understands.

If the child still does not understand, repeating the same answer loudly does not help. Change the words around, use other words—but do not give up! Help to understand and to exchange and further meaning. In doing so, you are demonstrating how explanations are made and how different combinations of words are used effectively. The child will go on to do the same with friends, colleagues, and eventually his/her children. Patience, like other good things, is contagious.

Attention Paid and Feelings of Lovability

Feeling loved by the parent is of great potential value to the child. *But* it is of much greater value and potential becomes fulfilled if the loving is expressed and conveyed to the child. Taking it for granted that he/she knows and that demonstrations are not necessary is missing the full boat.

Expressions of love not backed up by substance—real caring actions in which security in all forms is provided—come across as hollow stuff and generate distrust. Love for children is largely determined by our own past experiences and to a great extent is directly influenced by love we received as kids. Where it was missing and is missing between parent and child, treatment for the parent is valuable and even more valuable if applied before the birth of the new baby.

Attention paid to the child is interpreted as love being exercised. Of course, I'm talking about appropriate attention—the antithesis of either foolish fawning or perfectionistic demands. Attention includes care, interest, and participation with.

No child is oblivious to appropriate care. The child knows, without verbal explanation, that he/she is being properly housed, dressed, and nurtured. This is interpreted as being important enough as well as loved enough to warrant proper care.

Interest—real interest—in the child's daily activities and change and growth in all areas of his/her life is likewise conveyed as love to the child.

182

Participation with the child in household activities—cooking, cleaning, shopping—is excellent. The same is true of shared activities in relaxing, playing, and in appropriate areas of enjoyment—the circus, zoo, movies, music, theater, etc. Of course, playing games with the child that the child enjoys and reading to and with the child are invaluable. These are interpreted as loving activities and the adult will look back and feel these participatory events in childhood as loving moments.

Time spent alone with the child by each parent as well as with both parents is invaluable. This is especially true in participating in activities the child likes. It is also true in discussing problems, especially with adolescents—over lunch and with full seriousness. Children also feel a good sense of themselves in spending time with parents in adult activities as helpers in the kitchen, in the office, helping to repair the house, pump up the car tires, etc. They will all accrue to both feelings of self-esteem and lovability.

But remember, please—talking is invaluable. Talking—good, mutually interesting talk of a substantial nature—says, in effect, "You are intelligent enough for us to talk. You are valuable enough for us to talk. You are lovable enough so that we talk and we share. You have value and through talk I show you respect and dignity." Of course, this talk precludes talking down, up, or being short with, arrogant or patronizing. It is patient. It is encouraging. It is helpful. It is loving. I will have more to say about this all-important talking business as we go along. It is still, after all, the best way we have of conveying our feelings—as long as it represents real feelings and is backed by appropriate action.

Embracing, hugging, kissing, all appropriately shared and expressed, are forms of talking. Laughing, crying, cheering together are also forms of talking—loving talking.

But saying *"I love you"* in so many words is invaluable. This pinpoints, summarizes, and symbolizes what we feel. If heard and used in childhood, the expression has so much more meaning later on when we grow up. No, its use does not make it meaningless—unless it is said without backing by real feelings. Otherwise, it has much meaning and is symbolic all of our lives of our feelings of being lovable and of our ability to love others. Remember, we are highly symbolic creatures. We think and feel through symbols and use symbols to express who we are.

It is valuable to fight expressions of self-hate in children and expressions of hate to children from the outside. "I hate myself" must be investigated (usually perfectionism and too many demands on self are at work here) and blocked. "Can't understand why you hate yourself—please explain—you are worth more than any issue, work, exam you are involved in—I love you."

It is also valuable to encourage the child's affection and expression of affection appropriately. Children loving dolls, pets, and people, and using words to express themselves helps them to feel that expressions of love are natural and good.

I am convinced that people who have not been able to say the words as parents during their lives have themselves not heard the words as children. Men who feel embarrassed by use of the words—either heard or expressed—either (1) have difficulty believing in their own lovability, (2) are confused about gender roles and have macho hang-ups derived from childhood, or (3) have not heard the words adequately applied to them as children and while they were growing up, or all three.

No! Narcissism, selfishness, concentration on self to the exclusion of interest in others do not come from being told in the many ways possible of being loved. Feeling loved and being loved make for a high lovability quotient. This means that we not only feel loved but can also be loving without the threat of depletion. We have enough love to go around—to give. There is no fixed supply that will run out, but rather the feeling—the true feeling—that love is constantly generated by receiving and giving love. Of course, I mean here, openness, tenderness, intimacy, trust, and caring.

Narcissism derives from exploitation and a feeling of depletion. It derives from being fawned over and being used rather than being loved. It is a result of overprotection, noncaring, engendering of sibling rivalry, and the other damages I spoke of earlier. It produces insatiability, requiring more and more attention, praise, admiration, and proofs of lovability, which are always inadequate. Narcissism derives from self-hate, feelings of unlovability, and enormous insecurity.

*Lovability—feeling loved—*derives from self-esteem, security, and a history of being loved and told by action and word of being loved.

High lovability quotient is of paramount importance in further adding to self-esteem and the feeling of hopefulness, optimism, and the approach to lending one's self to intellectual and creative endeavors. When we feel lovable we feel substantial and we feel that what we have to give will be well received and cherished. This encourages production on all levels, making all kinds of enterprise possible.

Equally important, high lovability makes constructive relating, especially intimate ones, infinitely more likely. Trust and openness are natural ingredients here, as is the ability to express love to others, especially in intimate relationships—mates and children. This makes for cooperative and creative relating (of which I'll say more later) and healthier and satisfying lives all around.

Low lovability quotients—feeling unlovable—make for difficulty on every level and are invariably related to low self-esteem and self-hate, which I spoke about earlier. Unfortunately, no amount of reassurance or accomplishment helps. The individual here, having been so imprinted in childhood, goes on feeling unloved, used, and abused, and relates accordingly. Psychoanalytic treatment can be helpful, especially in breaking this chain for the next generation.

Is there a difference between self-esteem and lovability? Yes and no. No, because they are inextricably interwoven. Yes, because self-esteem is how we view ourselves. Lovability is how we view ourselves and how we feel other people view us. In high self-esteem and lovability, we feel we are good stuff and we feel that other people can feel we are also. We love ourselves and believe that other people can love us, too. Equally important, we know we can and do love other people. We know because our parents told us.

Please remember that talk conveys feeling. It also exercises feelings. It brings them out and helps to develop them—to feel more. This is especially true of loving talk.

When we love, we talk honestly. We tell how we feel—good, bad, indifferent, jealous, altruistic, generous, happy, etc. This is loving talk and its contribution to further emotional development and intellectual development, too, is truly unparalleled.

Feelings Exchange, Especially Love

A child who grows up in a household in which from day one feelings are freely, openly, and honestly exchanged (expressed to each other) is fortunate indeed. This child is not shocked or hurt or reticent about feelings or repressed later on. This child has the example and participates in feeling and telling of feelings. This is a child, unlike people of emotional vacuums, who is not alienated from feelings later on in life.

Exchange of feelings must not be confused with hysteria. Hysterics act out feelings for effect on others in order to manipulate them. Feelings exchange takes place as an effort to communicate and to teach others what we feel. One is often melodramatic. The other is rational, reasonable, and often done or said relatively quietly.

This telling of feelings is one of the most important and basic kinds of talking we can do. It removes guesswork. It prevents feeling one's parents as being ephemeral/enigmatic. It makes parents solid, real people and defines them in time and place. It makes them much realer and solidly palpable as role models. It makes relating so much easier as well as the development of one's own emotions. This is so because one's own emotions are seen and felt as natural aspects of self rather than as undesirable foreign bodies. In this way, the exchange of feelings aids self-acceptance and self-esteem. It also enhances feelings of security because really knowing who our parents are through how they feel makes their presence so much stronger and so much more supportive.

Honest, open, trusting feelings exchange is an excellent bulwark against cynicism, suspiciousness, and paranoia. It aids trust because it aids openness. There is never a pervasive air of apprehension attached to well-guarded secrets, revelation of which may bring on impending disaster. Feelings exchange contributes to an ambience of mutual trust and confidence in participants. It says, in effect, "I trust you with my feelings—me—because I know you are worthy of my confidence and of even the deepest information about me—what I feel!"

So many of my patients have told me how they really never knew what their parents felt—about each other, about them, about other people, and about all kinds of issues and things. Those who suffered the most in this area, that is, with their own feelings, came from families in which "keeping a stiff upper lip, not complaining, keep it to yourself" was seen as a virtue and a sign of strength. I see it as a sign of lack of trust.

The exchange of feelings also informs children early on of this most important area of the human condition. They begin early to learn of the complexity of people through learning how people feel, what they feel, what they think, too, about so many things and how all this is transmitted. This is an invaluable head start in a most important educative process. He/she learns about hurt feelings and the invaluable lesson of the value of talking about them. He/she will learn about clearing the air and the give-and-take that restores contentment to participants rather than the sullen coldness characteristic of repression.

All feelings expressed are important. These include feelings about issues, opinions, tastes, events, etc. A tearful response to a tragic event is a million times more valuable than so-called self-control. It teaches by example appropriate response. It dignifies feelings and makes them valuable, acceptable. This is a form of self-acceptance. In so doing, repression is minimized and future stress and psychosomatic manifestations are avoided.

Repeatedly asking a child how he/she feels relative to events, observations, perceptions is valuable; for example, going to a museum, looking at a painting, and asking the child how the painting makes him/her feel. The same is true of asking the child about tastes—"Do you like red better or green—the smell of the salt air? country air?" etc. This both extends and dignifies the value of feelings and aids aliveness and inner enrichment. It also contributes to talk of a substantial nature and to intimacy, which are valuable exercises for the future.

Tears are especially important because they convey so much feeling so quickly and so clearly. Parental tears, particularly father's tears, are especially helpful and more so to boys. In a "feeling" household they may mean sadness, and this is good— feeling sad is part of living. But they are also an indication of strength of feelings, ability to empathize and sympathize, and to identify with and to relate to—all evidence of humanity and human strength. This counters confused, false, idealized cultural versions of strength and masculinity.

Worries, regrets, and, yes, feelings of despair and then hope— the full range of feelings—conveyed to the child so the child knows that feelings change and situations change but love for him/her remains constant are all of value.

Anger, expressed warmly without sadistic ploys and vindictive manipulation, is very valuable and prevents fright of this emotion in the future. I wrote about anger in a book totally devoted to it—*The Angry Book*—because there is so much misunderstanding in this area. Unexpressed anger is the dangerous stuff. Expressed anger (not the explosive kind born of repression) clears the air for better communication and love.

Love is a wonderful emotion, especially when it is expressed through words, touch, a look, a smile between parents and from them to children. It conveys the message of security, solidity, family cohesiveness, and value. It says, "You were born of our love. We love each other a lot and that's wonderful. We love you a lot and that's wonderful."

Laughing, never the derisive kind, but warm, voluble, laughing together as a response to humor and fun, is simply invaluable. It is difficult to sustain pomposity, arrogance, and feelings of depression, morbidity, and hostility when laughing takes place. It further serves to destroy false idealization as it puts everyone, parents and children, on an equal emotional level.

Joy! Joy expressed at home and being brought up in a largely joyous, smiling, laughing household is a blessing indeed. It provides the lesson to the child. It gives endless, wonderful memories. It is the gut stuff of self-esteem because in being joyous we tap all of our inner resources, integrate them, and feel them in this most human way of all. I will discuss the joyful household at greater length later on.

Love All of the Child—
Especially Gender—
Regardless of Gender

W hat I mean here is love the child for his/her being a human being in the fullest sense of that word. This means love the child's total being even as shortcomings and imperfections are perceived. In this regard I mean love the child unconditionally, regardless of performance or conformity with cultural standards.

This kind of unconditional love by parents makes self-hate, self-rejection, depression, and hopelessness virtually impossible. Of course, there will be "correctable faults," but the approach to correction, to growth, is constructive through acceptance, love, and patience rather than through judgment, recrimination, and punishment.

Parents who have difficulty in this area do well to confront aspects of themselves they feel are less than lovable and to look to causes of rejection in their own childhood histories. Parents also often have difficulty in this area because of neurotic pride in child abilities and development and destructive competition with other parent friends.

Let me point out that competence in toilet control, reading, writing, walking, standing are usually equally good in people by the time they reach age twenty. This means that regardless of how we do in many areas of child development relative to age standards, most of us do all right by the time we are young adults.

Richness of intellectual, emotional, and creative development will be augmented enormously by parental acceptance, especially unconditional loving acceptance. Keeping up with other children, anxiety, and rejection, too, because of early backwardness, are harmful to the process. Rate of physiological development varies among children and has little or no significance in terms of self-realization unless it is used to make a parent self-hating and apprehensive, or worse, lacking in confidence regarding the child.

Of course, love of the boy for being a boy and the girl for being a girl—complete and loving acceptance of the child's gender—is a great aid to the child's image and self-identification in all areas. In fact, this parent can't envision the child otherwise. His/her gender is an inextricable part of the child and that child is experienced as a boy/girl person from the time sexual identity is revealed. This, of course, is the antithesis of "but I really wanted a boy or a girl!"

In terms of good gender identification, providing a strong role model is very helpful. This means a parent who likes being his/her own gender, likes the opposite sex, and gives ample opportunity for the child to identify. This opportunity consists of acceptance and attention. Time spent with the child—good quality time—attention-paid time, which I spoke of earlier, is very helpful.

Gender identification, clarity, and acceptance is important beyond the area of the child's future sexual relating life. It has great relevance to our interests here because it is a crucial part of the entire self-concept and contribution to total self-acceptance and self-esteem. Rejection of one's own gender constitutes profound self-rejection. Accepting human characteristics, which, aside from gender, physiological, and a few psychological differences, are the same for both sexes, is invaluable. We all feel all feelings and we need to accept this regardless of gender. But acceptance of our human characteristics is augmented by acceptance of our own anatomies and anatomical destinies as human beings in the area of sexual identity.

We are brought up in a family and to date there is no substitute for family upbringing to best develop our potential. Family is perpetuated by strong, clear gender acceptance and clarity and the relating and heterosexuality that ensue. This is also true of self-esteem. A girl who likes being a girl already likes an important aspect of herself (as does the boy), and this is a cornerstone of self-esteem and all that high self-esteem contributes to well-being. A boy who likes himself, and especially likes himself when he likes a girl and she likes him, adds another contribution to the perpetuation of self-esteem.

Despite new and good constructive views of homosexuality, I feel that parents—event homosexual parents—largely prefer their children to be heterosexual. One of the good reasons is because they know that life is easier for the heterosexual. This is true not only because of society. It is true because self-acceptance and self-realization are easier in heterosexuality.

Then why are so many homosexual people—especially men—so talented?

I don't believe heterosexual people are less talented than homosexual people. But I believe that heterosexuals are more inhibited. This is especially true of the male population, in which confusion and fear of homosexuality run high. The result is repression of much that is considered less than altogether masculine and even feminine. Thus, many proclivities and talents involving cooking, color, poetry, dance, language, etc., are suppressed and become stunted. Men who accept their homosexuality accept these aspects of themselves and therefore do not suffer in these areas and can realize their talents and development of these interests.

But heterosexuals can realize development in these areas, too, because basically talent is not confined to either group, no more than it is to either gender. People are not homosexual because they have particular abilities nor are they accordingly heterosexual. They are what they are, largely due to early influences already described.

I believe that full development will be lacking if we as parents reject aspects of our children that we confuse with being of the "wrong gender." Therefore, I say love them for what they are in toto. Love the boy as a boy and his interests in "boyish things." Love the girl as a girl and her interests in "girlish things." Love the boy's girlish interests and the girl's boyish interests. Help them both to be interested and to develop their interests and any special talents they may have, regardless of gender. These interests may include: athletics, logic, math, philosophy, cooking, colors, art, decorating, knitting, music, sailing, medicine, engineering, law, social work, psychology, etc. Don't cheat them of at least half of what is possible because they are either one sex or the other.

Whole people are happier people. People who are totally accepted tend to accept the totality of themselves. They are better integrated. They have a better inner organization and ability to focus their assets in desirable directions. Of course, they have more assets to focus. These *whole* people (no aspect or characteristic of whom, including gender, has been rejected) are better integrated into the family. They relate well with members of both sexes and with people of multiinterests both in and out of the family. These people relate well to people of both sexes because they share areas of development and interests. Later on, in living with a member of the opposite sex, they do not separate into inviolate, encapsulated interests and activities. They participate together, enjoy their commonality, and continue this nonsexist participation relative to their own children. They have respect for each other's work and responsibilities as well as mutual respect.

Total acceptance of the child is, I suppose, a form, or perhaps *the* form, of love that most characterizes unconditional cooperative relating characterized by nonpatronizing, nonjudgmental attention. The child feels this and responds accordingly.

Let me close this chapter by saying that so much depends on parental acceptance of the child as a real, whole, separate, unique human being with individual potential. This acceptance largely determines the kind and outcomes of our children's parental and self-fulfilling prophecies.

Loyalty: The Sacred Alliance

Loyalty to children is a form of love and is the antithesis of overprotection. Let me list some ingredients I consider important under this important enabler of self-esteem and that the child unconsciously and consciously feels as evidence of lovability.

(1) Respect and inviolate cognizance of the child's particular state of development at different times. The child is not pushed beyond his/her capacity—to keep up with anyone. I remember my father saying that I would learn arithmetic later than other kids but eventually I would learn. He was right and he recognized that I was a slow starter in this area.

(2) Appropriate protection at all times. Protection from outside sources of persecution or bigotry of any kind—antireligion, sexist discrimination, teachers who dislike redheads, and any ideas, concepts, or practices that are ultimately destructive, etc. We must not expect the defenseless child "to stand up for" him/herself.

Know and protect the child's needs, appetites, and proclivities. I'll talk more about this at the end of this chapter when I discuss the sacred alliance.

Even as self-assertion is encouraged, indicate to the child that self-preservation has greater priority than self-assertion. Glory seeking is destructive. Asserting one's self against anyone or anything in any form who or which is ten times stronger than one's self and bent on destruction is self-destructive.

(3) Recognition, acceptance, and appropriate patience and steps taken in problems that come up. Bed-wetting, stammering, reading problems, physical problems, etc., are never, ever to be treated in any kind of rejecting, punitive way. They are always to be treated with optimistic compassion and with expert intervention. This is especially true of bed-wetting, in which first a pediatric urologist must be consulted; the body image—the physical image—and the sense the child has of his/her self is crucial to self-esteem. That image is affected greatly by proper treatment in this area. Of course, left-handedness, eye color, hair color, etc., as personal characteristics, all deserve nothing but total acceptance.

By the same token, let me caution that hysterical, hypochondriacal parents must make a special effort not to overprotect by dragging the child to a doctor for every sneeze. This is damaging to body image (the child's image or his/her physical self).

(4) Protect the child from participating in activities that may be damaging either by virtue of development or by the nature of the activity itself. Cautious children are often giving the message that they are not yet ready for gymnastics, diving, etc. Pushing before they are ready can lead to getting hurt. Zealous parents must not push children to activities designed for their own vicarious satisfaction. Protect the child from participation in activities that are totally antithetical to his/her well-being and dangerous. Frail boys gain nothing but fractured bones or worse on the football field. This is a form of protection of individual proclivities. Chess can be as exciting as football and more valuable to some children. But do allow the child to take appropriate "first steps" as participants in everyday life—no overprotection please!

(5) Never tolerate punishment in any form from a stranger! I am not happy with punishment in any case, but allowing punishment from a stranger is felt by the child as parental weakness, disloyalty, not caring.

(6) Stand up to self-hate in the child whenever it is perceived. "I hate myself for being scared," or "I hate my looks." These and similar statements must be taken seriously and addressed and countermanded at once.

(7) See that the child gets proper treatment and appropriate praise and compensation relative to jobs and work done.

(8) Be supportive and lend strength, wisdom, and compassion in times of need and crisis. This is especially applicable when new places and situations are confronted:

> new neighborhoods
> new schools
> examinations
> first dates
> first dances
> love affairs, and especially ones that are terminated
> first business ventures—selling newspapers, magazines, to investments
> first jobs
> any first attempt—from bowling to swimming to singing or dancing lessons.

(9) Avoid odious comparisons, especially with relatives and friends, and when the child participates in them in the service of self-hate—"John is a better player than me"—counter them with things your child is good at and unique at and discuss the valuelessness of this kind of competition.

(10) Get help for the child when needed—especially if he/she requests it: medical help, counseling, therapy, teaching help, physical training help, self-defense, if necessary, etc.

(11) Comfort and reassure the child who has problems with temper tantrums and poor self-control.

(12) Consult professionals at once if you suspect undue shyness or depression or anxiety. This one is different from (10) only because these areas are so important and common.

(13) Expect no more of your child than you do of yourself in terms of integrity, honesty, manners, self-control, religious dictums, fairness, optimism, people acceptance, especially those of different cultural and religious persuasions.

(14) Never embarrass the child.

(15) No admonishment in front of other people.

(16) Speak praises to him/her directly so that he/she doesn't have to hear it from other people to whom you told it.

(17) Share your possibly so-called secrets about family eco-

nomic status and where appropriate (age and developmental-wise) problems you may have.

(18) Respect the child's messages to you and especially secrets. Never trivialize his/her communications, however childish they may seem to you.

Remember back when you were a child and consider feelings you had about loyalty to you and caring about you at that age. That is a very valuable way to reestablish feelings at various times of one's own development, which can be used to further understand the child. The recollection of actual memories is very helpful. We do this in psychoanalysis to trace back to the origin of problems in order to clarify and to help with solutions and new directions. In doing this, we almost invariably add to compassion for ourselves because we usually have tender feelings for the innocent, vulnerable children we used to be. The same process aids our feelings for our children and restores sensitivity to their needs at a time when it is most useful—while they are still children and while we still have a major effect.

Believe me, this recollection of childhood and resuscitation of our own memories is no small thing in its constructive possibilities. We often repress all of it because it was painful and because we are terribly caught up in a world of daily affairs that runs roughshod over real needs. But if we can relax long enough, let it come, it will—the memory and feeling of how it was. This has an integrating effect on us—hooking up the various aspects of ourselves that may have been lost along the way at different times. More important for our purpose, it also provides a valuable bridge—a deeply involving, healthy bridge (involving does not mean inundating, exploitive, or overprotective) between parent and child.

This bridge constitutes the *sacred alliance*. The sacred alliance is the special, unique relationship only possible between parent and child. Its basis and substance simply are *consistent loyalty regardless of adversity, success, happiness, or sadness.* It largely determines the basis for constructive adult relationships. The *sacred alliance* provides a special sensitivity to the child's needs and proclivities—talents, abilities, potential. It is never perfect. It requires work. But consciousness of its existence and possibilities makes it much more likely to exist and to flourish for a lifetime.

The Incomparable Value of
Straightforward Messages

The title of this enabler almost tells it all.

This is a way of talking that is the absolute antithesis of sarcasm, wise-guy talk, soap-opera one-upmanship, adolescent ranking, manipulative talk, etc. Of course, there are no double-binds here and no talk that is made for performance. Indeed, the message, the substance, is what it is all about. There are no hidden meanings and nothing is left to the imagination. All transmissions are clear, to the point, and explicit, leaving minimum possibility for misunderstanding. When this does take place, the message is straightened out at once. These messages are not subtle. We tell it the way it is—compassionately, gently, but in so many words.

This kind of talk is particularly valuable in conveying feelings, opinions, and desires. Of course, talk involving straight information or directions of any kind is more valuable when conveyed well. This takes place when the child does not have to struggle to understand how a parent feels about a particular subject.

Displeasure, anger, pleasure, contentment are better conveyed by simple words—"I like that," or "I don't like that," or "That makes me angry," or "That makes me feel good"—than by silences, food treats, etc. One of my patients knew that his mother was angry only when she dusted so furiously that she invariably broke something.

Straightforward messages convey information clearly and

thus help in the education of the child. They also give an excellent example of how to talk so as to get along better in the world generally.

But most of all these kinds of messages prevent bafflement and confusion in the child. He/she knows where things are at—where a parent stands on issues—who a parent really is. This adds immeasurably to a sense of security.

Straight talk is a hallmark of cooperative relating. It is the principal vehicle for helping one another through the honest exchange of information of all kinds. Its design is for this bridging across to take place with ease, efficiency, and benefit for all concerned. It is the antithesis of talk used to gain an upper hand and admiration.

In this kind of talk the other person (the child) is the all-important object. His reaction to the giver of the message (parent) is not important. The parent is not looking for submission, admiration, respect, etc. What is important is that the child receive the message clearly so as to be able to absorb and use the information.

Of course, it is valuable to talk in terms accessible to the child relative to age and development. If the child does not understand, patience and compassion are mandatory to aid this kind of talk. As I said in the chapter on "Talk," talking louder does not help! Blaming the child does not help. Repeating the same words (as people tend to do with foreigners) does not help. Try other words. Try another approach. This talk is not a test of parental ability. It is a means of conveying information to the child.

Of course, insistence on clear messages from the child is enormously helpful. Do not settle for sulks or pronouns or sloppy use of words if you can help it. Do not tolerate wise-guy, one-upmanship sarcasm between siblings. Try, whenever possible, to convert this kind of talk to straight talk.

When a child sulks because he feels hurt or angry or both, do your best to draw him out supportively—to get him to talk about it. If she says, "I just don't want to talk about it," respect her sensitivity for now, but indicate to the child that you do want to talk about it later. Tell her how important it is—how advantageous it is—to talk about it in words rather than through sulks. Explain that sulking is talking about it but is not a good way to talk about it.

When the child says, "Basically, I'd rather go to the movies today than the game," ask him what is basic about it. Why use the word *basic?*

When the child says, "Jane told Jill that Mary wanted skates and then she said to her . . .," point out that you have no way of knowing who *she* and *her* are unless you are told.

Give the example and encourage the use of words—proper words—to convey straightforward, clear messages. Explain as soon as the child can understand how misunderstandings take place because of:

(1) sloppy language;
(2) ambiguities of all kinds—the child must come to understand that we are separate persons and that because he/she understands who or what he/she is referring to, we do not if we are not told; and

most important,

(3) When manipulation, being a wise guy or a martyr or attempting to make someone feel guilty, becomes more important than conveying understanding of how we feel.

Through example and instruction, teach the child that the best communication between people and the best way problems are solved between people is through the use of compassionate straight talk. Straight talk is aided when messages are clearly stated through the use of proper words and consideration that the other person is a separate human being. Demonstrate to them that although it is often a struggle to help the other person understand, it is one of the most important and rewarding struggles. Tell them that you are more than willing to share in the struggle to convey understanding, to understand, and to help them to do the same. I shall say more about struggle a few chapters from now.

Proclivities and Rhythms

Some parents are blessed with the ability—the happy ability—
to be able to *read* their children—some of us are not. But
we can all improve this important ability if we are open to
our children, if we *listen* and perceive without prefixed notions,
prejudices, and resistance. We can then avoid pushing against
impossible odds—changing our kids to what they are not and
neglecting the development of what they are. It is so much
easier to provide meaningful support to a natural flow and real
possibility.

We are not all born the same and the environment from day
one is not received by any of us in identical ways. Therefore,
there are always major differences and unique qualities even
in children of the same parents. If we are attuned to these
differences and uniquenesses, we dignify their proclivities and
rhythms.

It is of great value to avoid "training" a child, that is, to
make him/her conform to a preconceived pattern. It is of great
value to recognize natural tendencies that exist and to aid them.
This enhances self-acceptance and individuality and counters
the dulling effect of useless conformity. This eventually enhances uniqueness over superiority. I mean that what one feels
about one's self and outside issues becomes more important
than what others think of us and than being ahead or better
than other people. Self-esteem comes of our good evaluation
of ourselves as a function of self-acceptance. Momentary shots

in the arm, resulting from victories over others or being higher in the competitive hierarchy, constitute pseudo-self-esteem.

Children do not require the same amount of sleep, the same amount of food, nor do they have the same food tastes. I never slept more than five hours. I am grateful that I was not forced to sleep eight hours because an eight-hour norm was established by well-meaning experts of that time. There are variations in needs within the parameters of satisfying healthy requirements. Respect for individual differences has great value. Indeed, the child who has slept enough, who has eaten enough, is far less irritable than the child who is forced to conform in these and other areas. Unfortunately, many fights, breakdowns in communication between parent and child—perfectly well-nourished and rested children—often take place relative to these issues. The issues themselves are fed by the parents' own conventional training that eventually deteriorates into a destructive power play.

Different children fatigue more or less easily. Some children need naps, some don't. Some have very sensitive skins and can't stand too much towel rubbing—some don't and love to be washed and rubbed down.

Some children have superb body awareness and control and therefore can chance certain activities requiring excellent reflex action early on. Some are very limited in this area and wisely act very cautiously in any kind of gymnastic attempts. The former do well with encouragement and even training in this area. The latter must neither be pushed or mocked but supported in enjoying activities limited to realistic possibilities. I believe that respect for one's own bodily needs and possibilities reduces stress or even avoids the formation of stress in later life.

Children early on demonstrate different perceptive sensitivities and these must be respected if our goal is self-acceptance and full development. My nephew was always acutely vulnerable to loud sounds. As an infant, loud, discordant music made him twitch and start and cry, while my own children were not "bothered" by noise or cacophony at all. My nephew is now a graduate of The Juilliard School of Music.

Some children show early proclivity to body movement relative to music—not to be ignored. I've actually heard children like this being told, "Don't fidget! Sit still," when they were moving in perfect synchrony with music played in the background that the parent didn't hear at all.

Some children are acutely vulnerable to smells of all kinds and suffer when someone blows smoke in their faces. Some of them love the smell of flowers and early on show an easy interest in identifying flowers and plants and associating them and their names with individual scents. They may not go on to be horticulturists. But they will be fuller, richer, more alive, and self-accepting people.

Some children need solitude more than others.

My granddaughter and grandson—she is twelve, he's nine—both love to play together and with other children. Neither of them is shy. But Jacob periodically goes off by himself and plays alone. Nathania seldom does that. I believe his need for solitude is very important. He needs time alone to absorb and integrate what he has experienced with other people. He needs it to get a feel of himself and to use his imagination in games he plays alone as a means of stretching his creative possibilities and growing.

Nathania integrates the goings on even as she plays and is generally more gregarious. Neither is healthier than the other. Neither is better. They are different. Fortunately, neither is expected or pressured to conform to a direction or pattern that is not natural for them and therefore they remain healthy.

People who are gregarious are not manics and people who need more solitude than others are not schizoid. Respect for different requirements is of paramount importance. Jacob falls asleep early and gets up early. Nathania goes to sleep late and gets up early. There is no attempt to convert either or both to another pattern and no message conveyed that one or another pattern is better.

To summarize very simply, I suppose I am saying that it is greatly enabling to listen to the child's music, to enjoy the rhythm, and to join in his/her songs as you encourage him/her to go on composing.

Struggle and Work

I have talked about struggle before in different books and in different contexts, but none is as important as applied to young children as well as young adults. To encourage struggle and to help the child to value struggle and work is giving him/her one of the most valuable enablers of all. This is so because struggle and work—and they are for me synonymous—are necessary for any kind of worthwhile stretching and growing.

Our society often deprecates struggle and demeans accomplishments that are the results of hard work. Too often prestige is ascribed to goals reached through crafty manipulation, luck, outsmarting the other guy, being a good examination analyzer, etc., none of which increases either real self-esteem or intellectual, emotional, or creative development. "Any dope can work hard and break his neck to get what he wants" is not a rare attitude. But demeaning struggle not only prevents deep change and growth; it also prevents real enjoyment of accomplishment gleaned through the use and full awareness of inner resources—self.

Struggle to learn, to change, to adapt, to find, to understand, to teach, to develop, is often confused with suffering. This is understandable if a large cultural influence exists that demeans anything antithetical to the quick road to quick results.

It must be kept in mind that neurotic suffering takes place in the service of self-deception, self-stagnation, and false self-idealization. Struggle is the major ingredient, the vehicle through which healthy growth and self-realization—real self,

real spontaneity, the antithesis of neurotic compulsive rigidity—
take place.

I have a patient who is a physician, who could not understand
why none of his four children have gone into medicine. But
he remembers demeaning his own efforts to get through medical
school—"the awful struggle to learn all that stuff," as well as
the struggling he did to get started as well as the daily practice
of medicine. "Must be an easier way to make a living," he
admits was practically a theme song in his home while the
children were growing up. Struggle is also demeaned when hard
work is put down; when speed is extolled over thoroughness;
when quick understanding takes precedence over deep understanding; when attempts to grasp, to learn, to understand are
met with derisive impatience; and whenever compassion is absent relative to efforts made to extend one's parameters.

A parent's attitude toward his/her own struggles as well as
the struggles of others is of paramount importance. But the
parental attitude toward the child's struggles is crucial! This
will largely determine the child's attitude. Dignifying the child's
struggle by parental participation is always constructive.

I was waiting for a train in Grand Central Station some months
ago and watched a young mother and her two very young daughters. One was trying to tie her shoelaces. The other was trying
to tell the time. The young woman was utterly gentle and patient
with her daughters and was obviously enjoying their struggles.
She went over the process of lace tying again and again, and
as the little girl tried, she helped the other child to tell time.
She used both the big clock in the station and a drawing the
child made on a big pad with her mother's help. On several
occasions the children wanted to quit. Their mother gently,
very gently, encouraged them to go on and skillfully guided
the small child's fingers and hands through the lace-tying process. The children succeeded after many trials and errors. Success was far from perfect. But standards were appropriate to
their skills and limitations. The mother praised their efforts—
"That's wonderful," she said, "keep trying," and she stopped
a while and kissed and hugged them, especially when they became impatient, annoyed, and frustrated.

In this process she accomplished several very important
things, some of which I will discuss at greater length later.

(1) She demonstrated and gave and exchanged love through a joint effort—the effort to learn something new.

(2) She helped to increase attention span—a wonderful characteristic that aids all efforts at every stage of life and makes attention to detail and complicated work easier. Attention span and frustration tolerance are different for different children. But with parental patience they can grow. It is constructive to help the child to participate in pleasurable activities, preferably of his/her own choice. If he can't choose, then introduce him to tasks and games. Don't overload! Keep her at a task just a bit longer each time around and have as many in-between rest periods as needed. Attention span can be stretched in this way, imperceptively at first, but eventually enough to take on complicated activities and to see them through. The struggle to persevere, not to give up, extends attention span and hope, too. *But* it is also important to help the child to surrender inappropriate tasks, at least temporarily, until he/she is better prepared. Preparation itself can be viewed as a struggle and as a component of delayed gratification, which I will talk about in the next chapter.

(3) She helped to increase frustration tolerance.

(4) She demonstrated hope and optimism in terms of fulfilling the possibility of learning fruition. She showed them she believed they could learn to do it and in so doing helped them to believe likewise.

(5) She dignified and respected struggle, effort put out, and work done. She appreciated accomplishment *but* not as much as she appreciated effort—work, stretching, growing. The process must always be more important than the product; indeed, the process is the principal product. Please see *Compassion and Self-Hate*.

(6) She helped to teach the important lesson of the value of postponement of gratification. Had the mother tied the shoe, the satisfaction of doing it herself, which took time, would not have accrued to the child.

Remember—every new effort, new experience, requires struggle and hard work at every stage of life. Knowing this can spell the difference between hopelessness and defeat and optimism and success. I had a patient who was a first-year medical student. She was terribly discouraged, I learned, because in reading physiology and anatomy, it took her hours to go through a page so that it made sense and so that she would remember it. She had always been a fast reader and a fine student. While she realized she could not read and absorb this kind of material as quickly as a novel, she was chagrined and felt increasingly hopeless because technical material of the past had gone much more quickly.

I pointed out to her that in effect she was learning a new language and that this took a great deal of time. I told her that everyone—myself included—took hours with each page at the beginning. I recalled to her my reading internal medicine (easier than the earlier subjects) and for the first month having to consult the medical dictionary every few pages. I indicated that struggle here was absolutely appropriate and that the work does get easier as the language is learned. She did it. She enjoyed it. She is now a physician involved with other important struggles appropriate to her stage of development.

Help appropriately (don't do it for them unless it is necessary; don't expect them to go it alone when it is not possible). Help them with love, patience, respect, dignity, participation, encouragement, fun and enjoyment, to struggle when:

—The child attempts to hold his bottle, reach her rattle, babble her message.

—The child attempts to stand up, to walk from one supporting object to another.

—Struggles to utter first words, to pronounce them better, to form phrases, sentences, to frame ideas, to play more and more complicated games.

—To read—how hard it is to read—especially for people whose earliest struggles were met with derision.

—To play, to socialize on any level.

—To learn anything at all on all levels.

—To express feelings and to articulate about them.

—To work at jobs—selling papers to first adult job interview, to learning new work skills, to taking on large responsibilities.

—To stick to programs involving training or any kind of goal directions.

—Struggles to leave home for the first time and eventually to make it on his/her own.

—To encounter social and sexual experiences—first parties, dates, kisses, infatuations.

—To encounter harsh realities—sickness, injustices, limitations, prejudices.

—To participate in special new experiences—swimming, athletic events, speech making, debates, acting, singing, dancing, skating, bike riding (which can take time but then gives great satisfaction in newfound self-controlling mobility).

—To participate in any and all creative efforts, from finger-painting to writing short stories; from Tinker Toy inventions to building tree houses to drawing architectural plans.

—To sustain relationships as well as to terminate counterproductive ones.

—To understand more and more about the human condition.

—To achieve and to sustain humility and self-confidence in a world often pressuring otherwise.

—To learn more and more about him/herself. This help can only be extended productively if it is offered generously and gently, without moralistic, judgmental criticism.

—To help to accept rejection with equanimity.

—To help your children to be helpful in the struggles of their children.

—Struggles with understanding money and financial realities.

—Struggles in any and all training or school programs.

—To learn new languages of all kinds.

Of course, this list goes on and on. I'm sure there is much you can add of equal or more importance than the areas and activities I've listed.

The point again is to support struggle in any and all human manifestations and activities. Lend complete endorsement to the belief that struggle—work—is a highly satisfying activity that leads to self-esteem, self-development, self-realization, and gratification unmatched by any shortcut maneuvers born of craft, gamble, or manipulation, however clever.

Remember please:

(1) The process—the struggle—is living and is the product and more important than the achievement itself.

(2) Winning time contests is not as important as quality work and learning "well."

I remember one surgeon who was slow but meticulous. His results were infinitely better than those of speedy confreres—to whom speed became the principal goal.

(3) Each child, each human being, finds some areas more difficult than his/her confreres do. This is not a cause for abandonment of the attempt. On the contrary—most often the greater the struggle, the better the stretching or growth process and the greater the satisfaction.

This is an important corollary of (3):

(4) Pacing and timing are different for all of us. A "job" that a child can't do today, he may be able to do a month from now. I have known this to be true of connecting with poetry, music, and especially learning to play an instrument. Don't delay unnecessarily, but delay where appropriate without "giving up."

(5) Parental attitude toward their own struggles, toward other people's struggles, and especially toward the child's struggles, is terribly important.

But helping the child struggle is love and doing it with loving support—verbal encouragement and demonstrable love, hugs, and kisses—makes struggle pleasurable for all concerned and aids the process immeasurably.

The Postponement of
Gratification

This is one of the key enablers in life at any age and is especially valuable if parents help to establish it at an early age. The postponement of gratification—being able to put off immediate satisfaction in order to have larger rewards later on—is in its way a form of elongation of attention span. If we put off gratification in a particular process, then we sustain attention to that process at least until the goal is achieved at a later date. This permits engaging in long-range activities, plans, preparation, and training required by ambitious goals involving maximum self-realization. This is a struggle of enormous practical value.

In overcoming indecisiveness, I wrote that procrastination and avoiding commitment are the antithesis of the knowledge that "solid results require time." In the former, time is used poorly and is truly wasted in endless rationalizations. In the latter, a decision is made and a long-range plan is initiated, commitment to which is usually obvious by appropriate work done.

Postponement of gratification gives an appreciation for what time and its use can do in terms of achieving goals. It makes for respect of time as it increases patience. For me there is nothing in life as valuable as time. The time of our lives and how we use that time tells the story of our lives. Postponement of gratification honors time, uses it well, and psychologically—

211

in our feelings—gives us a good sense of time and its value. This is especially true when we learn to wait at an early age. Let me say at once that I do not advocate deliberate frustration of the child—making him/her wait for a bottle when he/she is hungry, etc. This sadistic contrivance is counterproductive. He/she must learn about waiting through productively gratifying experiences that grow in complexity as the child grows older.

As I've said in other books, training, experience, and development, especially in an ever-increasingly complex world of specialization, takes time. An inability to wait is a virtual guarantee of small or no rewards and often frustration, resignation, and hopelessness. Rewards are usually geometrically and directly proportional to the ability to wait. The rewards I speak of here include a lifetime of interesting and well-paid work; a satisfying and prevailing feeling for one's own professional expertise; sufficient development to enjoy good music, art, performing arts, good books, and sustained relationships with interesting people.

To become a surgeon, lawyer, diplomat, business administrator, musician, or writer takes time. So do relationships. Struggle and work are necessary, but there are many initiation fees to pay along the way before great gratification takes place. Of course, humility paves the way and neutralizes feelings of humiliation as we become freshmen again and again after each graduation—elementary school, high school, college, medical school, first-year resident, etc. The postponement of gratification is an ongoing and renewable process and is part and parcel of serious self-development. As students, little money is earned and recognition of work done and energy expended is minimal. But joy in work is possible if acceptance of the necessity for postponement is present. The rewards come later in the form of doing expert work and other rewards that this usually brings. It is gratifying, after all, to be a useful, contributing member of a community of fellow human beings.

Again, here, as in other enablers, parents' own attitudes are extremely important. Impatient parents do not make for good contribution to providing or enhancing this enabler. And parents do convey patience to the children if they themselves have it, along with a sense of the value of time and a sense of well-being in being able to wait for what they want.

I have a patient who always remembers her lawyer father working patiently on "big cases" for years, knowing that the rewards would eventually be "enormous." They led to great financial rewards, much prestige, and the personal satisfaction of participating in landmark, precedent-setting cases.

I know a woman who admired her mother because she would wait and save up for a "particular" coat she wanted rather than get one *now* that she didn't want. She did not suffer as she waited. My friend said that her mother waited patiently and never seemed in a hurry or deeply frustrated by lack of immediate gratification. These "lessons" are important for the child, who seldom fails to pick them up. He/she knows how parents feel about time.

But what about active application from parent directly to child? Again, this application will be rendered ineffectual if the parent takes on the maxim of "Do as I say, not as I do" as he/she goes about depressed because a swimming pool, etc., can't be built at once.

There is no reason why a parent cannot tell a child, as soon as he/she understands, about the value of time and waiting in so many words. "You have to read a book to enjoy the book and to enjoy the outcome fully you must read the whole book before you read the last page." A discussion about this example and others, as well as about geometrically high satisfactions in constructive waiting (using time in behalf of the goal while waiting), is of great value. It also provides a good subject for constructive communicating between parent and child.

Younger children understand these discussions, too, if the parent is patient and not patronizing. Examples, especially those parents participate in, are very good to get the point and philosophy across, as well as interesting questions and answers.

"Do you know how long it took Dr. Brown to become a doctor? Why? The schools he went to? The stuff he learned, etc.?" "But do you know the kind of work Uncle Frank does and the money he makes, the people he meets?"

Discourage statements and attitudes like, "If I can't have it now, I don't want it."

I saw a young mother and small child in a restaurant. The child said he wanted ice cream. His mother said it would spoil his appetite but he could have it later. He said he didn't want it if he had to wait. She replied, "You will want it later." She was teaching him about waiting.

Participate in and help with all kinds of waiting activities and experiences leading to enriched satisfactions. Some examples follow:

—Learning to thread a needle with increasing efficiency and then mending a sock.

—Fishing—enormously gratifying for even the youngest children and also aids in the experience of tranquility. Waiting brings rewards.

—Putting together a jigsaw puzzle—from the simplest to the most complex—and watching the picture as it reveals itself.

—Acquisition of any skill that takes time and then leads to increasing satisfaction and pleasure—games, jacks, pick-up-sticks, tennis, etc.

—Collecting and watching collections grow—coins, stamps, buttons, etc.

—Building from erector sets.

—Saving up to buy anything at all, especially if one's own earnings are involved.

—Learning how to knit, crochet, needlepoint, and then following through to completion and use of the finished product.

—Cooking a meal, especially for several people.

—Painting a room or a picture or building from wood.

—Learning how to use clay and then making something with it.

—House-training and obedience training for a dog.

Of course, the acquisition of taste for complex music and art takes time. I recommend a very gradual approach of small exposures, gradually lengthened relative to the growth of attention span.

There are many other possibilities. Parental patience is not only a virtue here. It is crucial.

The Joyous, Healthy Household

To be born into and to live in the joyous, healthy household is to have an overall enabler of enormous influence. This enabler provides so much of the germinating ground for all of the other enablers. Let me list some of the principal characteristics comprising this family milieu.

(1) Reality orientation is excellent and is not experienced as a burden but rather as an acceptable state of being. This means that imagination of members may be rich but illusions about self and the family are minimal. The family's image of itself is not aberrated by a fantasized mystique.

(2) Self-satisfaction—the sense of secure, comfortable membership in the community—is almost ever-present. This includes the family community as well as various segments of social structure—neighborhood, city, country, human species.

(3) The family makes use of appropriate skills in day-to-day living of its various members. In the sick family, the loudest voice prevails, however sick and unskilled the individual owning that voice may be. In the healthy family, leaderships are "assigned" as a natural consequence of individual abilities. If the mother is good with money, she governs the family bankroll, etc. If the sister is good with career counseling, she helps her siblings in that area.

(4) The family members eat, exercise, and take care of themselves appropriately. The members are not given to hypochondria or to life-threatening risks.

(5) The family makes extensions into the surrounding social milieu easily.

This occurs as a consequence of family-member interest and involvement in community affairs, including educational institutions (PTA, school boards, etc.), political organizations, cultural institutions (museums, music halls, etc.), religious or subcultural groups, charitable groups, etc.

This family also has "people over." They entertain extended-family members—uncles, aunt, cousins, nieces, nephews, as well as nonfamily friends. They welcome and aid the children's invitations to friends and help to use their home as a warm, entertaining place.

(6) The family shares enthusiastic joy in partaking as a family—especially from early on in the lives of the children—in zoo trips, picnics, extended family affairs, weddings, parties, etc. The family enjoys trips and vacations and in some cases lectures, concerts, and educational experiences—taking courses together—photography, fashion, cosmetics, economics, psychology, childrearing, etc.

(7) The family especially enjoys celebration of joyous events—family births, weddings, confirmations, birthdays, graduations, achievements, completion of projects, etc.

(8) The family enjoys the commonplace—eating together, talking, walking, going to a movie, working in or on the house together, visiting, and all the activities that comprise the everyday stuff of life—the nonpeak, adrenalin experience—the valley activities where we do so much of our living.

(9) This family laughs a lot out loud. "Letting go" with abandon is a welcome phenomenon here.

I mean this literally, but even more important, figuratively also.

The happy family has fun together and they demonstrate it with laughter and conversation. Good times and being together and experiencing everyday life, within realistic expectations, are felt by all. This being part of a happy family is a contagious morale booster. Coming home from school or work is experienced as a lift. This is true whether people are feeling convivial or feel like being alone to do their own thing. Members of this family are also capable of happiness when they are not within the confines of the family.

Members of this family do not have to be in the presence of their immediate relatives to feel they "belong." That feeling provides background music regardless of where they are or what they are doing. It contributes appreciably to security, self-esteem, and optimism. These people, without trying, provide a therapeutic effect wherever they go. People feel better for being with them. Their way of relating is to engender and to sustain happiness both in play and in work. This kind of approach to work makes it so much more productive and satisfying, aiding the cause of realizing one's potential.

Good Sexual Orientation

$\mathbf{B}$y sexual orientation I mean how people feel about sex. This includes their own and other people's sexuality as well as information about sex or sex education. Indeed, from this point of view these cannot be separated. Feelings about sexual encountering and activity on any level are as much and even more a part of one's sexual education as is formal knowledge about sex. This is why the most important aspect of sex education occurs in the home, and this happens from the very beginning of one's life.

Sexual orientation is a very important enabler in at least several crucial ways:

(1) How we feel and what we come to know and believe about sex will have great influence on how we feel about ourselves as well as how we relate to people of the same sex and especially to people of the opposite sex.

(2) Clean and healthy sexual orientation helps to prevent internal sexual conflict, disturbed sexual relationships, guilt, frustration, rage, confusion, and, indeed, it promotes healthy relating on all levels.

(3) Sex on all levels is a basic relating instrument. This means that it largely motivates us to get together, to live together, to form families, to have children. It also means that sex is an effective instrument to express affection and in so doing to develop strong feelings for other people. Used fully, sex, as an instrument of conveying affection, also aids the process

218

of emotional investment, caring about and for someone else. This produces the full development of emotional ability used for the process of sustained relating we call love.

(4) Healthy sexual orientation contributes to strong gender identification—a very important and basic component of self-identification and self-esteem.

(5) Sexual feelings can be strong feelings and as such are an antideadening and antialienating (alienation from our feelings) device. This makes us feel vital and alive, connected to the rest of humanity; puts us in touch with other feelings, and contributes to joy.

(6) Sex provides the possibility of sharing much pleasure both in terms of physical gratification and intimacy. Intimacy, while expressed physically, can be an extension of deep feelings of closeness born of the deepest trust and shared lives.

How does a child develop a sexual attitude that is healthy, spontaneous, free of guilt, and full of potential for the expression of deep love? Nearly all of it happens at home.

Of course, the home that produces this kind of enabler is free of exhibitionism, narcissism, gender prejudice, sadism, seductiveness, sexual exploitation of any kind, constriction, guilt, and sexual hang-ups and disorders. Obviously, I am saying that parents themselves—that is, how they feel about sex and what their sex lives are like—exert an enormous influence. The child is aware! Make no mistake. He/she is learning lessons in sex constantly. And I'm not talking about viewing sexual intercourse between members of the family or farm animals.

He/she notes the respect, consideration, sensitivity to the needs of Mom to Dad and Dad to Mom.

He/she notes if and how affection is transmitted—hugs, kisses, words. He/she knows if they are perfunctory or if they convey real feelings and meanings. "I love you" has great meaning when parents say it to each other, mean it, and follow it up with mutual care and sharing of important tasks, responsibilities, and problems.

Reactions to affectionate gestures and moves are duly noted. Are they repelled? Are they accepted with gratitude because they are so rare? Are they accepted and returned in a mutual expression of love and pleasure? Are they contrived gestures used to please, to mollify, or to manipulate? Or are they natural, spontaneous, and generous giving of one's self and one's love? The child knows. He/she is uniquely tuned in and responsive to parental feelings as well as to words. Tones, movements, and subtleties do not escape him/her.

The child knows if opinions rendered by parents and feelings expressed by parents are taken derisively or with interest, dignity, and respect by the other parent. Yes, this, too, is an attitude toward a sexual partner and conveys a sexual attitude.

The child also comes to know about delicacy, privacy, and discretion as regards self-comportment, dress, as well as open family displays of intimacy—without stilted behavior or prissiness.

While gratuitous information is not pressed on the child, his/her curious questions are answered forthrightly and are fully informative. They never give the impression that sex is a taboo subject. Answers and discussions—such as the connection between sex and emotional involvement—are appropriate to the development and age of the child.

Child self-exploration and self-stimulation are never viewed with horror. They are accepted as the natural phenomena that they are.

Misinformation, especially that involving the opposite gender—physiology, anatomy, etc.—is straightened out at once, clearing confusions and preventing prejudices and distortions.

I have known adults who believed:
—Women don't have real sexual desires.
—Once a woman has sex she craves it all the time.
—If a man has sex with a woman of another race he will never want it with a woman of his own group again.
—Fondling a woman's breasts will permanently enlarge and distort them.
—Women need orgasms to become pregnant.
—Women with small breasts are more difficult to excite.
—The size of a man's penis determines his potency.
—People go crazy if they have sex too often or too seldom.

The list of misinformed nonsense is endless—yes, even in this enlightened age. All of it can be traced to childhood and to misinformation as well as to extensions of one's own prejudices and fears.

Healthy sex between the sexes does not begin with overt, concrete, physical sexual activity. It begins with healthy mutual respect and *social* intercourse. It is important for parents to encourage children of both sexes to play together. As a consequence of the familiarity born of this play, children recognize members of both sexes as quite human and of this earth. Later on, attendance at parties and dances needs encouragement. This prevents the development of painful awkwardness as well as frustration, confusion, self-hate, and anger. It also prevents idealizing the opposite sex, which invariably leads to damaging disappointments.

Bringing both boys and girls home as friends helps enormously to make matters between the sexes smooth and open and comfortable later on. But this can only happen as a natural consequence of parents' encouragement and parental warm acceptance of friends of both sexes. Of course, parents themselves associating with members of both sexes is very helpful.

These applications of natural socializations to children of both sexes help immeasurably later on in serious heterosexual relationships. Many adult couples are never friends, having had no experience with heterosexual friendships as children. Some have greater difficulty as a result of prejudice against members of the opposite sex experienced as children, induced by apprehensive and bigoted parents. Sexism in any form is very destructive in this connection.

It is obvious that good sex evolves from good sexual education in all its ramifications. Good and healthy sex is largely the result of early familial experience and education. It is also the result of one's own mental health generally and all the factors that led to that state of mental health. Good sex, in turn, contributes to mutual satisfaction in terms of relating on all levels as a vehicle for conveying deeply felt emotions.

The Success Habit

Struggle and the postponement of gratification become especially meaningful if they lead to the satisfaction of success.

Of course, continuing success in all things is impossible. We all learn this soon enough.

But defeat after defeat can become a habit that leads to resignation and hopelessness.

In keeping with the psychology and philosophy of compassion and what I said earlier, I would describe two kinds of success experiences. One, I would call *process success;* the other I would call *accomplishment success.* Both are relevant. The first is subtle and more important. The second, often an offshoot of the first, has relevance especially in our society and is obvious. Let's take a look at both since both are contributing members of the enabler—*the success habit.*

In *process success,* success may be measured by the degree of interest in, involvement in, tenacity (attention span), commitment to, satisfaction from, and joy derived from engaging in the process—the actual doing. This means that the child, if successful, is giving himself as totally and wholly as possible, with rapt attention and enthusiasm, to drawing, painting, writing a composition, walking up and back from one end of the playpen to the other, or crawling to her goal. The crawling is the process and in this kind of success, reaching the goal is not relevant. In this kind of success, the crawling itself (the process) is the goal and requires your support. She receives your support through your interest, praise, and gratitude. Your fuss about her *attempt* to reach the goal aids the philosophy of the process being the product.

Repeated "process successes" of this kind and recognition through you that *trying* and *doing* represent success is a worthwhile enabler in several ways. It eventually encourages attempts at complex problems in all kinds of endeavors in the future, without the inhibiting blockages of worry over potential goal failure. It makes for raising of self-esteem early in life by just doing and especially in doing fully. It provides pleasure in doing regardless of outcome. It gives respect and honor to all life's processes—the everyday stuff of living—obliterating the need for adrenalin highs derived only from huge achievements.

And this feeling of success through involvement (and we may use any of the examples to exercise this kind of success listed in the chapter on struggle) makes for a commitment that gives the greatest chance for *accomplishment success* and satisfaction therein derived, too.

The processes the child may get involved in may not interest him/her at first and they often need repeated parental stimulation to get involved. This may be true of crawling or of complex photographic work, etc. I'll have more to say about some aspects of this later on in the chapter on home enrichment. But it is important for parents to know that interest usually follows involvement and not the other way around. Early in life, big interests do occur and I'll have more to say about this later, but with much that we get interested in we must be sufficiently involved before interest takes place.

It is difficult and often impossible to like to do something before we've tried doing it. This is particularly applicable to unfamiliar and complex activities. This is why parental suggestions and their own enthusiasms are important in order to get the child sufficiently involved so as to become interested in order to become further involved. This is particularly true of activities that do not have common, ordinary excitement, like ball games or network television's constant stimulation. Thus, taking the child to the ballet, concerts, theater, planetariums, movies of quality, botanical gardens, aquariums, and art museums can have enormous value. That value is increased immensely if the parent is excited enough to share with the child enthusiastic conversations about music, botany, and their ramifications, painting, etc. When the child becomes interested and shows it by his/her enthusiasm, both parent and child have experienced success in this kind of *interest-extending* endeavor. We will discuss this more in the chapter on home enrichment.

But what about sure-bet successes of the accomplishment variety, the kind that helps the child to experience the pleasure of accomplishment?

Start small! Don't overload! Praise through joining in at fruition time with enthusiastic joy—"Wonderful"—but don't be patronizing! Be supportive and encouraging but don't take over and complete the task yourself because of impatience! Stay within the child's parameters appropriate to age and skills.

The goal completions, met by praise, are the same as those listed in the chapter on struggle, but here completion and joy in completion are associated and linked through parental pleasurable response. There are many successful possibilities:

—Fetching an object, the name of which is recognized by the very young child.
—Helping to close a door.
—Closing draws completely and thus successfully.
—Winding a clock completely.
—Sweeping a floor.
—Shelling peas.
—Helping with selection of food to be bought, buying it, preparing it, serving it.
—Helping in the family business. Arranging merchandise on shelves to eventually making sales and ordering and buying new goods. Helping a lawyer mother to gather material for depositions and to write briefs.
—Swimming a length of the pool.
—Playing a simple tune.
—Writing a letter, composition, paper, story.
—Buying and selling anything at all in an effort to earn some money.

Obviously this list is endless and extends from the simplest tasks to the most complex and refined. In the execution of success-oriented endeavors, the individual combines optimism as well as an appreciation of realistic limits. The first prevents hopelessness and the second prevents failure leading to further hopelessness and resignation. A large part of the process depends on and also feeds good judgment. Success, even in the smallest and simplest attempts, provides incentive for more of the forthcoming rewards and thus further promotes *doing* rather than *stagnation*. This doing increases experiential knowledge, which is increasingly used to enhance good judgment. This judgment is used to choose endeavors that have a good chance for success—saving much time and energy as a constructive cycle is established.

If full engagement in the process (process success) leads to maximum satisfaction, while goal completion offers satisfaction, too, failure to fully reach goals is never catastrophic. This means that further attempts are made because the attempt itself is satisfying. This markedly reduces feelings of hopelessness when difficult criteria cannot be fully met. I remember one man who hardly ever "felt down," regardless of outcome. He would get up and try again or try something else. His most vivid and telling recollections involved activities (sailing, rearranging his father's drugstore stock more effectively) through which he shared a great deal of pleasure with one or both of his parents. Familial struggles, including making limited income do during hard times, were viewed as successful and shared by the entire family, who participated in the process. This early sharing of endeavors, which were felt as important, gave him much success orientation as well as identification with family, contributing to self-security and optimism.

Finally, the family that freely enjoys successful involvements, small and large as well, as accomplishments (both the process and the product) links joy and success. This prevents the reaction of pseudojoy that many people experience through martyred failure—"losers" who revel in being "losers." This curtails feelings of sustained abuse that lead to failure in every area, especially in relationships. The simple truth is that it's fun to be with someone who enjoys success in any of his/her struggles and achievements.

Curiosity

Curiosity is a great enabler and I believe a natural inborn asset. It can be enhanced and may become a constructive inner resource. As such it can be a powerful motivator for self-development in all areas and in healthy change and growth throughout one's entire lifetime. It can also be stunted and destroyed and when this happens a stimulus to healthy growth is lost.

There's a story I've told about my son Jeff and a fishing reel.

One day, when Jeff was about ten years old, I found him at a table trying to put together my favorite and very expensive fishing reel. He told me that he had taken it apart—completely, down to nuts and bolts—some hours earlier and had been trying to get it back together since without success. I was enraged and really let him have it—about his being callous, grandiose, not caring about money, etc. Neither of us had the slightest notion of how to get it together. But he did have all of its parts—at least sixty or so of them. We brought the whole mess, in a paper bag, to my friend Joe, who owned the local gas station. Joe patiently put it together—perfectly—in under an hour while I continued to rant at Jeff. After we were done, Joe took me aside and told me that he really believed that Jeff was an unusual boy and that what he did with the fishing reel proved it. He said that Jeff in no way engaged in malicious destruction but rather exhibited great curiosity and was challenged about how the reel worked. He pointed out that my reaction was appropriate to the former and not to the latter.

To lighten the incident he also told me a story about a grandfather and small boy who asked many questions.

"Grandpa, why do people die?"

"I don't know," said the grandpa, "but it's a good question."

"Grandpa, why does the world keep going around the way it does?"

"I don't know, but it's a good question."

"Grandpa, how high is the sky?"

"I don't know, but it's a good question." And then the grandfather said, "That's the way you learn, by asking questions."

Joe helped me to work on my humility and to become curious about curiosity and as a result I started to think about it.

It occurred to me that psychoanalysis is in a way a process in which we help the patient to become curious about him/herself. We help the patient to want to find the real truth and connections between feelings, motivations, actions, life events, yearnings, conflicts, anxieties, etc. In so doing, the patient becomes interested in whats and hows and elucidations and clarifications and real meanings. Patterns, sequences, causes and effects begin to emerge as insights become formed and usable. Thus, the patient learns that his/her life and behavior is not haphazard but has designs of which the individual had little or no knowledge. As these are revealed, the person becomes increasingly in charge of his/her life, and real free choices and decisions can be made constructively.

The psychoanalyst is not as interested in giving answers to curious questions as he/she is in helping the patient to find answers and to go on being curious about still more issues. Thus the analyst makes more use of the words *when* and *how* than *why*. *When* and *how* lead to descriptions of feelings and still more opening up. *Why* leads to intellectual or logical thinking answers that tend to close up, to terminate the process. The analyst is interested in further exploration—and still further exploration—which adds to curiosity and still more growth.

"*When* that happened, *how* did you feel?"

"*When* you felt like that, *how* did you respond?"

"*How* do you feel about it now? *What* would you feel like doing about it now?"

This is not unlike what we can do to make children's curiosity an even greater enabler than it is. Of course, we must not crush their curiosity by vindictive tirades such as mine or by ignoring their curiosity or in any way treating it in a perfunctory, disrespectful way, indicating that they and it are nuisances.

From my point of view, we may divide curiosity into three subgroups that may ultimately interconnect.

(1) *Primary curiosity.* This is self-starting and is an extension of the child's earliest encounter with the world he/she is born into. The healthy child perceives, unconsciously and consciously, and asks questions about, explores for answers and wants to know more. As he/she learns, new vistas keep revealing themselves, knowledge acquired to date is applied, newer and deeper and sharper perceptions take place, more questions, explorations, and answers are provided, interconnections are made, stimulation continues, and the process of development goes on as a vital part of living.

The main characteristic of primary curiosity is that it starts with the child him/herself. Further stimulation and messages go up and back between the child and the child's environment, including the very things and issues he/she is curious about. And this may include messages between parents and other people and the child, too, making for elaborations and extensions of the original issue he/she was curious about. But the main thrust here is that the child is the starting place for the subject of interest.

(2) *Secondary curiosity* is the curiosity about new areas introduced to the child by the parent or other enabling person.

Secondary curiosity is very simply the result of parental introduction and stimulation.

When we take a child who knows little or nothing to the planetarium, we are engaging in the production of secondary curiosity.

The possibilities for secondary curiosity production are endless and wonderful. They provide superb vehicles for communicating with the child through an area of common interest. They are a very effective way of demonstrating and practicing care, involvement, love. They also help parents to develop new interests.

—Showing the child a ball bouncing.
—Trips to zoos, aquariums, botanical gardens.
—Examining a grasshopper or frog or fish.
—Taking pictures and developing and enlarging them.
—Chemistry set experiments.
—Microscope work.
—Physics experiments.
—Nature walks.
—Bird watching.
—Map reading.
—Looking at travel books.
—Navigational chart studies.
—Visiting and discussing various ethnic areas.
—Games: chess, word games, psychological games.

The list goes on and on. Success in secondary curiosity is an evidence of continuing interest on the part of the child as well as continuing curiosity. Sometimes the child goes on to get the parent who started it all even more involved. I've seen this happen several times, with high-fidelity equipment and computers. The parents made the child curious, who then became more knowledgeable than the parent and extended the parents' involvement and interest and further curiosity.

(3) *Extended curiosity.* This is primary or secondary curiosity developed and extended to collateral areas of curiosity. This extension of curiosity, which has much in common with what goes on in psychoanalysis, has great value in promoting self-development.

Asking questions, as the grandfather said, is in fact very important. The process of questioning is itself a form of opening up—as takes place in psychoanalysis—and also provides stimulation. Questions and answers that lead to more questions and answers are, in fact, a form of associative process—one association leading to another. This, psychoanalysts know, leads to ever-widening visions of one's self and the human condition. We also know that it is through associations that we remember things and call them up from memory when we need them.

Answers to questions are obviously of value and provide satisfaction. *But* answers that are only satisfying often produce information relative to the question and little or nothing else. This does not augment this all-valuable *extended curiosity.* Thus if the question is asked, "How much water is there in that aquarium?" and is answered, "Twenty gallons," this gives information but may end the conversation and effect a closure. The answer, "Twenty gallons—the same as the car gasoline tank," may extend the dialogue to all kinds of containers—rivers, oceans, as well as to different kinds of liquids—water, gasoline, chemicals, and also to chemical reactions (combustion engines), fish that live in the sea, etc.

Thus, satisfaction answers are extended so that collateral areas of curiosity are broached. This is an opening-up process and a process that stimulates associative production—thinking and feeling. It also encourages and extends valuable discussion experience. This provides practice in being articulate, expressing, and conceptualizing ideas clearly as intimacy through the exchange of exciting ideas takes place. The tank *discussion* also provides a collateral benefit that often takes place in stimulating extended curiosity. Here ideas and feelings take place that may be out of consciousness but that are nevertheless registered, of the relative size of things. Here—tank to ocean, etc. This kind of information is seldom forthcoming in giving simple closure answers and is often of greater value in terms of mind stretching and applied usage in judgment of all kinds than the material of the original subject.

Discussion leading to answers is always better than simple answers. Of course, some questions, in some circumstances, require quick, short answers. But where circumstances permit, discussion as a response is of great value. To the extent that all thoughts and ideas—however irrelevant they may seem at first—that the child has are given free and respected rein, we are aiding creativity and originality. As in psychoanalysis, meaning may not at once be apparent but being encouraged to associate—one thought leading to others—is usually revelatory and enriching.

The analytic response to questions can be of great value in this connection for all the reasons given and can also give more information than direct factual answers.

"How big is the ocean?" The answer, "A million, trillion gallons," may have some meaning to a young child even on a feeling level, but it would have more value after an analytic dialogue takes place.

"How big does it feel?"

"Big, very, very big."

"How does it make you feel?"

"Small."

"How does it make you feel small?"

"When I stand here and look at it—it's so big. I'm so small."

"Are there other things that make you feel small?"

"Houses."

"Anything else?"

"Elephants."

"How come?"

"They are bigger than me."

"Are they as big as the ocean?"

"The ocean is bigger."

"Is there anything bigger than the ocean?" the child asks.

A discussion of the size of the earth, stars, universe may ensue, depending on the child's attention span, which is valuably extended in the process as well as his/her ability to absorb information relative to development. Obviously this answer led to opening up discussion and to enrichment of and through associations as well as to extension of attention span. It gave the child early feelings about relativity, in evaluating things and concepts (size). It demonstrated caring.

Let's say a child asks questions about sex. This is a wonderful time to extend his/her curiosity about areas as diverse as relationships (how people feel about each other, etc.) as well as to biology (sperm, egg, botany, and life itself). There are few children who do not at once develop interest in living things and how they function. Simple physiology, such as blood circulation, is fascinating (usually more than sex) to even the very young child—seven or eight.

The promotion of extended curiosity is an enriching experience for all concerned—adult as well as child—but is of greatest value to the young mind. The process of opening up and enrichment through discussion leading to association production and linkages is invaluable to development in all areas.

In closing this chapter may I suggest that all activities embarked on by parents and children to find answers are highly constructive. This includes trips to museums, the planetarium, the zoo, the aquarium, and mainly the library.

Engaging the child in the search for information in a library containing vast information is an infinitely more exciting venture—and has much greater value than almost any other activity. Early education in the use of the library for finding answers is invaluable over a lifetime. The school that provides education in library research is providing a wonderful service. I shall always be grateful to my father, who in response to many questions I had, introduced me to the public library when I was seven years old. This began a love affair with books and great adventures, which is not yet over. Libraries still provide me with a feeling of inner peace and connection to my fellows, past and present, which I cannot parallel with visits to any other places.

Home Enrichment

The best educational enrichment programs take place at home as a natural consequence of a home rich in interests.

When I was a child and even later on into my early adulthood, my friends used to love to come to my house. It was a pretty modest place but it was fun. How?

There were always exciting discussions taking place and everyone present, including the very young, was invited to participate. These were almost invariably lively and often passion-filled discussions.

My father very frequently had friends drop by, but even when they didn't he chaired discussions. What did we talk about? Everything!

I was very fortunate in several ways. My parents didn't much care when I went to sleep. In fact, my father felt that partaking in discussions was just as important as sleep—which he believed I'd catch up on, in a natural way, when necessary. I was also fortunate because he always saw to it that I got a chance to say something—even only a few words—or more, or to ask questions. *And* my father attracted interesting, verbal people who loved to exchange ideas and information. There were writers, musicians, businessmen, a politician, an opera singer, a few workers from the clothing industry, a poet, a rabbi, and still others. Some were prestigious, others enjoyed no special community status, but all were special to me and to my friends who visited, too. This is because people talked substantially— they told what they really felt about all kinds of things and they listened well, too. I still remember some of the subjects:

—Should children listen to the radio whenever they want to and what kind of programs are good for them?
—Should Mayor LaGuardia permit the neo-Nazi Bund parade to take place on Fifth Avenue?
—Many discussions about Shakespeare's work, Tolstoy, Chekhov, de Maupassant, Hemingway, Hardy, Mark Twain, Nietzsche, Gogol, Thomas Wolfe, etc.
—City politics and national politics.
—Socialism and capitalism.
—The Stalin-Hitler pact.
—Business ethics.
—Friendship and what it means.
—City living versus small town life.
—The Old Masters, Picasso, current modern painters.
—The value of advanced formal education.
—Anti-Semitism and bigotry.
—Beethoven, Bach, Haydn, Vivaldi.
—Women's role in society.
—Looks and the role of immediate impressions.
—Nutrition and its effects on well-being.
—Loneliness.
—Natural ability, acquired ability, prodigies, and genius.
—Possibilities of systems other than reward and punishment.
—Capital punishment and imprisonment.
—Talmudic arguments and ethics.
—The Jewish people and their role in society.
—Mussolini, Stalin, Chiang Kai shek, Rasputin.
—Forgiveness and understanding.
—*Death of a Salesman* and other current plays.
The list goes on and on, just as there were so many nights and sometimes days, too, of involved discussions. There were some I started, too.
—My teacher said that heredity was more influential than environment. That sparked some passionate argument.
—The purpose of living. Lin Yutang's book, *The Importance of Living*.
—Gandhi, Einstein, Jesus, and their theories and ideas.

—The value of money and what purpose it could serve.

—Abstract art. This provided enormously passionate diatribes, much of which went over the heads of my friends and myself, despite my father's attempt to simplify and clarify. He was usually superb at boiling things down to understandable conceptualizations.

—The need to be liked and its value, if any.

—Franklin D. Roosevelt.

—Joe Louis and Jackie Robinson.

—Possessions—the need to own things in lieu of just using them or seeing them as in museums.

—Why children got sick and died—this one when I was about seven years old.

—Catholicism and the rituals involved—this one as a result of going to church with some Catholic friends.

—The idea of heaven, hell, purgatory, God, the Devil.

—Life on other planets.

—How thoughts are formed and how the mind sees things. Much talk here—few answers, and I'm still questioning. My father had some surprising ideas, which he said came from the Talmud.

—Parades, uniforms, guns, patriotism, and war.

I made my contributions. But mainly it was fun and the result of this kind of fun was a continuing interest in all aspects of life so that high motivation for development existed as a natural consequence of "home enrichment." I was very fortunate in this regard and my friends envied me—but they benefited also. There were side benefits to this intellectual and emotional stimulation. I felt close to my father. I came to love books. I liked being home more than being on the streets. The benefit of "mind and language exercise—clarification and use of ideas" I appreciated years later when these were used in direct and practical application to my work.

Not every child has the opportunity for the special kind of experience I had.

But, can we expect children to have interest in life's real substance—in the arts, books, politics, philosophy, etc.—if parents have no interest? I think the odds of overcoming parental lack of interest are enormous. The odds of overcoming parental indifference are incalculable. It happens, but this is rare, and where it does we usually find that the child was fortunate to find an enabler outside the home—a friend, a friend's parent, a teacher.

Why are the arts relevant to the issue here—to the stuff of this book's purpose? By *the arts* I really mean *art* in the broadest aspect: literature, including poetry, nonfiction and fiction, music; painting; sculpting; drama, the performing arts, and the art of conversation, too—conversation of substance, and yes, the art of medicine, and architecture and engineering and the beauty of the pure sciences. All of the arts are related—get at the guts of human existence and tell us on a gut level what life is all about.

(1) Appreciation of the arts is fun—it gives new dimension for having fun through satisfaction of both intellect and emotionale, which art helps to integrate healthily.

(2) It stimulates our own ideas and feelings—making us more alive and vital. As we relate to artwork we become more alive.

(3) It inspires new ideas, thoughts, and conceptions as it inspires us to be creative, and this helps make artists of us all.

(4) It connects us to the time and culture of artwork. This helps us to feel and to be part of that time and in modern works this time—the present—now. This gives a sense of the continuum of human history and evolution.

(5) Art connects us on the deepest level—on a feeling level—to humanity. This has a therapeutic effect because it makes us feel less alone, more connected. On a gut level we feel the commonality of all human beings through the ages. Even as we appreciate the uniqueness and individuality of the artist and of ourselves, our humility remains intact as we also feel ourselves as being part of the whole.

Parental attitude is crucial. It will determine the nature of the development of interest in these areas—fun and healthy struggle or burdensome tasks designed to promote child suffering. The parent who is genuinely involved and interested or struggling with healthy curiosity and interest to become involved will convey his/her interest to the child. Family-shared activities provide a natural evolvement of interest for the child in lieu of contrived interest used as an attempt to seduce the child.

The earlier the child is exposed to and immersed in the rich substance of art (discussions and literature, etc., included), the better. This makes the material a natural part of growing up and becomes nourishment to the growing child, as does food and air. It also prevents cultural mediocrity (especially media inundation, television) from drowning the child and building resistance to "good stuff."

Making outings to the museum, library, etc., real fun by accompanying them with picnics or nice restaurants and lively family discussions makes for pleasant psychological associations so that concerts, etc., are felt and thought of as pleasurable acts. I remember my mother and sister taking painting lessons together and having nice lunches in small restaurants as a fun activity.

Have books around—lots of books. I remember reading them because they were there and because everyone else was reading them, too—children are imitative and suggestible. A family project of reading and discussing the works of a particular author can be fun, inspiring, and supportive—giving a great sense of belonging.

I also remember "writing" a book when I was very small and my parents and sister pitching in. Yes, a family project of writing a book, particularly one involving family history, can be highly constructive on all levels, and if perfectionism doesn't get in the way, is a highly gratifying process. But, whether writing or reading or both—the discussion that takes place draws children into an exciting intellectual, emotional, creative, and family-identifying experience of great value. Discussions of this sort must not be judgmental and, of course, it is imperative that children are heard and encouraged to speak and to comment about what they hear. Their free-associative processes are stimulated in this way and nothing they say should be met with derision or harsh criticism. This must not become a competition of any sort, but rather an exercise in more and more exploration and accumulation of information and mutual exchange.

Remember, enjoyment is contagious and this applies to listening to and playing music, going to plays and movies, seeing fine art and painting, etc. *But* it must be done to be contagious. What good fortune it is to come from a household where good music is commonplace—and where people talk about it enough to know the names of pieces and composers!

Of course, if the child shows the slightest inclination to play an instrument, support in that area is invaluable. I would be wary of coercion, though—and this applies to dancing, art lessons, etc.—lest it turn the child against the enjoyment of listening to good music, etc. A household replete with this kind of activity makes childhood interest a natural evolution. Interest and involvement here are almost inevitable. In a family with no such background, a concerted effort must take place—a beginning. In this connection I suggest that the start ought to be gradual and relatively easy. Going from reading and discussions of books like Jack London's *Call of the Wild* to eventually Leo Tolstoy's *War and Peace* makes it easier than the other way around. The same is true of symphonic music and esoteric chamber music—of representational art and abstract art.

Of course, children have different attention spans. Don't wear them out. When they get restless, take a break. The goal here is enjoyable struggle and not punishing suffering. *But* it is important to begin and to continue the process without any hiatus that is too long. In time, attention spans will increase, as will interest following involvement. In time and with family participation, books will be sought after and as satisfying as pizza, ice cream, baseball, and even more important, TV.

Do not become discouraged, especially if family enrichment programs are embarked upon after the child is born. Time and struggle are always necessary when the household members have not been brought up in an enriched household themselves and embark on a program after the parents are grown up.

But the struggle couldn't be more worthwhile and it does get easier. Eventually, the contribution to joy for all involved is enormous and the gift to children's children will come as a natural consequence of interests established before they (the grandchildren) were born.

Independence and Privacy—
Fun Together and Apart

Togetherness in the form of cooperative relating and team-work that promote family and individual well-being is a great enabler. But obsessive togetherness and the obliteration of individual identification and action are monstrous. The family is not a multiheaded monster. It is a nourishing group for the promotion of individual growth and self-realization. Healthy togetherness is not forced. It is a natural and spontaneous outcome of enjoying each other's company, mutual activity, fun together, and the propagation of self-realization and individuality—uniqueness. Individuality and self-realization support the well-being of the family as a natural consequence of having learned the lesson of empathy, sympathy, human identification, and emotional investment on a gut level. Real individuality and real independence, unlike detachment, preclude the fear of inundation. Getting lost and drowned in the muddy emotional waters of contrived and forced family togetherness, however, must be prevented.

Therefore, even as we extol, and we do, the value of family cooperation and family fun together and identification, we also promote healthy independence. Of course, healthy independence is the antithesis of morbid dependency and therefore in large part will spring from all healthy input that promotes self-esteem. As the child becomes increasingly adequate through intellectual, emotional, and creative development—unblocked by overprotectiveness and other damages, he/she will become increasingly independent. Independence will in turn contribute to further development in all areas.

The goal here is to develop a full, separate, unique human being. *Full* means having the complete set of human, adult characteristics necessary to cope. *Separate* means to be able to get along apart and away from the family. This is the antithesis of being a family appendage. *Uniqueness* means individuality— all healthy human beings combine characteristics in ways that are different from all other people. No two people are exactly alike. When they are, it is because conformity has been forced on them or because they are emotionally ill—uniqueness is in large part linked to spontaneity. Fixed, forced, compulsive behavior tends to be the same. Thus, in emotional illness, symptoms are almost identical, making diagnostic categories possible. This, in part, occurs in physical illness, too. Advanced leprosy destroys features and produces victims who look alike. Malignancy does the same. In health we retain our individuality— and independence, too.

In this connection I want to point out that separate, full selves are necessary for real relating to take place. Healthy exchange is not possible with appendages and extensions or with immediately compliant and conforming pseudoselves. Real relating and emotional as well as intellectual exchanges can only take place between separate selves. It is a natural consequence, then, that individuals of families in which separateness has been obliterated in the name of forced togetherness and because of severe mutual dependency remain stunted and impoverished. Families comprised of nondetached, empathizing, sympathizing, cooperative, mutually concerned but separate, independent, unique people with strong personal identities will contribute the most to its members. This will in turn provide strong and contributing individuals who can give to each other in *different* ways.

This individuality and independence I speak of here is a very special enabler in several ways.

(1) I've already mentioned its contribution to self-esteem and to relating effectiveness. The ramifications of these enhancements are virtually limitless.

(2) This enabler provides the possibility of making independent choices and decisions instead of being swayed by the crowd, which is often wrong, or by convention or by the compulsive need to be either liked or admired. Independent people are usually able to exercise better judgment on more objective levels.

(3) Being a full, separate person makes it possible to be alone. This is extremely important because there are times when we must be alone. This prevents the compulsive need to seek out people to be with constantly in order not to be depressed. This also makes it possible to do work that demands solitude and is thus a great aid to all areas, especially to creativity. Any self-contemplative activity—writing, studying, composing, planning, painting, etc.—often requires separateness and being alone.

(4) This enabler makes loneliness much less frightening and burdensome. The self is not sacrificed in order to "have someone around—anyone." I have known any number of people who stay with sadistic partners for fear of being lonely. Without someone there, they feel they themselves do not exist.

(5) *Independence*—true independence makes all kinds of mobility and necessary changes possible. Adaptation to different locales, friends, jobs, and ideas, theories, principles, and concepts is enormously enhanced. With this enabler there is minimum clinging to the familiar and the status quo when these may be highly destructive because there is terror of letting go, of "being on one's own."

Beyond all the healthy measures represented in this book as well as avoidance of the damages, are there specific contributions we can make in behalf of this enabler? I think there are a few important ones worth mentioning. *Privacy* is a key factor in these contributions.

(1) If the child is on occasion having fun alone—let him/her have fun alone. Of course, we are not talking about chronic seclusiveness, which requires investigation. But if the child likes to do things alone, this is good and he/she should not be pulled away to play with friends or used to mitigate the loneliness or boredom of a friend or relative. Lonely parents, especially dependent parents, tend to exploit children in this way. Narcis-

sistic parents often "show off" a child to a visitor, thoroughly oblivious to the child's desire to continue in the solitary activity he/she was engaged in before the visitor's arrival.

Yes, encourage and welcome friendships and friends—from early on. But also respect the child's need and desire to be alone, often expressed by young children by walking off and going to a separate part of the house. Indeed, helping them to do it—suggesting and encouraging it—is constructive.

I have watched small children and friends who finally have had enough and want to be alone. Parents who provide this aloneness are tuned in. Parents who insist on further sociability, despite the obvious fact that the social attention span has run out, produce crankiness, guilt about wanting to be alone, and are hurting this enabler.

(2) Some corner of the house—room, if possible, but a curtained-off area, if necessary—should be the exclusive area of the child. For a very young child it is not possible for "his/her space" to be inviolate. But as much privacy as can be given should be given. This is especially true for adolescents, whose space must be regarded as virtually inviolate. Bursting into a teenager's room without knocking on the door is highly destructive.

Privacy of place is extremely important relevant to independence as an enabler. The ability to be alone is greatly enhanced by the opportunity to be alone and to be in a place where outside disturbance is unlikely to impinge. *But* it goes further than that. Having a place of one's own that is obviously respected by parents and family members produces respect for one's self, for one's desire and ability to be alone, and also for other people's privacy. It also provides a secure place for undisturbed self-contemplation.

Of course, parental attitude toward their own privacy teaches a mighty lesson. That they have their own inviolate province and need time alone together is a lesson not wasted on the child. The insistence that a child knock on a bedroom or study door has great value. But this value is undermined and diluted if the child's space is violated without ample justification. It also helps if the child is taught to respect the privacy of brothers and sisters, who are taught the lesson as well.

(3) While it is constructive to encourage a child to share

possessions, especially toys, forcing him/her to do so all the time is destructive to our goal here. The child must be allowed and even encouraged to feel that he/she can own objects without feeling guilty. He/she must be given at least some opportunity to decide about sharing and to turn down the possibility without fear of incurring parental disfavor. This sense of ownership of place and object makes the child feel worthy of ownership and responsibility for ownership of object as well as self. In fact, I believe that the child who really does own things is usually more ready to share them than the child who always feels that ownership is not real. In later life, the people who feel more secure about themselves find it easier to make loans and to share what they have, particularly themselves.

A word of caution here—it is destructive to our purpose to threaten or to take back as punishment an object given to the child and identified as his/her very own. If taking it away must take place—never as punishment (especially because he/she refuses to share it) but because it is dangerous—then another object must be substituted as recompense at once. If a family object is to be used by several siblings, it must be clearly and repeatedly stated that *it* will remain a shared family object. This prevents confusion and despair.

(4) Whenever possible and appropriate, it is superb to elicit a child's taste as regards of choice of clothes. If that taste can be implemented by a purchase (when shopping is appropriately taking place; I do not advocate clothes-buying frenzy and addiction to be visited on children), so much the better. The same is true as regards room furniture, wallpaper and paint, etc.

Whenever possible, the promotion and exercise of the child's particular tastes have value in teaching respect for tastes, feelings, choices, self, and promote independence. I have seen parents ask a child if he/she wants a frankfurter or a hamburger, and when the child without hesitation says "a hot dog," the parent insists on a hamburger. This is usually an attempt by the parent to have it both ways—to exercise parental choice while making it seem that the child's taste has relevance. This is duplicitous and destructive and makes the child feel that his/her own taste and appetite count for nothing. Do not ask, if you do not intend to use the information given constructively.

Of course, where possible, it is good for the child to have his/her own clothes, toys, etc., but if they must be shared, this must be done on the most equitable basis possible. With hand-me-downs it is important that the child who relinquishes clothes is ready to do so and that new ownership is complete. The new owner must not be reminded that these are not really his/her own or taunted in any way.

(5) Eliciting the child's own feelings, ideas, opinions, etc., and respecting them, is wonderful.

But insistence on wanting to hear them—for the child to tell when he/she is not ready to do so—indicates lack of respect for the child's unique self.

Of course, I do not promote seclusive or autistic behavior and I am all for communication. *But* there are times when people—children, too—have not yet formed their ideas adequately enough to share them. There are other times they want to own them alone for the time being. There are still other times when sharing might be embarrassing.

Respect and sensitivity to private needs in this area are enormously enhancing to our purpose here. Every thought and feeling need not be shared if we are indeed separate people. Unfortunately, there are families in which if someone gets hurt, everyone screams out, "I'm hurt." This lack of separation of identities is highly maladaptive.

(6) I remember a friend who used to bring a child a jigsaw puzzle (simple and then complex), get her started, and then walk out of the room. This is a good idea. Encourage reading and studying alone from very early on. This improves both cultural enrichment at home and the ability to be alone. Later on, after a book is read, discussions can bring togetherness as well as the enrichment of exchange of ideas about the book.

I remember the thrill of going out and buying and owning my first book—hardcover: *Twenty Thousand Leagues under the Sea* by Jules Verne.

I don't feel that children should be forced to learn to read too early. But they can be helped to learn when they desire it. I believe it is a good idea to go from picture books to reading-together books and then reading-alone books as rapidly as they demonstrate the desire and the ability. The desire is largely motivated by the parents' input. Having fun recognizing pictures and the words the pictures represent and then reading simple stories is an excellent start.

Library clubs in school and at home, too, are wonderful, as is a child collecting his/her books, especially with his/her own money. This gives value to a book—which can be lent out—while others are borrowed from siblings, other relatives, and friends. Reading is an exciting alone venture and the book not only provides companionship but stirs the imagination and self-ignition, making it still easier to be alone.

(7) The child must be allowed to have his/her own friends. This simply means that a friend must not be "stolen" by a parent or older sibling. If the child brings a friend home to play, others can join in that play if the host child invites them, but must otherwise respect the exclusivity of that relationship. Having friends stolen or seduced away is a particularly bitter experience for adolescents. It leads to lack of self-confidence as well as intense and destructive sibling rivalry. Older patients, often with bitterness, recall this happening when they were younger and always having the feeling that they never had the chance to have anything of their own, "not even a friend."

(8) If an adolescent or older child is in psychotherapy, it is imperative that, if at all possible (and it usually is unless the child is severely disturbed), the parent stay out of it.

Adolescents value privacy more than any other age group. This is particularly true regarding their therapists, to whom they tell their most intimate feelings, problems, and experiences. They want the therapist to be their own and no one else's in the family. This privacy must not be violated by well-intentioned parents. Meetings, telephone conversations with the therapist are felt as a breach by the adolescent. The therapist and parent destroy therapeutic exclusivity and confidence in both therapist and parent, and this is followed by counterproductive results. Of course, this does not apply to family therapy, in which from the start it is understood that the therapist is treating the family as a group.

(9) Dates, contacts, and relationships with members of the opposite sex must be dignified and respected regardless of age. This is especially true of adolescent first dates and dances.

Privacy must not be violated either because of constructive interest, a desire for voyeuristic entertainment, or a need for vicarious identification—to feel one's youth again. This means that prying must not take place. The child will tell you when and what he/she feels comfortable about telling. The child will usually tell more if no embarrassment has taken place due to inappropriate prying. Usually the child whose privacy has been respected and has maximum confidence in parental respect and is relatively independent will comfortably share the most. Of course, the parent wants to know how a child makes out socially in initial adult encounters, but it is best in this connection to simply be an available listener. In this way more will be learned. Real friends learn to wait and know that some information always remains private and only one's own.

Let me close this chapter by saying that just as we must not use the need for communication to inundate with obsessive and forced togetherness, we must not polarize the other way either. This simply means that parents must not use the need for privacy to rationalize and justify their own detachment.

Let appropriate common sense prevail and remember, it's good to be able to have fun together as part of the joyous family experience—and fun apart.

Beyond Attention Span and Struggle

As the child is growing up there are certain insights we can impart to him/her that are invaluable enablers and that are related to and extensions of constructive struggling, good attention span, and the ability to postpone gratification.

I discussed aspects of some of these in other books and contexts, but they are particularly pertinent here. Let me say again that the child learns by example, by good teaching—telling him/her about it compassionately—and by parental response. Thus, parental response to a job seen through to completion, for which responsibility has been taken following dedication and motivation, is extremely important. A parent who responds with gratitude and satisfaction is teaching the lesson well! Parents who give their children doable jobs, as described in the chapter on the success habit, are making a good contribution here. Parents who bring the young child back to the job after he/she wanders off to complete it (filling in a drawing) are contributing.

I remember a patient who said, "I could always get out of anything; all I had to do was complain enough—now I still complain about everything and finish nothing." He, too, learned a lesson from parents who did not want to be bothered—a bad lesson. Now let me list and discuss some of the key messages we must try to deliver from early on.

247

—Procrastination usually leads to never getting anything done. In children it is often due to fear of not being able to complete the job satisfactorily. Instead of condemnation, discussion leading to what it is that makes for anxiety in tackling the job is valuable. Does the child feel unduly coerced? Lack of confidence? Afraid of disapproval?

—The need for perfect results makes for inhibition and paralysis. The child must be taught that perfection is not expected, possible, or desired. Doing the job fairly well to completion is desired.

—Try to teach them that popularity contests are not worth winning. Peer acceptance is not worth rejection of personal values and feelings. Rejection is commonplace and once we can accept rejection we are free to attempt all kinds of enterprises, including asking for dates.

—Tell the child that it is not possible to satisfy all options and desires. Homework cannot be completed at the same time as ball can be played. But there is the possibility of doing some things sequentially.

—Teach him/her that there are priorities that count. Health is more important than pleasure that is dangerous. Responsibility to a job taken on is more important than an urge to see a ball game. Prioritizing is one of the key ingredients to success in life.

—As a corollary of the above two enablers the child must learn that everything in life requires a price. Expertise must be paid for with time and study. Food must be paid for with money earned. Friendship requires at least some self-sacrifice. Success is paid for with hard work. Total freedom is paid for by lack of training and little or no economic success and prestige, etc.

—Teach the child what I have discussed as the main insight in the book *Overcoming Indecisiveness*. Given several choices, dedication to a choice is almost always more important than the choice itself in making a decision. This means successful outcome of a decision has less to do with the substance of the decision than the commitment to it. The power of commitment is enormous. Change of mind where appropriate is all right but must be done only if conditions have changed and warrant a change and not as a rationalization to destroy a commitment.

—Teach him/her that taking on an obligation that involves the well-being of other persons is a sacred responsibility. While our lives must not be predicated on being universally liked and admired, respect from people we do business with is important and hinges on how seriously we take responsibilities.

—I have taught my children that time is the most valuable commodity we have after life itself and therefore should be treated well. Time spent for good leisure and fun, with people we enjoy being with, for self-growth, for helping others, is using time well. Allowing ourselves to be bored is using time poorly. Boredom is, I believe, largely the result of not using our inner resources well, blaming others for our discomfort, and spending our time wastefully, chronically complaining.

—Teach children that concentrating time and energy on a particular task results in a tremendous amount of work getting done relative to that concentration. Teach them, too, that increments of work add up with time but only if there is sufficient respect for the increments so as to get them done. Writing three pages a day (without failure to do so) adds up to three hundred pages in a hundred days. Three hundred pages is about ninety thousand words—a considerable amount. This constitutes a book but it is a book only if the commitment to doing three pages (a seemingly small number of pages) a day is adequate.

—It is very difficult but an enormous enabler if you can teach children to profit from other people's experience, expertise, and help in contributing to their own development. Truly independent people can do this without suffering self-hate through attacks of hurt pride. To be able to listen openly and then to make one's own mind up and to integrate information acquired and to use it is valuable indeed.

—Teach them that it is easier to quit than to stick it out, though, of course, there are times when leaving a place, person, job, etc., is appropriate. But, let them know that it is always easier to leave a situation than to find one to go to.

—Of course, having realistic expectations is highly constructive. This enabler prevents disappointment, self-hate, and depression, as well as the danger of selling one's self short. Much
of this one will depend on the child's reality view of the world
and people as gleaned from his/her family experience. I shall
discuss expectations in the next chapter.

Appropriate Expectations

It may be apochryphal, but it is said that Sigmund Freud's mother called him *"mein goldene Ziggy"* (my golden Ziggy), and that he said she believed he would be a great man. It is said that he could not resist that combination—her love and her expectations. We are not all Freuds nor do we need to be great, but we do need—all of us—a measure of self-realization. Parental expectations and self-fulfilling prophecies are related.

Expectations parents have of their children are extremely important for two reasons. First, they will in large part determine the quality of the relationship between parent and child. Secondly, these parental expectations will eventually become the expectations children have of themselves.

Before I get to specific effects, let me say that parental expectations are largely based on expectations—fulfillments and disappointments—they have had of themselves. They are also based on feelings—conscious and unconscious—they have of their children, often different for each child and each gender. Much depends on the degree to which they identify with each child and the displacements of how they feel about different people in their pasts that they've unwittingly transferred or displaced to the child. Expectations of the child, at least in part and sometimes fully, remain unconscious on the parts of both parent and child, but the effects are always extremely powerful and their influences of great importance. But before we get on to these effects, let me explain a bit about what I've already stated.

Parents who are disappointed with themselves and have felt lack of parental approval and acceptance are more likely to foster inappropriate expectations in their children. Unfortunately, we are the victims of victims and those of us who have been treated less than fairly often unfairly look to our children to redress wrongs inflicted on ourselves. This kind of vicarious living through children often makes for exorbitant expectations and even claims for perfection in various areas. The expectations here, as in all situations of relative lack of health, evidence a tendency to have nothing at all to do with the real abilities, assets, and limits of the child. They are usually direct projections of parental needs for self-compensation and forms of child exploitation. The reverse is true of healthier situations in which parents view their children with greater objectivity. They are then viewed as separate and unique people with their own characteristics and proclivities.

Parents who view themselves as impoverished to the point of hopeless resignation will often have few or no expectations of their offspring. This outlook is fostered by the belief that anybody and anything in any way connected to themselves are incapable of fulfilling any desirable activities or goals.

I cannot stress enough here that viewing the child as a separate entity, however much related and a member of the family, is a great antidote in combating destructive self-fulfilling prophecies. Of course, further prejudicial expectations—often present long before the birth of the child—come from fixed ideas about gender as well as ideas about certain relatives. You can readily see how different expectations will be of a girl and a boy if a parent is preconvinced that boys are more logical, that girls are more emotional, etc.

I knew one stunning, redheaded, extremely intelligent and talented woman (a gifted painter) whose father had himself and her convinced that redheads are unstable, unable to see a job through, potentially wild, and not very bright. She lived up to these expectations of his, which were pounded into her head from infancy until they became her own, until psychotherapy revealed and changed these self-fulfilling dictums.

Fulfillment of these dictums represented a kind of resigned, predetermined hopelessness because she unconsciously felt that her situation was genetic and therefore unchangeable. Fulfillment of these expectations was also an unconscious attempt to please her father. This was a classic destructive double-bind situation. She could not please him. He hated her if she fulfilled these disastrous expectations, which were born of his self-hate and hate of his own origins. He hated her if she took any constructive route away from these expectations because she then did not comply and fulfill his dictums and satisfy his perverse psychological needs. When she came fully and consciously to understand the trap she had been in, she extricated herself and lived up to her own healthy expectations, light years removed from his.

Interestingly, it came out that his view of his daughter was totally based on his mother, with whom he had a love/hate relationship of considerable intensity. His mother was a beautiful redhead. She was also "wild," having done everything to excess in her life, including six marriages, scrapes with the law, etc. His mother also swung from times of overprotection of him to complete neglect—disappointing him again and again. His daughter remembered him saying repeatedly, "You just can't trust crazy redheads." His own hair was red.

Appropriate expectations are an extremely important enabler. Their appropriateness is directly proportional to (1) the parents' recognition of and respect for the child as a separate, unique individual, albeit a family member, and (2) the parent knowing, really knowing, the child and having minimal distortions about him/her. This is largely based on hearing the child—really hearing the child—from birth onward.

Expectations are transmitted from the time we hold our finger out and expect the child to grab it to the time we expect the child to read (different for different children), to the expectations of the child to have at least some sensitivity to the needs of others, to the expectation that the child will, under normal conditions, be able to fulfill him/herself on a socioeconomic basis, etc.

In these expectations we convey our esteem for the child, our hopes, possibilities, encouragement, even as we tell him/her

what society expects in the way of manners and human considerations. These expectations connect the child to the family and
society and the species. This happens even as they start the
process of his/her forming expectations of him/herself that will
determine patterns of behavior leading to varying degrees of
self-realization. This self-realization will in large part reflect
and be proportionate to the reality or appropriateness of the
self-expectations.

As I described earlier, exorbitant expectations are destructive
and often lead to depression and resigned hopelessness.

But I have found in my own practice that impoverished and
even in some cases virtually no parental expectations lead to
a chronic loss of goal direction of any kind. I have encountered
this very damaging effect considerably more in women than
in men and I believe this is a prevalent condition in our society
that parents, especially of girls, must guard against.

So many talented people I have seen in practice, especially
women, lived resigned, unhappy lives with very little evidence
of self-realization. They were not happy and some of them
suffered from bouts of acute self-hate and considerable depression. Close investigation repeatedly revealed that their parents
had little or even no expectations of them beyond that of creating
as little disturbance as possible—being "good people." In many
cases the prime concern for men was "to be able to make
a living" and for women to marry a man "who could make
a good living" or otherwise to be able "to make some kind
of living" for themselves. Some of these parents really hated
to be "bothered" and most of them really didn't know their
own children at all.

My own exploration invariably revealed talents, intelligence,
and long-hidden aspirations that had been lying dormant for
years. Attempts to open these up to the full light of consciousness were almost always met by enormous initial resistance.
Suggestions about possibilities for training and careers to be
used as vehicles for self-development and self-realization pro-
voked anxiety, amazement, and disbelief. But I persisted and
I also indicated that I had expectations of them—appropriate
expectations—which they, too, eventually found to be appropriate. In time, these expectations became their own. I believed

in them and so they, too, came to believe in themselves. As I indicated at the beginning of this book, many of them became doctors, lawyers, and psychoanalysts. More important, they feel infinitely more independent and fulfilled and are doing so much more for themselves and other people.

Why did they feel so anxious at the prospect of change? Why did they offer so much resistance? Because they were still enslaved by the dictums of their parents, by the lack of belief in and expectations of themselves. Relative to these beliefs my suggestions seemed grossly inappropriate and frightening. Imagine asking a nonswimmer if he/she would care to dive fifty feet into the water and swim the English Channel. Also, deep down I stirred hidden desires and needs and hopes that had been put to sleep years ago. These coming awake would and did produce considerable conflict—between healthy, alive yearnings and hopeless, abject resignation. This kind of conflict produces great anxiety, which must be worked through before a reality-based assessment of self can take place.

The simple fact is that once a status quo familiarity is established, it is very difficult to change it. This is especially true of how we see ourselves vis-à-vis the world. How much easier it is, as a result of appropriate parental expectations, to have so much that is constructive about us as the status quo.

School Must Be
a Wonderful Place

W hen the child experiences school as the wonderful place it ought to be, we have a very constructive and powerful enabler. School must be a wonderful place! If it isn't, something is radically wrong and must be immediately investigated and remedied.

Loving school from the very start contributes enormously to a continuing love affair with education throughout one's life.

School offers so many pleasant and enriching possibilities:

(1) It provides a warm, cheerful, secure place away from home. It thus serves as a transitional link between home and the outside—a first step toward healthy independence. If this first step is experienced pleasantly—with relatively little anxiety—significant contribution is being made toward individuation (feeling as a separate self) and future separation and independence.

(2) It is a new experience with place and people who are not home and family. Again, this early experience will effect future encounters with unfamiliar situations. Good early experiences in this area will contribute to healthy curiosity and a sense of adventure in expanding one's horizons. This is the antithesis of clinging to the status quo for fear of generating anxiety in new encounters—as one may have as a child. In this connection there is the experience of meeting nonfamily

256

members as well as members of different subcultures for the first time.

(3) School offers the possibility of social activity with one's peers without parental supervision. This is a real exercise of give-and-take with one's peers in antinarcissistic activities in which consideration for other people's needs is mandatory. This is a time when good manners, respect for others, respect for self (not to allow one's self to be used poorly or to be taken advantage of) learned at home will be directly applied and exercised.

This is the first time repeated contacts with one's classmates will permit the formation of relatively grown-up friendships—sustained relationships in which emotional investments are made in other than family people.

(4) This is a place to learn new games, jokes, and ways of having fun, and as one child I heard put it, "laughing a lot."

But mostly this is the place where, if all goes relatively well, fun is associated with learning, communicating, sharing ideas, having new ideas, and sharing in creative enterprises of all kinds.

(5) School is mainly the place in which keys are delivered to those who work, which open the doors to enrichment—a process already in motion at home.

School delivers the most to those whose curiosity remains intact. It makes available at least some of the knowledge already accumulated by the species.

Much of the success of the educational enterprise depends on the relationship between student and teacher as well as fellow students. Openness to learning and motivation is promoted by benevolent, compassionate interest as well as teacher-subject competence. Cooperative relating among faculty and students is infinitely more productive than adversarial, let alone antagonistic relating. This is especially true for very young beginning students, who usually are dependent on adults for nearly everything. These children are extremely sensitive to knowing which adults and teachers like children and which don't, as well as those who do and don't enjoy teaching. They are also sensitive to peer acceptance and have a great desire to be able to communicate with confreres once they reach school age.

Is there anything parents can do to enhance this enabler, to increase the chances of school being the wonderful place it ought to be? I have a few comments and what I hope are practical suggestions.

First, please realize that much that will determine the outcome has already happened and is in motion long before the child begins school. Much depends on the security, self-esteem, and emotional well-being of the child—established up that point and related to everything we've already discussed. But there are specific points, too.

(1) Do not despise your own school experiences, schools, and teachers. Your own attitude is crucial here. A positive parental attitude toward formal education pays off relative to elementary school as well as later on—the motivation to go on for higher learning.

(2) Introduce the child and have him/her talk to other children just a little older than him/herself who already have had a positive school experience.

(3) If possible, find out who some of his/her classmates will be and try to arrange for them to meet and even to get together several times before the school term starts.

(4) If possible, choose a school or at least check out the school for safety, warmth, cheerfulness as well as the competency and humanity of the teachers and the adequacy of the curriculum. Of course, small classes, good equipment, and individual attention are constructive where possible. But compassion and sensitivity are most important. If possible, the child must never be embarrassed by loss of self-control (bladder, weeping, fright, etc.), inability to speak, etc.

(5) Join the Parent Teachers Association and develop rapport with administration, teachers, and parents so that your own input is possible and counts. Of course, this doesn't mean being obstructive or destructively critical. There are limitations even to teaching situations.

(6) Bring the child to the school at least several times before school starts so that familiarity is established. This ought to include the route to the school; actual rides on the school bus

in advance is good; lunchroom; school smells; sounds; school grounds; gym facilities; school layout—getting from one place to another; bathrooms; classrooms; nursing office, etc.

(7) Meeting school personnel in advance—especially his/her own teachers—is valuable. Some teachers come to the child's house on a visit before school opens. This is extremely constructive, especially when the child views good rapport between parents and teacher.

(8) Feeling comfortable rather than apprehensive about the child beginning school is a great enabler here. Much here will depend on the parents being able to let go and not be overprotective.

(9) Talk about school—telling of its being a wonderful, exciting, nice place—has value.

Having the child talk about early school experiences has great value in demonstrating continuing interest. It also provides the opportunity to learn about any problems that may require remediation.

Of course, interest in homework by parents is helpful on all scores—showing how parents view education as serious and good. But this interest must be as a participant rather than as a judgmental monitor.

What if school is not a wonderful place?

Look for where the problem is and remedy it as soon as possible. Let me list several possibilities.

(1) Has school become a place for performance rather than for participation? Many children who develop much anxiety relative to school feel themselves to be in a highly competitive, insecure position. Consciously or unconsciously they are (like Ida in the section on damages) attempting to please perfectionistic parents. Performance needs not only create anxiety, they destroy fun. The focus on goals (grades, class standing, etc.) destroys the process of education, the fun of learning itself. The most constructive process here is full, open, cooperative participation without consciousness of how one is performing. Parental satisfaction in the child's growing interest, curiosity, fun with reading and facts is of great value. Sure, a good reaction

to good grades is valuable. Bad grades indicate a need for investigation of problems, but grades must not become the focus here.

But, you may ask, what if a child eventually wants to go to medical school and needs the grades to get in?

Good study habits that produce high grades start with early ease and love of studying, rather than apprehensive attention to grades. This is especially true of very young children. In high school I told my son Eugene, who knew that he wanted to be a doctor, that "Grades, unfortunately, are necessary in our current system. So try to get them but do not forget that the substance of what you are learning and fun in learning it is more important (so even though you are caught in the need for grades, try not to let it spoil the fun or seriousness of studying)."

(2) Is the school or the grade level wrong for the child? Some children require a more permissive environment. Some do better in a traditional, more organized routine.

Some children develop slowly and may be in a school or class that is currently too advanced for them. Parents often must deal with their own pride to cope effectively with this situation. Most kids do catch up—if their self-esteem is not permanently impaired. It is important that a failure habit and a hatred for school are not established by standards that are currently too high to meet.

Is the child bored? Is more rapid advancement required? Should the child be in a school with richer programs? Are there extracurricular activities that would be enriching and interesting for children who are more advanced than their chronological age indicates? Is there too much devotion to sports for a child who is not physically inclined? Beware of making a child live up to any parental standard, either intellectual or physical, in order to satisfy vicariously the needs of a parent or anyone else.

I prefer coeducational schools for obvious reasons. We live in a world of both genders and experience with both sexes from early on is invaluable. But if a school is so special and so fit for the needs of a particular child, an all-boys school or an all-girls school may then be preferable. In this case it is important that the school arrange meetings with students of other schools so as to make natural contact with the other gender possible. These may include cooperative productions of plays, operettas, discussions, debates, parties, trips, dances, some shared classes, etc.

(3) If a child complains about being bullied, always listen and always investigate and take remedial steps. If a child acts frightened or seems to be threatened, consider the possibility of bullying by another student, a child who is not a student but hangs around the school, a teacher, a bus driver, etc. There are adults who are verbally sadistic to children. Here is one area in which easy and open communication with a child is invaluable. Remember, bigotry of all kinds still exists!

Do not—*do not!*—inappropriately take the position that a young child must defend him/herself. This flagrantly breaks the loyalty contract a parent has with the child. The child usually rightly interprets parental lack of intervention as not wanting to be bothered and/or as weakness (self-effacement) on the parent's part. Parental investigation and remediation are correctly interpreted as parental loyalty and strength with which the vulnerable child can identify and use as he/she becomes older and more experienced in these matters.

(4) Has the parent unwittingly contributed to a double-bind situation? Some parents want their children to go to school but also want the child to stay home. This is characteristic of possessive, overprotective parents who tend to foster great dependency in their children.

The child in this situation picks up the double message unconsciously and responds accordingly. They are unusually ambivalent, conflicted, and even feel guilty about being away from home. Anxiety is generated and even though the parent in part wants his/her child to leave home, he/she rationalizes the child's staying home by believing the child to be too underdeveloped to go to school. Thus, parental anxiety generates child anxiety and school is felt as and interpreted as the origin of this difficulty. In effect the parent says, "Go to school—you are grown-up enough and this will please me, but if you go, you will miss me too much to stay away because you are not grown-up enough." Unfortunately, some highly narcissistic parents, whose

desperation to be missed is the prime mover in their relationships, never allow the emotional umbilical cord to be cut.

When this happens, or for that matter when a child "cannot
make it at school," outside help with a child analyst is often
indicated. Family therapy often helps in these complex situations, especially if it is sought out early when the child is very
young and just begins school.

(5) Some children come to believe that they do not like or
even hate school and some even become fearful and phobic
about school because of what is, or they believe is, happening
at home. Opening this up to the light of day and talking it
over and clarifying can be very helpful. Let me give you several
relatively common situations.

—A new baby has been born recently and the new school
child believes that his/her place in the parental heart will be
usurped, that he/she will be forgotten if he/she is not there.
This is particularly true in households that are very adversarial
and competitive and engender sibling rivalry. It is also true
where the enthusiasm for the baby has all but obliterated attention to the school child.

—The child is afraid of being forgotten—feeling out of sight,
out of mind. This sometimes occurs in children who make too
good an adjustment, so to speak, They do not miss home and
suddenly come to believe that the folks at home may not miss
them.

—When there is much parental fighting and talk of separating,
the child fears he/she may come home and find him/herself
fatherless or motherless or both.

—In which the child fears that all kinds of wonderful things
are happening at home that will be missed forever by being
away at school.

—In which the child has been convinced of his/her being
unusually fragile and vulnerable and in danger away from home,
that *only* loving parents can bestow the care and attention
needed. This is fairly common where overprotection exists.

—In which the parent or parents are so hysterical and emotionally overwrought at the child's leaving and growing up (and
their own aging process) that the child feels that he/she is a
participant in matricide and/or patricide in going to school.

These are just a few situations. There are others that are usually easily revealed on investigation. School phobia must not be allowed to continue for any length of time without professional intervention. It can become an insidious habit and can be highly destructive in its neurotic implications and ramifications. It contributes to reclusivity and fear of relationships generally as well as occupational involvements. It is a symptom, and if the problem or problems producing it are not easily revealed and resolved, expert help must be applied—the sooner, the better.

(6) In older children who "hate school," look for a peer group that hates school. Groups form in which the *"in thing"* is to hate school. Extricating the child from that group is very important. If it can't be done, it may be very wise to change schools.

(7) As an addendum to the above, there are children who are very conforming and particularly vulnerable to destructive influences of peer pressure. This can produce conflict with home values, anxiety, hatred of school, and worse. In the case of drug-influencing groups, radical measures may be needed. I know one family who moved out of the neighborhood they were living in with great success. Both their children are now practicing attorneys.

(8) Many depressed children are not ready to be away from home in either boarding schools, prep schools, or colleges. They must be brought home for serious, professional consultation—and the possibility of attending school near home—without recrimination or any engendering of any self-hate whatsoever. I've known lives to be saved because parents acted wisely and without sick pride in this matter.

(9) If the child seems to be without friends in school, without joy, picked on or teased more than is usual, investigate at once.

If you cannot bring objectivity to the problem or find the cause of the problem, get expert consultation. It can save years of worry and heartache and help to put the child back on a track of self-realization and joy.

Money as an Enabler

Money represents time and energy and the exchange of work or one's time and energy. But money has much more symbolic value than that, too—in all the cultures of the world. Money for great numbers of people represents accomplishment, prestige, power, acceptance, and, in magical ways, expertise (in areas unrelated to those in which the spurious expert made his/her money), longevity, and even immortality. "If I can't take it with me, I won't go." This is funny. But so many of us really come to believe that money confers a kind of immortality. "So-and-so died—he was so rich"—as if the rich don't die. So many families confer with the richest member of the family on all kinds of matters in which he/she has no expertise.

We are often so surprised to find out that even enormous money does not produce a Shangri-la existence in which there are no sicknesses, emotional difficulties, or problems with children. Yes, money has its limits—mankind remains mortal and limited, after all!

But money and the way it is handled and who is in charge of it—as I've written in a book called *One to One*—often quickly tells us much about family relationships on a level that is not at once perceived. "You could be easily fooled. He is a rather expansive, blustery guy. She is quiet, reserved, says very little. But then I did business with them. She made all the money decisions. She is really the one in charge." "My parents always held money over our heads as a kind of emotional blackmail. They tried to buy compliance and affection with it. Even now, my mother, who is a widow, is constantly threatening to change her will."

But money can be a constructive enabler in several important ways and that's what interests us here.

Money can and does, in fact, buy some very nice and important things in life. This is a reality. Children who are brought up knowing it are not exempt from also knowing that money does not buy everything. A nice place to live, good food, entertainment, interesting toys are possible with money. Money does not buy love, feelings, humanity, appreciation for beauty, humor, etc. But money does buy books, good music (recitals and records), paintings, etc. Pointing out to the child that earning money to buy what one wants is directly proportional to struggle and training and to the postponement of gratification is constructive.

Allowing the child money responsibilities and decisions in a respectful, dignified way commensurate with his/her age has value. This is true of allowances and especially true of money the child has earned him or herself. Giving the child a well-meaning but sanctimonious lesson about money when he/she has saved ten dollars baby-sitting and then taking the family out to a two-hundred-dollar family dinner in a restaurant is tasteless. It also demeans the child's time and effort and makes it difficult to understand parental refusal when an object costing twenty dollars is refused, no matter what explanations about age and skill are offered.

At appropriate ages relative to individual development, it is valuable experientially for children to own their own money. Whatever the amount, whether an allowance, a gift, or earnings, ownership is important here. This means that, short of destructive decisions, the child must have control of the money without coercion or any kind of manipulation. He/she can choose to save it or to spend it, but the decision rests with the owner, otherwise ownership is unreal. Of course, I am talking about appropriate sums and not about trusts, inheritances, or educational funds.

Giving suggestions and teachings—without manipulation—that money spent is money gone; that there is satisfaction in buying things for other people; that a given amount set aside regularly accumulates; that money earns money, is constructive. These are realities and we do live in the real world.

Teaching the child the relative value of services, objects, and especially necessities in terms of actual money—practical pricing and shopping—also has value. This is especially so if applied and related to payment for skills. This again demonstrates to the child the value of training and the forthcoming rewards of the postponement of gratification and the struggle for developmental skills of all kinds.

A deal is a deal! Once the child is given an allowance, do not punish by withholding it. It is manipulative and a poor lesson in ethics.

But the most enabling process the parent can provide directly with money as representing the application of his/her own efforts, energy, and time is direct spending on the child's education. This has more value than ten thousand trust funds and business partnerships.

This spending on education, and I use the term education here in the broadest sense, is the direct application of money to the child's permanent self-development and practical ability to take care of him/herself with maximum satisfaction.

Trusts disappear. Businesses vanish, and so does money. Skills do not vanish except in grievous disease or death itself.

Money used for education is the parent putting "his/her money where his/her mouth is" in terms of struggle, postponement of gratification, price to pay, etc. It is a direct contribution to the child's real adequacy in coping in this world.

Jews have known this for generations. Being chased from country to country and often arriving at each new place penniless, they knew the value of having a skill. "Doctors are needed all over and they can't take my training away from me."

But by education I mean anything and all things that contribute to the child's adequacy and potential for self-care and fun:

—Music lessons.
—Art lessons.
—Tennis lessons.
—Good schools.
—University and professional training. It is virtually impossi-

ble to both work and go to medical school or law schools these days. Financial support is necessary.

—Dancing lessons.

—Crafts of any kind—carpentry, pottery, ceramics, etc. Of course, any of these activities extended into the home and shared as a family enterprise has great home enrichment value. I remember building model boats and airplanes with my sister, mother, and father when I was very young. It was great fun and a source of much satisfaction for all.

—Chess clubs.

—Drama lessons and clubs.

—Singing lessons and clubs.

—Bridge lessons.

—Typing and speed-writing courses.

—Foreign language conversational courses.

—Swimming lessons.

—Automobile driving and mechanics lessons.

—Library usage and research and paper-writing courses.

—Museum appreciation courses.

The list is virtually endless. Money spent for personal growth is money extremely well spent. Investment in training that leads to professional expertise and to ways of making a living interestingly, as well as to making a significant contribution to human betterment, is an invaluable enabler.

Understanding versus Reward and Punishment

By understanding, I mean taking the pains to understand the child when he/she is contrary, rebellious, or so-called lazy or destructive. I also mean conveying that understanding to the child, which requires great patience and often considerable struggle.

I believe that for the most part children behave badly as a symptom rather than as any kind of willful act out of evil intent. If they eventually act badly consistently, this is evidence of serious maladaptation and even serious emotional disturbance. If they become highly manipulative, it is because limits were never adequately established and/or they were taught early on by parental response that manipulation pays off.

Make no mistake. I believe in the preservation of the family. If a young adult is destroying the family through manipulative, sociopathic acts—no matter what the origin of his behavior— the family must stand tough and protect the other members. See the comment on liability—lack of conscience—in section 2. If necessary, he must be sent away or ostracized. But even in these kinds of extreme cases, it is good to remember that this, too, is a sickness—albeit a sickness dangerous to others. Even here I caution that cruel punishment makes matters worse. Restriction and restraint and setting absolute limits has value but is not easy. Understanding, in these cases, is made easier by remembering we are not dealing with the enemy, but it is still very hard.

But what about children who are not ill, who are not antisocial but quite ordinary in their behavior? Before we go farther, I must point out that all children must be taught limits. This, too, is part of extending understanding and helping them to know who they are vis-à-vis other people.

I do not believe any child is "just lazy," or "just spoiled," etc. I do believe that some children get fatigued easily; some get discouraged easily; some do not get adequate praise for what they do; some feel unloved and do almost anything to get attention; some have infantile impulse control—they are slower to develop than others; some imitate screaming, yelling parents; some have poor frustration tolerance; some feel hopeless and give up easily because they have poor self-esteem; some feel themselves to be the victims of favoritism or intolerance; some feel like strangers and even unwanted in their own homes, etc. For some there is a kernel of objective reality as the basis of their feelings. For others their feelings are solidly founded on objective reality. For others their difficulties are based on fabrications but, nevertheless, fabrications over which they have no control or insight as to origin.

There is never difficulty due to too much love. By definition, love—unselfish love—in which the child is never sacrificed for vicarious needs of the parent (overprotection, etc.) can never be excessive.

Reward and punishment produce no light, no insight, and only on occasion do they produce significant behavioral changes. From my point of view, punishment produces some limitations but not really solid ones. Restraint and understanding are more effective. I remember my wife telling me how when she had chicken pox as a four-year-old, she was told that scratching her face would bring scars. The itch was intolerable. Knowing that it was best not to scratch helped but not enough. Her mother distracted her with toys, games, and lots of conversation. She also, when necessary, held her hands as she kept talking to her, once through a particularly long and awful night. She never punished her. There was no talk of being good or bad. Understanding and restraint demonstrated love—significantly rewarding and never forgotten by my wife—who also gave of herself unselfishly and self-rewardingly to her own children years later.

Children, as I've indicated earlier, are remarkably receptive to understanding. They really don't understand themselves when they "act badly" due to excessive fatigue, hunger, frustration, etc. They really do want to understand and want help in understanding what they are doing wrong and where it comes from. Parents are good at understanding children, provided they are interested in understanding, listening, really listening and talking. Parents who understand themselves are usually particularly gifted in this area. Punishment stops understanding. It closes off! If the child is given no chance to talk, it makes him/her very frustrated and eventually extremely bitter and hostile, contributing to more bad behavior. The use of power over the powerless produces extreme rage—often repressed and eventually becoming destructively explosive.

Constraint or restraint does not preclude communication and understanding. I don't advocate talk while a child is playing with fire (actually and figuratively). Removal and constraint must be exercised at once—even as talk is initiated. If the child is too young for verbal talk, he/she will usually respond to voice tone and manner, which should be appropriately alarming. If the child is not responsive, and few are not, medical examination is indicated.

Needless to say, parental responsibility dictates that the child is never left alone with fire or its equivalent. By the time the child is old enough to go it alone, hopefully sufficient communication has taken place to educate him/her about various common dangers. Much of this goes on constantly as a result of parental example. If the child is nonresponsive unless he/she is punished by a small, insulting pat on the behind, so be it, but this must be quickly followed by hugs, kisses, love, and conveyance of parental concern and, yes, with the cliché, but true, "for your own good." But again, understanding and conveying understanding combined with constraints where called for is, for me, the real thing.

Most parents who spend much time with their child know

an amazing amount about his/her reactions. They know that he gets wild "when he has to pee." They know she yells a lot when she is tired, etc. Those who don't know their child must observe more closely so as to make linkages.

With adolescents, understanding is best promoted by nonjudgmental, nonforced, noncoercive, nonprivacy-intrusive talk. Open, warm talk leading to insight in which nonparallel (see the early chapter on talk in this section), but rather responsive talk takes place, is most valuable.

Talking straight and compassionately reveals not only symptoms but makes possible understanding and a solution to underlying problems as well. This is not terribly different from what the trained therapist does. He/she has the advantage of nonjudgmental objectivity as well as knowing how to interpret what is said.

Talking about behavior is an attempt to understand, clarify, and remedy. It is also a lesson in compassion and an exercise in logic. Even as it nullifies untoward behavior, it adds to openness and intimacy and stretches and enriches both the emotionale and intellect.

The Announcement

Children make an announcement, I believe some time between the ages of ten and fifteen, age depending on their development and experience. Sometimes the announcement is delivered subtly, quietly, almost imperceptibly. Sometimes, in fact, it is only hinted at and really hard to hear. Some children make it loud and strong. The way the announcement is made is usually consistent with the personality of the child. If parents of a reticent, self-effacing child are not open to it and listening carefully, they may very well not hear it at all.

What is the announcement? It is the stated desire of what the child would like to do as a life's work. Parents who don't take it seriously—who don't hear it—are usually missing a key enabling opportunity.

The announcement is not the same as childish exploration of imaginary things to be—largely stimulated by TV, movies, comic strips, etc. The announcement is an inner calling and if supported properly it makes life so much easier in this highly complex, specialized world.

I believe parents miss the announcement for several reasons, most of which go on unconsciously and many of which overlap.

(1) They do not listen to their children seriously. They don't take their children seriously. They don't hear it when it is made.

(2) They are unaware that the child is not as childish as the parent thinks in this area of deciding what he/she wants

to do. This unawareness is particularly true of parents who have a need to subvert their child's growing up.

(3) The parents themselves are afraid of commitment and decision and project this to the child. They have never learned the value of commitment and the fact that in most decisions dedication to the decision is more important than the option chosen and determines its success.

(4) Some parents who have the notion that they themselves have "failed" want their children to "succeed" at *all things*. The announcement can lead to commitment to *one* thing, thus discarding other things and precluding universal success in all things.

(5) Many parents cannot imagine that the announcement exists—let alone for young children. They are sold on the idea that children don't make up their minds until they are in college or of college age. Therefore, they do not pay attention and operate on a closed basis in this connection.

Let me point out that gender identification and sexual preference take place in the first three years of life.

Personality and character structure are usually determined before the late teens.

I further want to point out that at an early age the child is often more in touch with his/her feelings and proclivities than at any other age. There is far less inundation by all kinds of money, glory seeking, popularity needing, competitive pressures.

(6) Many parents are unaware of the importance of enthusiasm and sustained enthusiasm in pursuing long-range goals requiring much struggle and work.

(7) Many parents are unaware of the campaigning—the planning and input involved in making ambitious goals come to fruition.

(8) Some parents have unconscious and even conscious ideas of their own and therefore have a vested interest in not hearing or paying attention. Some in this category will sabotage the announcement even when it is made consistently and repeatedly. Some will pressure for their own plans and goals, regardless of the child's proclivities, leanings, and desires.

I know one very unhappy young man who composed music as a child and who clearly stated his desire for a musical career from the age of four. When he was fourteen, his family "had it out with him." He was pushed into a premed program. Today he is neither a doctor nor a musician nor a composer. He is slowly making his way into the music world, but much time has passed.

(9) Some parents are so preoccupied with their own options, indecisions, and difficulties that they can't hear their children.

(10) "But they are only children, why force them to grow up?" Yes, some parents do not want to infantilize their children but they do not want to usurp their childhoods either, and they are right. But hearing and beginning to facilitate the announcement does not take away their childhood. They will go on being children, even though the announcement has been "heard" with all seriousness. Not to hear the announcement is to miss one of the most important enabling opportunities.

The child need not grow up prematurely in order to be taken seriously, to plan, and to begin to see to it that his/her education includes aspects that will be useful in pursuit of particular goals. For example, science can be a game as well as serious work. The same is true of music, literature, language, law, etc. But the simple fact is that most serious goals involve a great deal of preplanning and development—economic, incidentally, as well as educational.

One of the major points I'm making here is that motivation is crucial in pursuing a complex and difficult course in the development of a skill or profession to completion. Parents who don't hear or take the announcement seriously or don't know of its existence are in danger of destroying motivation and incentive at its very inception. Those who do hear it will recognize it as one of the few times in life when interest is there, along with healthy curiosity, even before large involvement has taken place. This is one of the few times in life this happens. In fact, it is a unique exception to the rule I've already discussed—that interest almost always follows involvement. Parents who *hear* will take advantage of this unique exception and opportunity to help sustain motivation, interest, and incentive by nourishing and helping to facilitate the announced ambition.

Some parents insist the child wait for more options before his/her mind is made up. Some inundate the child with options and drown his/her desire in a mire of confusion and newly generated self-doubt. They rationalize their stand with the argument that the child doesn't even know that certain fields that might be of interest exist. Some of the same parents realize that commitment is necessary for success and cannot understand children lacking commitment when they have consistently put down announcements made—both consistent ones, variations of the orginal one, and altogether new ones.

But what about fields that the child doesn't know exist or with which there is lack of real familiarity? The announcement need not be adhered to rigidly! In some cases the child is so gifted in a special area (music composing) that the specialty itself becomes the chosen course. But quite often the announcement points to a direction—a very important direction—which, if facilitated, can easily lead to one or another area which becomes familiar later on. Thus, the science announcement may lead to physics, chemistry, or biological research, regardless of whether the child says he is interested in being a physicist or a chemist, if his interest in science is supported and facilitated. Musical interest may lead to musicology, playing an instrument, composing, etc. Medicine may channel into surgery, internal medicine, or public health. I know that I wanted medicine from age four. I was never discouraged by my parents. When I was twelve I loved reading the *Merck Manual*. I thought seriously of internal medicine or surgery (which I still find very interesting) until college, when I took psychology. I then decided on psychiatry as a specialty of medicine.

How do we know that the announcement is *the real thing?* There is nothing more helpful in this regard than the parent knowing the child. A healthy, close relationship, in existence for a long time before the announcement is made, provides that knowledge of the child. But there are a few specifics, too:

(1) *Appropriateness.* The announcement must be appropriate

in terms of possibility based on assets. Obviously, a child who is severely handicapped physically is stating a wish rather than an announcement if he/she talks about becoming a professional athlete. *But* be careful here! A child who is a poor student may announce a goal that requires great study. Many poor students can and do become very good students after they make the announcement and it is *heard,* that is, taken seriously, demonstrated by parental support. Of course, the required intelligence and potential must be there as a necessary reality.

(2) *Repetition and consistency.* Does the child repeat the announcement again and again? A single announcement has little or no meaning. When it is the real thing, the child will state it over and over again. He/she will consistently come back to it without veering off course.

(3) *"Job" interview and interest and knowledge.* I mean that discussions with the child about the announcement will reveal considerable interest and more than usual knowledge (often surprising to the parent). Some children supply surprising logic and argument for their choice. To support their choice they will even bring in particular attributes they have in its connection as well as a history of long-standing adjunct interests. This is easier for parents who have had easy and ongoing discussions with their children right along.

(4) The child demonstrates an *absence of fickleness* and will not jump from one option to another and will *resist inevitable suggestions made* by other people.

(5) *Action.* Many children will have already implemented their decisions with action. I remember having played with a microscope set long before I used the real thing as well as having read and studied the *Merck Manual.*

Where does the announcement come from? I believe it is infinitely more important than it is there and that it is recognized (heard) and well used than in knowing where it comes from. But I believe it largely represents an amalgam of family professional history (identification with a parent or other relative); admiration for a mentor (often a teacher or one's own doctor or the family lawyer); an unconscious feeling for one's own assets; a push from an inborn creative ability and urge (art, music); and from familial experiences, especially those springing from family enrichment participations.

In any case, hearing the announcement and helping to facilitate it are enormously helpful to our endeavor. Being deaf to it or ignoring and neglecting it, or worse, sabotaging it, destroys a wonderful opportunity. This announcement deafness, despite the women's movement, is still particularly prevalent as applied to girls. Do not permit wedding bells to drown out the stated aspirations of your daughters. I am convinced that women are the single largest repository of untapped creative richness in our community. Fifteen of my women patients have gone on to become doctors, psychoanalysts, and lawyers in later life— *later* because there was considerable damage inflicted in childhood and their announcements went unheard.

I do not believe for a moment that hearing and implementing the announcement precludes marriage and children. It augments the possibility for those who want it. Most men welcome the help and the richness of the development of their wives' inner resources. Dependency is no longer the prized commodity our culture inflicted on women ruthlessly up until some twenty-five years ago. Occupational independence does not in any way dilute the importance or satisfaction of raising children any more than it hampers the possibility of enjoying a rich family life. How do we show that we hear the announcement and what do we do to facilitate it?

(1) We give it our heartfelt credence. We talk it over with the child and tell him/her that we take what he/she says seriously and with great respect.

(2) We gear much of what we do in family cultural enrichment programs to the child's aspirations. A child who wants to be a doctor is thrilled by conversations with family friends who are in medical schools, residencies, or in the practice of medicine. They like to watch the TV health channels with parents. Future architects like to look at books describing various kinds of building styles. Doing this is not difficult and pays off.

(3) Parental investigating and research—with the child's participation—into the prerequisites and requirements for entering the field in question has great value. For example, finding out

what subjects, backgrounds, extracurricular activities and interests medical schools or law schools require. Finding out how one goes about becoming a marine biologist or a sea captain. Investigating the need for high grades and in what subjects.

(4) Help the child to campaign for what he/she wants. Indicate the importance of grades even as you help him/her love the subject by entering into interesting discussions about it. Help to get jobs related to the subject (hospitals, law offices, etc.). Help to meet people who are in the field and who love the field.

Unfortunately, we do live in an age of high competition and specialization. High motivation and achievement are necessary in order to enter most fields requiring expertise. Active parental involvement in the campaign helps enormously. If grades are required and the child does not have the knack for getting them, tutoring by a capable and benevolent teacher helps enormously. This must not be seen as a put-down or an indication that a child is entering the wrong field. Many superb doctors, for example, have had a terrible time with premedical school and even with medical school. The practice of medicine has very little to do with premed subjects, *but,* unfortunately, grades in those subjects are largely the criteria used to determine admission.

Remember, the stakes are high. The world is complex. Vehicles are necessary for most people who wish to experience a high degree of self-realization.

To summarize some of the advantages of "hearing" the announcement:

(1) Self-esteem is enhanced by the child's observation of parental interest and participation—taking him/her seriously and demonstrating belief in the child's ability to function effectively in the adult world.

(2) Helping to integrate the child's assets and abilities and to bring focus to effective action in the use of inner resources.

(3) Providing the experience of commitment and involvement, thus adding immeasurably to the process of decision making.

(4) Providing the experience of cooperative effort and its benefits.

(5) Giving possibility to fruition in terms of serious self-realization in providing an area of practical, applicable, fully developed skills.

Can a child change his/her mind? Of course! But if one's mind changes constantly, even though conditions have not changed, chances are the announcement was not the real thing. *But* if it was the real thing and conditions or new opportunities of great value come up and there is a new announcement we can be certain that everything gained by the original announcement is still intact and will be used constructively for the new one. In any case, the announcement *heard* leads to involvement, to increased interest, and to sustained motivation of a quality infinitely better than the kind produced by a quest for glory.

Keeping Lines of
Communication Open:
Breaking Pride Deadlocks

This enabler must be viewed as an enabler to enablers. Yes, it is true that all the enablers tend to nourish one another and to multiply. But when lines of communication remain intact, only then is it possible to be fully supportive in the myriad ways possible as discussed throughout this section. Keeping lines of communication open means not permitting destructive silences (I discussed silence as a damage in section 3) to be maintained. It means talking over problems, feelings—particularly hurt ones—grievances, fears, and any areas that particularly need communication: diagnosis of difficulties involved, appropriate support, and remedial action.

Where lines of communication are open, constructive communication takes place. Where they break down, destructive silence and being cut off from help takes place. This seems apparent enough but I have seen any number of people who cannot understand why they know so little about their children even though they talk. Investigation reveals that they talk about "good things" gladly and easily, but have long ago gotten into the habit of retreating into silence when it comes to problematic issues. They also find that silences are and have been for a long time characteristic following arguments and even disagreements and are especially prevalent when these people sustain

280

any familial grievances. They have not learned the lesson that it is usually better even to scream than to remain distant, cold, and silent.

Noncommunication as a way of handling interpersonal problems between family members—"let him/her cool off and it will all pass"—easily becomes a habit and little that is worthwhile, like mutual clearing of the air and support, can flourish in this kind of chilly atmosphere, characteristic of adversarial families discussed in section 3.

But if communication breakdown is not permitted—and I hasten to add that this enabler must not be used as a rationale to pry and to invade privacy—even from the beginning, then it will not become an ingrained and habitual response to pressured situations and *the* family way of relating.

Again, as in all other areas, children learn from parents. If parents get into a "snit" and withdraw from each other when beset by outside (business) problems or personal problems, it is an exorbitant expectation to believe that children will act differently.

Communication, particularly when hurt feelings take place or when problems are encountered, can, if engendered from early on, becomes a constructive habit. Much here depends on response and general household ambience. Let me list a few enablers of this enabler of enablers in the prevention of silent sulking that prevents diagnosis or remediation of problems.

(1) There is no fear of embarrassment regardless of what is told by children on the part of parents who do not act sanctimoniously holier-than-thou. It is an excellent exercise for parents to review their own childhood and adolescent difficulties periodically.

(2) There is little or even no history of "I told you so"—the vindictive triumph response if there is an admission of having been wrong.

(3) There is little or no history and therefore no fear of degradation, punishment, harsh judgment, or recrimination.

(4) There is no history of fear of a breach of confidence.

(5) There is a history of fulfilled expectations of compassion-

ate analysis of problems and discussion of possible solutions and help to facilitate them.

It must be remembered that when a child feels aggrieved by a parent it takes enormous confidence in that parent for the child to be open and honest with this person, who is rightly seen as the source of nourishing dependency as well as transgressor.

(6) There is little or no history of parental arbitrary rightness or "I am right because I am older or because I am your parent." This is a sure closure to communication.

(7) There is awareness on the part of the parent that repressed anger leads to self-hate and to anxiety and depression. Warm anger—expressed—prevents explosive rages as well as chronic hostility and many somatic difficulties, including accident proneness. Anger expressed warmly and humanly does not hurt! It clears the air, making other feelings, particularly feelings of love, possible. But for this to take place, mutual confidence is necessary. This means that anger expressed will not be interpreted as lack of respect. It must be seen as a feeling message of displeasure delivered to a person who is felt to be important enough to receive it and strong enough and loving enough, too, to use it constructively.

(8) There is a history of apology for all concerned. This means that members of the family—parent to parent to child to parent—have apologized not because they were forced to swallow pride but because they wanted to, without being demeaned or feeling demeaned. "I was wrong. I am sorry" was and is not felt as a humiliation by the apologizer nor is it a source of vindictive triumph to the wrongly aggrieved partner. It simply says, "I can be wrong and that is all right. We are all human. We can all learn. I, too, can hurt people. I'm genuinely sorry when I do and I'll try to do better." This is the stuff of healthy and genuine humility. This teaches the child that it is all right to be wrong and that in apologizing we take healthy cognizance of someone else's feelings—a good antinarcissistic lesson that helps to be open to learning.

The pride deadlock is surely the most common cause and form of communication breakdown. The pride deadlock closes down communication and keeps it closed down. Therefore, the prevention and breaking of pride deadlocks are extremely important enablers of the enabler of enablers—of keeping the lines between us open. What is a pride deadlock?

Simply put, in a pride deadlock, each adversary—and they are adversaries at this point—puffs him/herself up with self-righteousness and clings tenaciously to his/her position with total implacable rigidity. It takes two to tango. In a pride deadlock both refuse to dance. Each contributor to the deadlock feels totally wronged and stands on his/her position waiting for the other to make amends. Since neither gives in—each now feeling that his/her very substance, let alone integrity and dignity, are at stake—they are both locked into a destructive, encapsulated, self-corrosive, noncommunicative position.

Pride in these cases, as in most cases, starts out as a device to protect feelings of vulnerability. For example, the man who really feels sexually inadequate takes pride in his sexuality, relegating himself to the pride position of sexual athlete. When his pride is hurt (let's say a failure in sexual performance takes place), he is put in touch with his real problem and his intolerable self-hate. By scoring a vindictive triumph, usually over his sexual partner, his pride position is restored. If he cannot score a triumph, he may withdraw altogether—as in a pride deadlock—with a "who needs you anyway?" stance, also in an attempt to feel proud again. Obviously, this kind of pride positioning does little except to produce damage to real truth and real self. It confuses, obfuscates, distorts real self and real living and hurts real communication. Pride is puffery, hot air, and produces pretense and affectation as well as high vulnerability, making communication on a real level impossible.

People kill out of hurt pride more than for any other reason. This is readily understood when we realize the intensity of the self-hate exposed when a chink in the armor (pride) reveals the real person in all his/her humanity (limitations) from which hiding has taken place. Crimes of passion and most wars are due to hurt pride and paranoid fears of being knocked down from false, exalted versions of ourselves. These are usually largely sustained by feeling falsely superior to others in a mythical hierarchy established in our own heads.

Unfortunately, here, too, children learn from parents. Yes, children—even the very young—are already capable of taking part in pride standoffs and deadlocks. I say standoffs because we do stand off by ourselves—alone and encapsulated—stuck with our own self-corrosive rage. Unfortunately, this kind of thing is very habit forming, and sustaining and protecting the pride position becomes more important than our real selves and our real and loving feelings for other people. Yes, pride, I believe, is the emotional cancer of our times and perhaps of all times. It is not territorial imperative that we must fear but the pride imperative. But this complex subject can fill volumes—volumes describing emotional pathology, at least to some degree common in all of us.

To be aware is already an enabler. To try not to confuse pride (that sullen, puffed-up feeling) with real self or self-realization (almost always connected to helping others rather than scoring over them) is an enabler. But what about the enabler, *breaking the pride deadlock?*

Prevention is very important here as elsewhere and is especially useful in not permitting the habit and its malignant consequences to form.

Talking—as described earlier as an enabler—prevents it. Talking also breaks the pride deadlock. To the extent that there has been a history—a continuum of talking, and I mean benevolent, *real* talking—there will exist a minimum of pride deadlocks.

But in households where talking of a serious, open kind has not taken place, pride deadlocks will usually be commonplace. Diagnosis is crucial. Remember, in very few instances is anyone completely right or wrong! Remember that arbitrary rightness is a disaster and, in this case, actually feeds pride and the deadlock.

As soon as the diagnosis is made—and this is easy—people feel aggrieved and hurt and puff up and take off and wait. *Don't* wait! An emergency exists. Talk or hug or bring out some goodies to eat for both of you or announce that you are both going to a movie and talk and talk through your actions—eating on the way to the movies and after the show, etc.—with words.

Parents are better equipped to talk and break the deadlock. Hopefully they will—after reading this—understand better. Remember—no matter who was hurt, how, and by whom, or by what—remediation is possible *only* if things can be talked over. Talk here must not be of the blame variety whatsoever or the feelings of abuse or self-justification. Initial talk, in fact, may be about subjects unrelated to the hurt. After both people feel easier about each other and themselves, they may address their angry feelings. When each talks, this is a time to listen. Here again, parents are better at it—hopefully—because children do not usually have long attention spans at these times or as much self-control. Try above all to stay with the subject on hand and to prevent personal attacks of any kind, which will only lead to another deadlock. When everyone has really come to feeling better, discussions about pride may be helpful. Let me recommend that you read Karen Horney's *Our Inner Conflicts* and the book I wrote, *One to One,* especially the chapter called "The Game," as well as a description of the *good fight.*

Let me close by saying that talking simply has no substitute. It is very difficult to sustain a deadlock while talking so long as the talk is not self-righteous or vindictive or of a "scoring over you" variety. Of course, apology and admission of wrongdoing where appropriate and only where it is heartfelt and not received and used to restore pride is a message of love and has a wonderfully balancing effect on all concerned.

Dogs, Cats, Fish, Birds, and Other Friends of This Kind

Small children and even older ones and adults, too, often feel that small creatures extend the family. Even more so, they fill out the family, providing a kind of warm, friendly, interesting, and alive ambience.

A household is unlikely to feel perfectionistically constricting and antichild, as described by Ida in the chapter on the damage of the perfectionistic home, when it at various times contains all or some of the following: dogs, cats, birds, fish, mice, gerbils, guinea pigs, turtles, plants, flowers, cocoons, chameleons, snakes, lizards, iguanas, grasshoppers, moths, butterflies, etc. I ought to know. We had them all at various times when I was a child and when my children were young. This kind of household usually feels like a free and congenial place to children—a place in large part oriented for their feeling comfortable and a place to grow up. But I believe living with members of species other than our own does more than that.

(1) I feel that on a deep level—out of conscious awareness and transcending ordinary logic—closeness to living creatures other than ourselves puts us in touch with nature at her most basic and that this in a mysterious way nourishes our creativity.

(2) Living closely with small members of the planet stirs our compassion, humility, and humanity.

(3) There is the contribution of exciting entertainment and education. There is little to match the child's interest and excite-

ment in watching a moth or butterfly emerge from a cocoon or the birth of live-bearer tropical fish, guppies, platties, swordtails.

(4) There is a growth of an aesthetic sense in living with beautiful birds, fish, plants, and flowers.

(5) Learning the life cycles, breeding, feeding, and living habits of all these creatures and conducting selective breeding experiments stirs both intellectual curiosity and creative urges. It also adds to intellectual stretching and growth.

(6) The above provides materials for joint discussion and education by parents and children, drawing them together in family projects.

(7) Philosophical areas involving life and death become meaningful subjects for discussions and exchange of intimate feelings among family members.

(8) Training animals gives great satisfaction, self-confidence, patience, and teaches the virtues of stick-to-itiveness and motivation.

(9) Responsibility for care of creatures is excellent experience, applicable to all areas of life. It also augments self-confidence.

(10) Emotional investment in animals is excellent practice for emotional investment in people as well as the practice of tolerance and compassion for those with greater limitations than ourselves.

(11) Small creatures militate against loneliness. It has been shown that having a dog reduces stress in old people and adds to inner peace. The same is true for children.

(12) Living with animals removes the fear of animals and I believe reduces anxiety when confronted with the unfamiliar.

Of course, parental supervision and participation must be appropriately applied. No unwitting cruelty must be permitted under any circumstances and no guilt precipitated.

Living peacefully and fruitfully with nature's other children provides a reverence for life, including one's own life. I believe it also provides an early experience with a kind of parenting. Thus, when one eventually has his/her children, he/she has a head start, even though the stirring of familiar feelings may not at once be traced to early care of household animals.

The Cooperative or
Enabling Household

No household is totally cooperative and few are totally destructive. But the cooperative household is mainly geared to the real well-being of all its members and particularly to those who are not yet self-sufficient.

In this regard, the cooperative household mainly feels safe, secure, and interesting. This means that one can be one's self, can express feelings, can exchange feelings, can make mistakes, can explore, and can grow to be uniquely one's self without fear of derision, attack, or reprisal.

The cooperative household is a place replete with nourishment: physical care, love, emotional nourishment through the exchange of feelings, intellectual nourishment through the exchange of ideas, and creative nourishment through family enrichment participation.

The cooperative household is one in which most of the enablers are practiced actively and encompasses the enabler—*the healthy, joyous household* that I described earlier. Much of the joy experienced here is through the aid and awareness of mutual development and self-realization. Rather than experiencing competitive feelings, individual accomplishments and satisfactions are felt as accruing to the entire household, that is, all of its members. But even as this takes place, there is no impingement on each other's unique individuality or needs.

Mutual acceptance runs high here and it is for the most part unconditional. There is little or no concern for even exchange or fair shares. The members of the household largely feel that they get what they do relative to their needs. Sibling rivalry, favoritism, suspiciousness, and paranoia are significantly lacking.

In this household the various members tend to contribute relative to their particular abilities, skills, and expertise. Sick households have the loudest shouter dictate policy regardless of ability. Cooperative houses have people spontaneously contribute their expertise appropriately, with joy rather than a fear of exploitation. Help is received with joy rather than with feeling demeaned.

Here, arrogance is significantly rare and humility, combined with real feelings of self, is much in evidence.

The cooperative household members have very strong family identification and derive strength from it. They tend to go beyond the nuclear family in their feelings and to transcend generational gaps, too. This feeling for members of other generations and extended family gives even more of a sense of belonging and strength.

The cooperative household members demonstrate strong feelings, values, priorities, and social consciousness. They are flexible. They can hear each other. They don't engage in contrasts or contests. They give of themselves and they can give without feeling depleted. Without conscious awareness, they *know* that love is not a fixed fund and then used up. Loving generates more love. They love each other and are enablers to each other.

The Enabler

Let me say at once—the enabler is not a self-sacrificing, abused, single-minded martyr.

The enabler is a *relatively* strong, self-fulfilling, self-nourishing person with a strong sense of self. A major satisfaction and form of nourishment comes from the contribution to the child's self-realization. But this in no way diminishes one's own needs and joys in other areas, too. Real enabling can only be done by a real person. Real people are multidimensional and have many needs requiring attention, neglect of which causes shrinkage of self and one's own values and feelings—providing less to relate with and to give. I am reminded of a story my own analyst, Nat Freeman, told me, which I think sums it up. A mother had six children. At 4:00 p.m. she went into the kitchen, locked the door, put her feet up on a chair, read the paper while she drank a cup of tea. The children pounded on the door but she ignored them. One of them demanded, "Mom, what are you doing?" She answered, "I'm busy making a mother."

The enabler is strong. This means he/she has strong feelings about values and priorities and has no difficulty saying *yes* or *no* appropriately to the well-being of the child. The enabler is also sufficiently flexible so as to be able to be wrong and to change his/her mind when appropriate. The ability to set limits, to say no, and flexibility are certain evidence of inner strengths, which is invaluable in application to the child. The same is true of being able to avail oneself of expert help if necessary without feeling at all demeaned.

The enabler is not a performer. He/she does little or nothing for effect. It is done because the enabler feels like doing it—because it is consistent with real self-values and priorities. The enabler makes use of insights and expertise but does not behave like either an autocrat or someone following directions. He/she is alive and spontaneous. He/she is not afraid of mistakes because he/she knows they can be remedied and that change and growth can come from them.

The enabler is tuned in to the feelings of the child. He/she knows who the child is and is enormously motivated to know him/her better. The enabler hears the child—especially the child's announcement. The enabler loves, respects, and dignifies the child—the real child—with a realistic vision of his/her liabilities, limits, assets, inner resources, and aspirations as a separate human being. The enabler uses most of the enabling processes I described in application to the child's development.

The enabler helps to convey what it means to be a real person in the real world. He/she helps the child to appreciate both the limitations and wonders of being human. People are envious, jealous, happy, sad, generous, acrimonious, confused, logical, and much else, and this is conveyed to the child so as to make real self-acceptance (not an idealized glory-bound self) possible. The enabler provides a home where healthy growth takes place and a bridge to the world outside the home is constructed through teaching him/her of the real state of being a real person. The bridge is further strengthened by the child's development and by the love given and the confidence invested in the child.

The enabler's major characteristic is the joy and satisfaction felt in contributing to the child's healthy development and self-realization. This is not contrived! This is the real thing! The enabler feels joyous in his/her own growth and his/her child's growth as well as that of other fellow human beings.

The enabler is not a perfect human being and not a perfect enabler. But the enabler mostly relates to the child in a loving, constructive way and his/her contribution goes mainly in the direction of the child's healthy, intellectual, emotional, and creative fulfillment.

Index